AMERICAN
HORRORS

AMERICAN HORRORS

Essays on the Modern American Horror Film

Edited by
Gregory A. Waller

University of Illinois Press
Urbana and Chicago

First paperback edition, 1987
© 1987 by the Board of Trustees of the University of Illinois
Manufactured in the United States of America
P 7 6 5 4

This book is printed on acid-free paper.

Library of Congress Cataloging-in-Publication Data

American horrors.

   Bibliography: p.
   Includes index.
   1. Horror films—United States—History and
criticism. I. Waller, Gregory A. (Gregory Albert),
1950–
PN1995.9.H6A39   1987   791.43'09'0916   87-5833
ISBN 0-252-01448-0 (alk. paper)

To Robin, Moby, and Graham

Contents

Introduction

The modern horror film is an extraordinarily diverse group of texts that epitomize the tangled workings of American popular culture, which is at once business, art, and purveyor of entertainment and ideology. In its adaptability and capacity for accommodating a range of cultural values and cinematic styles, modern horror is probably equalled among American film genres only by the western from the late 1940s to the mid-1950s. Today, with the widespread availability of video recorders and cable television, we can all become experts in horror in a way that was practically impossible ten years ago. (One such expert-to-be is the astronaut in *Lifeforce* [1985] who enters the domain of the space vampires and declares: "This is incredible! I hope you can appreciate the scale of this on the video"—a fitting reminder of how much horror loses when it is transferred to the small, rectangular television image with its relatively poor resolution and color quality.) An immersion in the genre reveals that the contemporary horror film encompasses big-budget, major studio productions like *Jaws* (1975) and *Jaws 2* (1978), as well as cut-rate, independent, regional productions designed for the drive-in (and now the home video) market like *Humongous* (1981). It includes the cinematically accomplished (*Don't Look Now* [1973]), the technically innovative (*Wolfen* [1981]), and the merely formulaic (*Mortuary* [1981], *Friday the 13th—The Final Chapter* [1984]); the unexpected wit and savvy of *Piranha* (1978), *Alligator* (1980), *Alone in the Dark* (1982), and *Halloween III: Season of the Witch* (1983); and the ponderous pretentiousness of *Exorcist II: The Heretic* (1977), *The Awakening* (1980), and *Ghost Story* (1981); the unremitting seriousness of *The Exorcist* (1973), *The Hearse* (1980), *The Hunger* (1983), and *The Keep* (1983); and the black satiric comedy of *The Texas Chain Saw Massacre* (1974), *Sisters* (1973), *Motel Hell* (1980), and *Strange Invaders* (1983).

While the box-office revenues and the production of horror films seem to have ebbed in 1983–84, the genre has by no means disappeared. In addition to the primetime television horror of certain episodes of "Amazing Stories," "Alfred Hitchcock Presents," and "The Twilight Zone," 1985–86 has seen a steady stream of sequels (to, for instance, *The Hills Have Eyes, A Nightmare on Elm Street, Poltergeist, Psycho II, Night of the Living Dead, Dawn of the Dead,* and *Alien*), as well as several variations on the "little" monsters of *Gremlins* (*Ghoulies, Troll*), more adaptations of Stephen King's fiction (*Cat's Eye, Silver Bullet, Maximum Overdrive*), latter-day vampire films (*Lifeforce, Transylvania 6-5000*), and, proof positive of the genre's continued vitality and heterogeneity, *The Company of Wolves* (1985), *The Stuff* (1985), and *Re-Animator* (1985).

What I refer to as the modern era of the American horror film began in 1968 — the year George A. Romero's *Night of the Living Dead* and Roman Polanski's *Rosemary's Baby* were released (and perhaps not coincidentally, the year of the National Commission on the Causes and Prevention of Violence and the election of Richard M. Nixon as president). Through the 1970s and into the 1980s the horror film remained on the whole commercially viable (unlike the western, for example) and repeatedly proved its affinity for the topical and the novel, and thereby affirmed its place as a type of storytelling particularly apt and relevant to post-1968 America. At the same time, however, the genre became increasingly reflexive and allusive, flaunting its own generic inheritance and its own identity as horror and as film. Thus, as Noel Carroll and others have argued, contemporary horror demands to be seen in the context not only of American life in the 1970s and 1980s but also of those classic texts that it quotes, parodies, imitates, and remakes — films like *Frankenstein* (1931), *Dracula* (1931), *King Kong* (1933), *Cat People* (1942), *The Thing* (1951), and *Invasion of the Body Snatchers* (1956).[1] These films are horror's collective memory, acknowledged by filmmakers and fans alike, yet what of modern horror's more immediate precursors in the years before *Night of the Living Dead* and *Rosemary's Baby*?

The 1960s provided a number of noteworthy horror films — still disturbing oddities like *What Ever Happened to Baby Jane?* (1962) and *Lady in a Cage* (1964); *The Haunting* (1964), with its restrained "adult" (i.e., major studio, quasi-Victorian) terror; *Two Thousand Maniacs* (1964) and Herschell Gordon Lewis's other notoriously violent drive-in movies; and from outside of America, Michael Powell's *Peeping Tom* (1960), Roman Polanski's *Repulsion* (1965), Mario Bava's baroque tales of witchcraft and repression (like *Black Sunday* [1960]), and Masaki Kobayashi's cinematic rendering of Japanese ghost stories (*Kwaidan* [1965]). Most important, the 1960s saw the release of two of the most accomplished American horror films, Alfred Hitchcock's *Psycho* (1960) and *The Birds* (1963), both of which would greatly influence the shape the genre would take in the 1970s and 1980s. The presence of *Psycho,* for example, haunts innumerable films, from *Sisters, Halloween* (1978), and *Psycho II* (1983) to made-for-television movies like *Scream Pretty Peggy* (1973), which features an apparently harmless young man who assumes the identity of his dead sister and murders attractive women. And *The Birds* lies behind *Night of the Living Dead* and virtually all post-1968 films of apocalyptic horror, as well as films like *Day of the Animals* (1977), *The Swarm* (1978), and *Savage Harvest* (1981).

Hitchcock also had his imitators in the 1960s (William Castle in *Homicidal* [1961], for one), but the decade was dominated by horror films much safer and more formulaic than *Psycho* and *The Birds,* films like American International Pictures' adaptations of Edgar Allan Poe stories and Hammer Studio's series of British-made monster movies that pit humankind against familiar antagonists like Count Dracula, the Mummy, and Frankenstein's creature. In different ways, Hammer and AIP both transformed the horror film into a colorful period piece (usually set in the nineteenth century) peopled by inspired, grandly theatrical, often middle-aged villains; well-meaning, innocuous, young male heroes; and buxom young women waiting to be ravished or rescued.

Hammer films like *The Reptile* (1965), *Dracula, Prince of Darkness* (1966), and *Dracula Has Risen from the Grave* (1968) place a premium on unobtrusive, nondescript cinematography, stylized performances, special attention to decor and set design as bearers of meaning, and utterly straightforward plotting involving perfectly legible scenes of exposition, confrontation, and resolution that announce the film's system of values. Blending an unambiguous style with easily decoded themes and "messages," these films are often small-scale social fables that reveal certain correctable flaws in the nineteenth-century worlds they depict. For example, *The Reptile,* a representative Hammer production, pictures the danger to a rural community as emanating from an upper-class manor whose owner, a forbidding and stern "Doctor of Theology," has looked too deeply into the mysteries of the East and so must eventually suffer for his sins (and so must the rest of this community, since the doctor's sins have social consequences). In the film's finale a fire of purification destroys the manor house, killing both the overreaching scholar and his victimized daughter who has been transformed by a "primitive" religious cult into a murderous, reptilian monster. As a result of this sacrificial destruction — in the guise of self-defense — the rural world is once again safe from imported evil, and the middle-class newlyweds who were the real targets of the monster can proceed with the all-important task of setting up a household and beginning a family. What virtually all Hammer's horror films of the 1960s — particularly Hammer's extremely popular vampire films — offer the viewer is a world in which religious faith, ritualized violence, and individual heroism defeat a powerful but easily identified threat. Thus quite unlike *Psycho* and *The Birds,* Hammer's films reaffirm what are assumed to be the "normal" values of heterosexual romance, clearly defined sexual roles, and the middle-class family and testify to the importance and the relevance of social stability and traditional sources of authority and wisdom.

In vastly different ways, *Night of the Living Dead* and *Rosemary's Baby,* the two films that could be said to have ushered in the modern era of horror, challenge the moral-social-political assumptions, production values, and narrative strategies of Hammer and AIP films. Though there were zombielike creatures and satanic cults in the movies before 1968, Romero and Polanski redefine the monstrous — thereby redefining the role of the hero and the victim as well — and situate horror in the everyday world of contemporary America. (The essays in this volume by R. H. W. Dillard and Virginia Wright Wexman explore in detail the moral and psychological implications of this process of redefinition in *Night of the Living Dead* and *Rosemary's Baby.*) Looking backward, we can now see how these two innovative, much-imitated, commercially and critically successful films helped to map out certain directions the American horror film would take in the 1970s and 1980s.

Romero's *Night of the Living Dead,* independently produced on a budget of $114,000 in the wilds of Pennsylvania, is a graphically violent and darkly ironic treatment of catastrophic yet fully "natural" horror. In its images of invasion and social breakdown, it follows in the tradition of *The Birds* and Don Siegel's 1956 *Invasion of the Body Snatchers.* And like later films such as *The Texas Chain Saw Massacre, It's Alive* (1973), *Carrie* (1976), and *The Hills Have Eyes* (1977), *Night of the Living Dead* offers a thoroughgoing critique of American institutions and values. It depicts the failure of the nuclear family, the private home, the teenage couple, and the resourceful individual hero; and it reveals the flaws inherent in the media, local and federal government agencies, and the entire mechanism of civil defense. Romero's first feature also is a prototype of the low-budget, money-making horror film produced outside the established industry. Following *Night of the Living Dead* come, on the one hand, cut-rate, utterly derivative exploitation films (including most of the so-called teenie-kill or slice-and-dice movies released in the wake of *Halloween* and *Friday the 13th*) and, on the other hand, idiosyncratic independent productions like the films of David Cronenberg, Michael Laughlin, and Larry Cohen — imaginative, disturbing, often outrageous films like *Rabid* (1977), *Strange Behavior* (1981), and *Q—The Winged Serpent* (1982).

In contrast to *Night of the Living Dead,* Polanski's *Rosemary's Baby* was produced and distributed by a major Hollywood studio and adapted from a best-selling novel. *Rosemary's Baby,* we might say, gave birth to highly professional, much-publicized, mainstream (and so somehow acceptable and authorized) horror films like *The Exorcist, The Omen* (1976), and *Poltergeist* (1982). *Rosemary's Baby* also has a different lineage than *Night of the Living Dead,* for it has ties to previous films about female madness, conspiratorial evil, and sexual repression, including certain of Val Lewton's atmospheric productions of the 1940s (like *Cat People*). If *Night of the Living Dead* draws upon age-old fears associated with invasion and the end of the world (and on what Sigmund Freud calls our fear of the dead as malevolent enemy), *Rosemary's Baby* brings up to date the theme of humankind's weakness and complicity with supernatural satanic evil. Furthermore, like countless subsequent makers of horror films, Polanski takes as his focal point an apparently defenseless young woman. With Rosemary we discover the terror that lurks in the heart of the familiar, the evil in the mundane and the banal. *Rosemary's Baby* tells us of an isolated, justifiably paranoid woman who attempts to become independent from traditional (which is to say, male, paternalistic, socially validated) sources of protection and strength. From *Rosemary's Baby* to *Demon Seed* (1977), *Eyes of Laura Mars* (1978), *Alien* (1979), and *Visiting Hours* (1982), horror films have proven to be among the most significant documents in America's public debate over the status of the independent woman in a society still dominated by men.

If 1968 could be said to inaugurate the modern era of horror, it is not simply because this year saw the release of *Night of the Living Dead* and *Rosemary's Baby.* More important, in 1968 the Motion Picture Association of America (MPAA) instituted its "Industry Code of Self-Regulation" as a response to (and an attempt to sidestep) public concern over the role of censorship in the media. From the late 1960s into the 1980s, the MPAA's Code and Rating Administration (CARA) has grappled with the status of the horror film—refusing to grant an R-rating to Romero's *Dawn of the Dead* in 1979, for example, and making a concerted effort in the early 1980s to restrain the tendency toward graphic violence in films like *Halloween II* (1981).[2] With few exceptions, the modern horror film has been an R-rated genre, and the MPAA R-rating has allowed for and perhaps even legitimized the presentation of explicit violence—the violence of decapitation and dismemberment, of needles to the eyeball, and of scissors, kitchen appliances, handtools, and shish kabob skewers as deadly weapons. Such violence, undertaken with an air of "top that!" ingenuity and lovingly explicit detail, is perhaps the single defining characteristic of gore movies like *Maniac* (1980). (It is equally important to note that the R-rating also allows these and all other horror films much more freedom than pre-1968 films in the explicit treatment of sex, nudity, profanity, and what are euphemistically called "adult" themes like incest, necrophilia, rape, and cannibalism.) By continually pressing the boundaries of both PG- and R-ratings, the modern horror film has violated taboos with a monsterlike ferocity unprecedented in the contemporary American cinema, and in the process horror has increased freedom of expression and affected the codes of commercial television as well as the motion-picture industry. Without *Night of the Living Dead* and *The Exorcist,* we would have had to wait much longer for made-for-television movies to bring child pornography and nuclear holocaust into our homes during primetime viewing hours.

There are any number of valuable and critically defensible generalizations to be drawn about the horror film — including, for example, James B. Twitchell's distinction between terror and horror ("the etiology of horror is *always* in dreams, while the basis of terror is in actuality"),[3] Robin Wood's definition of the horror film as a collective nightmare in which "normality is threatened by the Monster,"[4] and Dennis Giles's contention that "central to the strategy of horror" is "delayed, blocked or partial vision."[5] Yet given the diversity of the genre since 1968, it is impossible, I think, to define once and for all the essence of modern horror (or, for that matter, of the Hollywood musical, the post–World War II western, or the hardboiled detective story). Nonetheless, there is no question that violence is a major element in the genre, as it is in virtually all dreams and all narratives of fact or fiction that we would label as horror stories. The motion-picture industry's often predictable advertising campaigns for horror movies entice with the promise of escalating body counts and elevators filled with blood, the same blood and gore that lead the genre's many detractors to deem horror dismissible or damn it as dangerous. Like the characters on screen, the viewer cannot ignore the violence in these films, which is linked, as Philip Brophy argues, to a "graphic sense of physicality" and "Body-horror."[6] How, then, should we face up to or master or make sense of modern horror's violence?

Although it is essential to acknowledge the role of the individual viewer and the collective audience as elements of and in the filmic text, studies of the quantifiable behavioral effects of violence on the movie or television viewer seem to me to be beside the point. What horror films offer, after all, is the representation of violence — violence embedded in a generic, narrative, fictional, often highly stylized, and oddly playful context. Only by ignoring the precise terms of the context and the codes and conventions of representation (and of perception) can we categorically group, say, *The Texas Chain Saw Massacre, The Omen, The Burning* (1981), *Scanners* (1981), and *Slumber Party Massacre* (1982) together as interchangeable exercises in dehumanizing ultraviolence. Rather than validating our safe oversimplifications – about horror, genre films, and popular culture in general – these and other horror films insist on offering (and at times unsettling and interrogating) us with what Stephen Neale calls the "conjunction" of images of violence with "images and definitions of the monstrous."[7] What is most significant, psychologically and ideologically, is the precise way each horror film displays this "conjunction" and speaks about the nature and function of aggression and conflict. Taken as a whole, the entire genre is an unsystematic, unresolved exploration of violence in virtually all its forms and guises. Thus recent horror films return again and again to questions concerning the meaning of self-defense, vengeance, and justified violence, to myths of uncommon "masculine" valor and all-too-common female victimization, and to images of violation, sacrifice, ritual, and of life reduced to a struggle for survival. This much-maligned genre undoubtedly has its share of forgettable demonstrations of the fine art of murder, like *Happy Birthday To Me* (1981) and *The Prowler* (1981), but it also includes films like George A. Romero's *Martin* (1976) and *Dawn of the Dead* (1979), Stanley Kubrick's *The Shining* (1980), and David Cronenberg's *Videodrome* (1983), which are among the most noteworthy recent examinations of the role and the representation of violence in American culture.

One common response to the violence in modern horror is to praise or damn the genre simply on the basis of its preoccupation with state-of-the-art make up and special effects work. ("Fanzines" like *Cinéfantastique* and *Fangoria* are given over almost exclusively to articles and interviews that focus on production information and special effects.) More telling is the contention – voiced by Chicago movie reviewers Roger Ebert and Gene Siskel, among others – that modern horror has become what Morris Dickstein calls a reductive "hard-core pornography of violence made possible by the virtual elimination of censorship."[8]

The equation of explicitly violent horror with pornographic gore is often based on the assumption that truly effective horror is always indirect and suggestive, leaving the horrific primarily to the viewer's imagination. This assumption informs histories of the genre like Ivan Butler's *Horror in the Cinema* and Carlos Clarens's *An Illustrated History of the Horror Film,* as well as S. S. Prawer's 1980 study, *Caligari's Children: The Film as Tale of Terror.* These critics follow H. P. Lovecraft's distinction in *Supernatural Horror in Literature* between the "true weird tale," which offers "a certain atmosphere of breathless and unexplainable dread of outer, unknown forces" and the story that is merely "mundanely gruesome."[9] The prescriptive call for films of suggestive horror – and implicitly for films that valorize an unseeable, transcendent signifier – is generally linked with a nostalgic longing for the "golden age" of horror, from *Nosferatu, A Symphony of Horror* (1922) and *Vampyr* (1932) to Universal's politically and socially conservative classics of the 1930s and 1940s. (A reviewing of *Frankenstein* [1931] and *King Kong* [1933], however, reveals that these films quite clearly rely on images of explicit violence – as close to gore as was possible in 1930s Hollywood.) This approach to the genre unjustly serves the past as well as the present. We would do better, I think, to pay attention to films like *Dracula* (1979), *An American Werewolf in London* (1981), *The Funhouse* (1981), and *Re-Animator* (1985), which in modernizing and commenting on classic monster movies prove that the relationship between contemporary and golden age horror involves much more than simply the distinction between the graphically direct and the atmospherically suggestive. (*Invasion of the Body Snatchers* [1978] and *The Thing* [1982] perform a similar function for 1950s horror.)

The most important criticism of modern horror's so-called pornography of violence is directed more explicitly toward ideological rather than stylistic questions. For example, what are we to make of the genre's propensity for depicting sexually active teenagers and independent women as victims and for suggesting that the (male) monster is something of a superego figure, reaffirming through vicious murder the mechanics of repression so necessary for a patriarchal society? Seen in this light, certain horror films – "stupid, gory, sexist ripoffs," Bruce Kawin calls them – could be read as being of a piece with X-rated pornographic displays of rape and other male fantasies of sadism and exploitation. The question of how we are to assess the horror film's representation of violence against women is further complicated because the genre includes texts (like *The Velvet Vampire* [1971], *Friday the 13th*, and *The Hunger*) that picture the threat to normality as a female or that offer a narrative in which the besieged female victim is alone capable of destroying her psychopathic assailant. Through her independent actions, the woman in *Eyes of a Stranger* (1981) and *Visiting Hours* (and in *Alien* and *Aliens* [1986] as well) proves her capacity for self-reliance and self-defense, but has she simply switched roles in the ongoing patriarchal drama? Several essays in this collection make clear the important cultural/sexual issues at stake in the horror film's choice of victims and elaborate on the complex issues involved in the genre's representation of violence and (and against) women.

Examining modern horror in terms of what I have called its exploration of violence is but one – albeit important – way of defining lines of continuity and areas of emphasis within the varied field of modern horror. We can, for example, construct a typology of the monstrous; after all, without the disequilibrium caused by the monster, there is no story to be told. No doubt it is true, as Rudolf Arnheim declared in 1949, that "the monster has become a portrait of ourselves and of the kind of life we have chosen to lead"[10] and that, in Frank McConnell's words, "each era chooses the monster it deserves and projects."[11] There is, however, no simple formula that can explain the many shapes the monster takes in recent horror—not all monsters are embodiments of our repressed fears and sexual desires or personifications of social ills or adolescent anxieties. Yet certain distinctions should be drawn between, for instance, the monster as willfully, irredeemably Evil (*The Exorcist, Halloween, Damien—Omen II* [1978], *Christine* [1983]) and the monster as somehow beyond or beneath good and evil (*Carrie, It Lives Again* [1978], *Of Unknown Origin* [1983]). Overlapping these categories is the distinction between the singular threat— Count Dracula, the shark in *Jaws,* the extraterrestrial being in *Alien,* the psychopathic killer in *Friday the 13th*—and the multiple threat—Romero's living dead, the Manson Family in *Helter Skelter* (1976), the ghostly avengers in *The Fog* (1980), the werewolf colony in *The Howling* (1981), and the corporate Machiavels in *The Stuff.* While it would run the risk of reducing the horror film to a wax museum or catalogue of creatures, a fully developed typology of monsters would offer a valuable means of delineating the paradigmatic possibilities open to this genre and the sort of fears that it feels will suitably trouble its audience.

Furthermore, since modern horror—like virtually all popular art—tends to run in sequels and cycles or sets of texts (call this the principle of exploitation or imitation or safe investment strategy), a necessary critical task is to chart the course of specific cycles or subgenres or formulae. Charles Derry offers a good starting point for this project when he divides horror of the 1960s through the 1980s into three categories, which he dubs the horror of personality, of demonic evil, and of Armageddon. Elsewhere I have taken a somewhat narrower approach, by examining the interaction between convention and innovation in the many vampire novels and films of the 1970s,[12] as has Vera Dika in her analysis of the cycle of stalker films from *Halloween* to *Hell Night* (1981). To write the history of modern horror we would need to place the stalker film and the modern vampire story in the context of other overlapping cycles and subgenres, including, for instance, films that come in the wake of *Frogs* (1972) and *Jaws,* which pit humankind against a threat from the natural world; stories of hauntings (*The Amityville Horror* [1979], *Poltergeist*) and possession (*The Possession of Joel Delaney* [1972], *Ruby* [1977], *Amityville II: The Possession* [1982]); ecological nightmares like *Prophecy* (1979) and *Humanoids from the Deep* (1980); and films of visionaries and dreamers from *Deadly Dream* (1971) to *The Sender* (1982) and *A Nightmare on Elm Street* (1984).

Since such subgenres find expression in novels as well as movies, one unquestionably important context for the contemporary horror film is mass-market horror fiction of the 1970s and 1980s. From *Rosemary's Baby* and *The Other* (1972) to the spate of adaptations of Stephen King novels in 1983 (*The Dead Zone, Cujo, Christine*) and 1984 (*Firestarter, Children of the Corn*), the major studios have approached horror principally as a matter of adapting best-sellers for the screen. (The countless paperback novelizations of films are of no intrinsic interest, though they surely attest to the popularity of horror in the 1970s and 1980s and to the interdependence of the entertainment industries.) Like horror fiction, the made-for-television horror movie also provides an important corollary and counterpoint to films released since the late 1960s, both because filmmakers like Steven Spielberg, John Carpenter, Wes Craven, and Tobe Hooper have all directed telefilms, and also, as I suggest in my essay in this collection, because horror takes a vastly different shape when it is tailored for prime-time network television. In addition, "subliterary" comic books and, in the 1980s, "subcinematic" rock music videos have served as host for as well as parasite of horror films.

Paying due attention to the subgenres and cycles within the horror film and to the intermedia relationships within the larger field of horror underscores the variety and adaptability as well as the continuity of modern horror. When we place horror within the broader continuum of popular culture, which is in a perpetual state of realignment and renovation, ideologically as well as formally, the boundaries demarcating this genre become hazy at best. Spurred by the demands of the marketplace, the interests of the audience, the cultural and political climate, and the contribution of the individual artist, popular genres mingle, influence each other, and evolve through a cumulative process of repetition and variation.[13] One result of this process is a film like *Mommie Dearest* (1981), a blend of family melodrama, investigative exposé, and old-fashioned "bio-pic" that derives a good deal of its imagery and its thematic preoccupations from the horror film. Or consider the case of *Prom Night* (1980) and *Terror Train* (1980), which were unambiguously advertised as horror movies in the manner of *Halloween* and *Friday the 13th*. Though they do feature psychopathic killers, both of these stalker films are structured very much like classical whodunits, complete with a plethora of mysterious clues and a cast of likely suspects. *Prom Night* and *Terror Train,* in turn, have their analogues in the many recent detective films, including *Sharky's Machine* (1981), *I, The Jury* (1982), *Endangered Species* (1982), and *Tightrope* (1984), which match the detective against a monstrous opponent who seems to be an interloper from the realm of horror. As Leo Braudy puts it, "Understanding the appeal of horror films these days is crucial to understanding films in general because the motifs and themes of the horror film have so permeated films of quite different sorts."[14]

Finally, to situate horror in the context of contemporary popular culture, we have to take into account not only questions of adaptation, imitation, and "permeation," but also the relationship between horror and the other popular movie genres of the 1970s and 1980s. For example, the rise of the modern horror film should be seen in relation to the decline of the disaster story and the early 1980s reemergence of the story of nuclear war, both of which — like horror — dramatize a sense of vulnerability and the capacity for survival. And the many horror films that picture teenagers as survivors and monsters, but preeminently as victims, find their doubles in *Porky's* (1981) and other R-rated comedies of sexual misadventures and adolescent highjinks. So, too, the highly traditional dream of heroic valor and selfless sacrifice in a universe of absolute values and transcendent Forces, a dream embodied in *Star Wars* (1977), *Raiders of the Lost Ark* (1981), and any number of fantasy adventure films and space operas, is answered and undercut in different ways by the many horror films like *It's Alive* and *Dawn of the Dead* that refuse to present us with situations in which moral, political, and spiritual distinctions are perfectly clear. And as Vivian Sobchack so effectively proves, the many horror films since *Rosemary's Baby* that focus on the child and the family are best read as companion pieces to family melodramas like *Ordinary People* (1980) and science fiction films from *Close Encounters of the Third Kind* (1977) to *Starman* (1984). Taking the horror film as our guide we can and should begin to rethink the nature of "influence" and "imitation" and the meaning of "genre" and "formula" in contemporary popular culture — in so doing we will inevitably rethink our own understanding of horror as well.

Beginning, appropriately enough, with studies of *Night of the Living Dead* and *Rosemary's Baby,* the essays in this book reveal a good deal about the range and the significance of modern horror. These are by no means the only worthwhile considerations of the genre published in the past fifteen years. (See the annotated bibliography for an overview of criticism written about the genre since 1968.) And there are films (*Alien, The Shining*), directors (Cohen, Craven), and issues (the aesthetics of the sequel, the transformation of the genre between 1968–78) that merit more than the passing glances they receive in this collection. Much remains to be written, for horror poses questions and triggers anxieties that demand a response, intellectually as well as emotionally. Having attracted the attention of critics and general audiences alike, individual films such as *The Exorcist* and *Halloween* and the larger, evolving text that is the horror film will, I think, continue to teach us about the narrative art of the movies, the processes of popular culture, the workings of the motion-picture industry, and the peculiar pleasures we seek from entertainment.

While modern horror can be understood as but the latest manifestation of broad-based, post-Romantic archetypes and psychosexual myths (Twitchell in *Dreadful Pleasures* makes the best case for such a reading), it is at least equally important to keep in mind that the horror film has engaged in a sort of extended dramatization of and response to the major public events and newsworthy topics in American history since 1968: fluctuations in "key economic indicators" and attempts to redirect domestic and foreign policy; Watergate and the slow withdrawal from Vietnam; oil shortages and the Iranian hostage crisis; the rise of the New Right and the Moral Majority; and the continuing debate over abortion, military spending, and women's rights. Further, contemporary horror can and has been interpreted as an index to and commentary on what have often been identified as the more general cultural conditions of our age: its "crisis of bourgeois patriarchy," to borrow Sobchack's phrase; its narcissism, postmodernism, and sense of the apocalyptic; and its attitude toward technology, death, and childhood.

As much as any branch of contemporary popular art, modern horror mirrors our changing fashions and tastes, our shifting fears and aspirations, and our sense of what constitutes the prime moral, social, and political problems facing us individually and collectively. But "mirrors" is too limited a concept, for just as horror can run the gamut from the reactionary to the radical, so it can alternately underscore, challenge, oversimplify, cloud, and explain the facts, styles, and contradictions of American culture. If nothing else, this genre is ambitious—not least of all because, in Kawin's words, horror films "represent a unique juncture of personal, social, and mythic structure."[15] Horror defines and redefines, clarifies and obscures the relationship between the human and the monstrous, the normal and the aberrant, the sane and the mad, the natural and the supernatural, the conscious and the unconscious, the daydream and the nightmare, the civilized and the primitive—slippery categories and tenuous oppositions indeed, but the very oppositions and categories that are so essential to our sense of life.

NOTES

1. Noel Carroll, "Nightmare and the Horror Film: The Symbolic Biology of Fantastic Beings," *Film Quarterly* 34 (Spring 1981):16–25. See, among other works, James B. Twitchell, *Dreadful Pleasures: An Anatomy of Modern Horror* (New York: Oxford University Press, 1985).

2. See Robert E. Kapsis, "Dressed to Kill," *American Film* 7 (Mar. 1982):52–56. In this context, see also Martin Barker, ed., *The Video Nasties: Freedom and Censorship in the Media* (London: Pluto Press, 1984), a collection of essays on the debate in England over the video rental and sale of violent exploitation films like *I Spit on Your Grave*.

3. Twitchell, *Dreadful Pleasures,* 19.

4. Robin Wood, "An Introduction to the American Horror Film," in *American Nightmare: Essays on the Horror Film,* ed. Robin Wood and Richard Lippe (Toronto: Festival of Festivals, 1979), 14.

5. Dennis Giles, "Conditions of Pleasure in Horror Cinema," in *Planks of Reason: Essays on the Horror Film,* ed. Barry Keith Grant (Metuchen, N.J.: Scarecrow Press, 1984), 41.

6. Philip Brophy, "Horrality—The Textuality of Contemporary Horror Films," *Screen* 27 (1986):8–10.

7. Stephen Neale, *Genre* (London: British Film Institute, 1980), 21.

8. Morris Dickstein, "The Aesthetics of Fright," *American Film* 5 (Sept. 1980):33.

9. H. P. Lovecraft, *Supernatural Horror in Literature* (reprint ed., New York: Dover, 1973), 15.

10. Rudolf Arnheim, "A Note on Monsters," in *Toward a Psychology of Art* (Berkeley: University of California Press, 1972), 257.

11. Frank D. McConnell, *The Spoken Seen: Film and the Romantic Imagination* (Baltimore: Johns Hopkins University Press, 1975), 137.

12. See *The Living and the Undead: From Stoker's Dracula to Romero's Dawn of the Dead* (Urbana: University of Illinois Press, 1986).

13. For a sampling of contemporary speculations about genre in popular culture, see Neale, *Genre;* John G. Cawelti, *Adventure, Mystery, Romance: Formula Stories as Art and Popular Culture* (Chicago: University of Chicago Press, 1976); Thomas Schatz, *Hollywood Genres: Formulas, Filmmaking, and the Studio System* (New York: Random House, 1981); and Stanley Cavell, *Pursuits of Happiness: The Hollywood Comedy of Remarriage* (Cambridge, Mass.: Harvard University Press, 1981). Two recent works of literary criticism are also particularly noteworthy: Alastair Fowler, *Kinds of Literature: An Introduction to the Theory of Genres and Modes* (Cambridge, Mass.: Harvard University Press, 1982); and Adena Rosmarin, *The Power of Genre* (Minneapolis: University of Minnesota Press, 1985).

14. Leo Braudy, "Genre and the Resurrection of the Past," in *Shadows of the Magic Lamp: Fantasy and Science Fiction in Film* (Carbondale: Southern Illinois University Press, 1985), 10.

15. Bruce F. Kawin, "The Mummy's Pool," *Dreamworks* 1 (1981):292.

1

Night of the Living Dead: It's Not Like Just a Wind That's Passing Through

R. H. W. Dillard

This selection by R. H. W. Dillard was originally published as the centerpiece of the Film Journal's *special number on "The Art of the Horror Film" (2 [1973]), where it formed the final section of an essay that also dealt with Universal's* Frankenstein *and* The Wolf Man. *Dillard's discussion of* Night of the Living Dead *is one of the first—and is still among the most convincing—close readings of a horror film, and it is all the more noteworthy because George A. Romero's film has proven to be a seminal text in the development of modern horror. An examination of the "textual and structural elements" of* Night of the Living Dead, *Dillard suggests, will lead us to the film's "aesthetic identity" and "moral nature." His analysis of Romero's reliance on the ordinary, the sense of "human smallness and ineffectuality," and the undercutting of "most of the cherished values of our whole civilization" often reads like a preview of one course modern horror would take, via Romero, to films such as* The Texas Chain Saw Massacre, Last House on the Left, *and* Rabid.*

Dillard's other important contributions to the study of horror are "Even a Man Who Is Pure at Heart: Poetry and Danger in the Horror Film" (in Man and the Movies, *ed. W. R. Robinson) and* Horror Films. *A Professor of English and director of the creative writing program at Hollins College, Hollins, Virginia, Dillard is the author of four books of poetry (including* The Greeting: New & Selected Poems), *two novels (most recently,* The First Man on the Sun), *and a collection of short fiction (*Omniphobia).

Night of the Living Dead is in many ways a unique film. A low-budget ($125,000 to $150,000) production, the first feature-length film of a group of independent filmmakers in Pittsburgh, released on the drive-in circuit with no fanfare, it has managed to become a striking commercial success. Lines stretched around the block in so unlikely a city as Barcelona, and the *Wall Street Journal* reported that it was the top money-making film in all of Europe in the year of its release. In this country, it gained a large and committed audience and a rising critical reputation, so much so that the film department of the Museum of Modern Art invited George Romero to present it in a showing at the museum as part of a series devoted to the work of significant new directors.

The easiest explanation of the film's popular success would be to say that it has simply outdone all of its rivals in the lingering and gross detail of its scenes of violence and that its appeal has simply been to that basest of needs, the need for unrestrained violence. This is the explanation favored by the *Reader's Digest,* which ran an article denouncing the film for its bad influence on the minds of children, and *Variety,* where an early review of the film found that it "casts serious aspersions on the integrity of its makers, distrib Walter Reade, the film industry as a whole and exhibs who book the pic, as well as raising doubts about the future of the regional film movement and the moral health of filmgoers who cheerfully opt for unrelieved sadism."[1] And even the film's admirers were forced to admit that it is an example of "grainy Grand Guignol"[2] and that it possesses a "gluey, bottomless horror."[3] The film's horrific specifics are remarkably detailed — walking corpses fighting over and eating the intestines of the film's young lovers, a close-shot of one of them eating her hand, a child's stabbing of her mother on camera fourteen times or gnawing on her father's severed arm, to say nothing of the countless re-killings of the living dead, the bashing in of their skulls. One of the film's backers was reputedly a butcher, and its footage shows much evidence of his enthusiastic support.

Certainly the film's open-eyed detailing of human taboos, murder, and cannibalism has had much to do with its success. What girl has not, at one time or another, wished to kill her mother? And Karen, in this film, offers a particularly vivid opportunity to commit the forbidden deed vicariously. But the film takes the source of its horrors from another desire and a fear that lies certainly as deep in the human consciousness, if not deeper. This is a fear of the dead and particularly of the known dead, of dead kindred. Anthony Masters reports on some of the primitive ritual involving that fear in his study of the vampire: it was always absolutely essential to speed the spirit on its way once death had taken place. At all costs the late departed must join the family's ancestors without delay. Should there be a delay the spirit would take offense, would hover malignantly around and when it did reach its eventual destination would have singled out defaulting members of the family for retribution. Precautions for the spirit's escape include the opening of windows and doors, the putting out of the fire in the hearth (in case the spirit doggedly refused conventional exits and insisted on the chimney), and keeping careful watch on the corpse.[4]

The film is almost a reenactment of these rituals in reverse. The unburied recent dead stalk the landscape seeking the flesh of the living, and the only defense against them is the shutting of doors and windows and the use of fire as a barricade. All traditional methods of handling the fact of death fail: as Doctor Grimes puts it in the film, "The bereaved will have to forego the dubious consolation that a funeral service can give." The ancient fear is unleashed on the characters in the film and on the audience with a force that only savage violence can repel. The movie thrusts its audience into a situation of primordial fear and offers them neither rational nor religious relief. The apparently universal human ability to find pleasure in an artistic rehearsing of its worst fears is certainly at the heart of the film's popular success, and the film's unrelenting avoidance of all traditional ways of handling the fear it has called up must be at much of the heart of its critical success.

But the question of what the film really *is,* of its aesthetic identity, is poorly served by either of these answers. It is not simply a film that is more frightening (or disgusting) than its competition, because it has an impact that other films with just as much gore do not have, and that impact must be found in the film's successful expression of a fear even deeper than the overt fear of the dead. And its admiring critics have not managed to explain just what the film does *do* even as it rejects the traditional approaches to its themes and subject matter. Elliott Stein sees the film's horror and violence as an exaggeration in kind of that in *Patton,* and he goes on to equate both the living dead and the posse that hunts them down, "all of them so horrifying, so convincing, who mow down, defoliate and gobble up everything in their path," with "ordinary people, in all the trance-like security of their 'silent majority.' " In other words, he explains the film, as his use of *defoliate* is intended to indicate, in terms of the familiar political rhetoric of the later 1960s and thereby sells the film short. Joseph Lewis takes much the same position when he describes the film's impact as "cathartic for us, who forget about the horrors around us which aren't, alas, movies," and goes on to say that Lyndon B. Johnson might never "have permitted the napalming of the Vietnamese" had he seen *Night of the Living Dead.*[5] But the horror of war and a disapproval and fear of the American middle class do not, for all their being related to the central fear and horror of the film, explain it adequately. For if that were the case, a newsreel, on the one hand, and Nathanael West's *The Day of the Locust,* on the other, would be aesthetic equivalents of *Night of the Living Dead,* and they simply are not.

Richard McGuinness avoids the stock political response in his review of the film in *The Village Voice,* and he comes much closer to the film's real values when he praises its "crudely accomplished but spontaneous effect," its "manic overacting," the plot that "is unrestrained and incorrigibly kills all the characters in what, near the end, becomes an avalanche of atrocities," and the fatally attacked Helen's "shrieking inertia" that "happens simply because . . . things are so demonstrably bad, life is no longer desirable." He stops short, however, and turns from the film's unique qualities to praise it for its narrative technique: "These fervently acted out, numerous unpremeditated cruelties in the midst of situations already at an intolerable level resemble the comic building in silent movies; and [*Night of the Living Dead*] by its daring crudeness and while scaring the pants off the audience, rediscovers the silent art of story-telling."

Before these strands of McGuinness's reading of the film can be pressed convincingly on to their proper conclusion, an examination of *Night of the Living Dead*'s textural and structural elements is in order. Although it is a film radically different in kind from either *Frankenstein* or *The Wolf Man,* it is as thoroughly and carefully composed, and the nature of its composition is the key to its thematic and aesthetic values, to its moral nature.

The essential quality of the film's setting and of its characters is their ordinary nature. The graveyard in the film's opening scenes and the house where the rest of the film takes place offer an immediate and telling contrast with *Frankenstein, The Wolf Man,* and almost all of the American horror films of the 1930s and 1940s. Even the cheap horror films of the 1950s (*I Was a Teenage Werewolf, I Was a Teenage Frankenstein, Frankenstein's Daughter*), with all their insistence upon the everyday availability of their horrors, have a slick, adolescent, greasy glamour that seems flashy and fantastic compared with the dully commonplace settings of *Night of the Living Dead*. The graveyard is no neo-expressionistic set like that of *Frankenstein* with a painted sky and lighting that comments on the scene even as it functions within it; it is a small Pennsylvania country graveyard, flatly lit and unretouched. (I recently ran across a viewer who had the added horror of seeing one of the living dead lurch across his mother's grave.) And the house is an ordinary frame farmhouse, no book-filled castle overlooking the perpetually befogged forest of Lawrence Talbot's mind.

The night of the living dead is a Sunday night, the first after the time change in the autumn. The season, with its overtones of dying away and approaching winter cold, is symbolically significant, as is the Sunday, which emphasizes the failure of religion in a secular age. Johnny, the first victim of the living dead in the film, admits to his sister, Barbara, that "there's not much sense in my going to church," and the film offers no evidence to contradict him. Beyond these rudimentary symbolic uses of the setting, there is no further use of the landscape except in its ordinariness. Its bleak emptiness suggests the frailty and the hopelessness of the characters' situations, but is no desert or polar ice-cap—just ordinary, familiar western Pennsylvania countryside.

The farmhouse has its symbolic uses, too, but they are minimal. There are in one of its rooms several mounted animal heads, innocent enough in themselves, but that do take on certain symbolic overtones in the context of the equally dead but moving human figures around the house and the posse with its hunting rifles. But Romero's only functional use of these heads is for a cheap shock (one of the very few in the film that isn't genuinely integral to its narrative flow) when Barbara first enters the house. There is also a small music box with revolving mirrors that sounds, for one brief, lyrically photographed scene, a sad little note of beauty and sanity in a context of madness. But that scene, too, is actually out of place tonally in the film, despite the hollow loveliness of the tune and the pathetic fragility of the tiny instrument, its turning mirrors reflecting only themselves. The rest of the house is symbolic only in its functional uses. Its simple, daily, practical nature is transformed by necessity into that of a fortress, a last barrier against the forces of destruction, and the ease with which it gives itself to that transformation offers some symbolic comment on its always having been such a fortress even in its peaceful past. The cellar also gains a symbolic quality from its structural use in the film's narrative. But, otherwise, the house is a house—ordinary and real, practically unchanged by the filmmakers, symbolizing and meaning only itself.

Even the specific tonal quality of the image is ordinary. Elliott Stein says that "Romero was offered a budget for colour; he preferred shooting in black and white; the result is a flat murky ambience which is perfect for the ramshackle American gothic landscape where the events occur." Save for some echoes early in the film of the Gothic angles of James Whale's *Bride of Frankenstein,* the photography calls attention to itself, appropriately like the setting, only in its ordinariness. This ordinary quality is no confession on Romero's part of inadequacies of budget or of ability. He has chosen a photographic style to suit his setting, and he has chosen a setting essential to his thematic concerns.

The characters (the living characters) are just as ordinary. Stein is correct, whatever his reasons, in identifying these people with the American middle class, the "silent majority." A sociologist might worry about classifying some of them higher or lower, but they are indisputably ordinary people. There is no scientist here dreaming of the great ray, nor any wise gypsy ministering to spiritual hurt, no barons or knights. The scene is American, and the characters are democratically ordinary and American. Perhaps the only unusual thing about them is that no one of them ever comments about one of their numbers being black, especially in the light of his assuming a natural leadership. But even that lack of race prejudice in a tight situation may be more ordinarily American than we might suspect.

Barbara and Johnny, the first characters to appear in the film, are two ordinary young people on their way to place a wreath on their father's grave, unconsciously acting out an ancient ritual of ancestor worship and also of propitiation to the fearful dead. Barbara takes it seriously, but Johnny does not. He is a very modern and urban young man. When she suggests that they might say a prayer, he says, "Praying's for church, huh?" When he notices her uneasiness in the increasingly dusky cemetery, he frightens her — "They're coming for you Barbara" — his voice an imitation of Boris Karloff's familiar horror film tones. There is nothing particularly cruel or unusual in his behavior; he has always tried to frighten Barbara, and he remembers how their grandfather had warned him that he would be "damn't to hell" for doing it. He is not a particularly sensitive or pleasant fellow, but when the first living deadman appears, he struggles with him manfully and gives his life to save his sister. Barbara manages to escape, but when she reaches the house and accepts the protection of Ben, she retreats further into a state of shocked unawareness, into an amniotic inner self. Both of them are ordinary, "realistic" people, and they both respond in normal ways — Johnny mocks his sister but gives his life for her, and Barbara finds the strength to escape a danger, but her strength gives out abruptly and naturally when she finds some semblance of sanctuary.

The other characters who congregate in the besieged house are as familiar and as ordinary. Ben, the black "hero" of the film, is a working man. He is good with his hands, and it is he who turns the house into a fortress. He is also the most articulate and, to all appearances, the most intelligent of the people in the house; his long speech, which is the first indication of the scope of what is happening and which he delivers as he works purposefully to shore up the house's natural defenses, establishes him as a man who is fully capable of active thought and rational action. But, again, his heroic potential is shown in an ordinary context; he is just an intelligent and vital man caught in bad circumstances, trying to do what he can about it.

The Cooper family, Harry, Helen, and their daughter, Karen, are even more familiar. Far from heroic, Harry Cooper is nevertheless a strong man, but one whose strength expresses itself in abrasive opinion and nearly hysterical action. His response to the situation is to hide in the cellar and wait until the problem goes away by itself or is handled by someone else. His selfish certainty gives him a strength almost equal to Ben's rational activism, and their clash, ideological and personal, gives the center of the film its tension. Helen is an intelligent but bitter woman. Her marriage is a burden to her, and she appears to endure it only for the sake of her daughter. Her desire to save the child gives her the strength to use her bitterness as a weapon against her husband. "We may not enjoy living together," she tells him at one point, "but dying together isn't going to solve anything." The child is ill, having been bitten by one of the living dead, but seems otherwise to be a reasonably normal child. They are, in brief, a relatively typical modern family, if we are to believe the divorce statistics, living only by negative values, bitter and abrasive toward each other and others, separated from hysteria and violence only by a thin veneer of social necessity.

The two other characters in the house would have been the romantic hero and heroine if this had been a 1950s teenage horror film. Tom and Judy are a young couple, not yet married but very much in love. They are a simple pair, lacking the forcefulness of either Ben or Harry, but they do offer a contrast to the Coopers' failed marriage. "You always have a smile for me," Tom tells Judy, and her loyalty to him is strong enough to impel her to risk danger with him when he and Ben try to gas up the truck for an escape. They are, almost embarrassingly, typical teenage lovers — not very intelligent but genuinely in love.

The sheriff is a grotesque figure, but he and his posse are at least typical of a modern American image of what they should be, if they are somewhat exaggerated for the real thing. The posse is composed of residents of the area where the film was being shot, and they have all the authenticity of a newsreel. To add to that authenticity, the newscaster covering the posse's activity is simply playing himself — Bill "Chilly Billy" Caudill, a Pittsburgh television newscaster and host of a late night horror film show. In fact, the only two professional actors in the whole film are Duane Jones (Ben) and Judith O'Dea (Barbara). Both co-producers play roles (Russell Streiner as Johnny and Karl Hardman as Harry), but neither of them is a professional actor. The film is, then, the story of everyday people in an ordinary landscape, played by everyday people who are, for the most part, from that ordinary locale. The way in which *Night of the Living Dead* transforms that familiar and ordinary world into a landscape of unrelenting horror reveals the film's moral nature and the deep and terrible fear that is at its heart.

The living dead themselves are the active and catalytic agency for the release of all of the film's horrors. The idea of the dead's return to a kind of life and their assault on the living is no new idea; it is present in all the ancient tales of vampires and ghouls and zombies, and it has been no stranger to films. *Night of the Living Dead* derives from those countless tales and films, and, as Calvin T. Beck points out, it shares very striking similarities with two films in particular — *The Last Man on Earth* and *Invisible Invaders.*[6] All of these tales and films spring from that ancient fear of the dead, and that fear is the first upon which *Night of the Living Dead* touches.

The scene in the graveyard is based purely on the fear the living have of the dead. A certain amount of graveyard fear does spring from its forceful reminder of the universality and inevitability of human death, but a literal fear of the dead themselves does still exist in the most placid of human hearts. Johnny frightens Barbara with that fear, and it is the fear that the audience feels throughout that scene and up to the point where Ben kills the living deadman in the house. The effectiveness of the dead woman at the top of the stairs depends upon that fear. But after Ben shows that the dead can be killed again, the fear of the dead begins to lose power. The dead, unlike death itself, can be stopped and become a more ordinary horror, one to which there can be a practical response.

When the information about the living dead begins to be available, by direct experience and the radio and television news reports, the ancient fear of the dead is dispelled almost totally. The living dead are revealed to be neither supernatural in origin nor impelled by ideas of revenge upon the living. Triggered by radiation brought to earth accidentally by a Venus probe, the recently dead have arisen and attacked the living for no motive whatsoever other than a blind need for food. They have no identities and are really no different from any other natural disaster; Tom specifically compares them to a flood, and he is right. They are, as Doctor Grimes puts it, "dangerous," but they are "just dead flesh." Once their individuality is denied, they become no less dangerous, but they do lose that initial aura of ancient fear. They become, in a word, ordinary. "Beat 'em or burn 'em," the sheriff says, "they go up pretty easy." And he expresses the loss of that aura of fear most fully when he says, "Yeah, they're dead; they're all messed up."

As the traditional fear of the dead loses its force in the film, it is replaced by another fear, one less easily defined and far more difficult to overcome once it has been established. The dead characters in the film, like the living ones, are very ordinary people — distorted by death and the artificial life in them, but still recognizably ordinary. Some of them are fully dressed; one of them is rather fat and dressed only in jockey shorts; one of them, a young woman, is naked. They look vulnerable, and they are vulnerable, to a blow to the head and to fire. As their danger becomes more ordinary in the film, the other fear reveals itself. The living people are dangerous to each other, both because they are potentially living dead should they die and because they are human with all of the ordinary human failings. Ben kills Harry because his cowardice has risked Ben's life, and the clash of egos between Ben and Harry endangers the lives of all the others throughout the film. But even more frightening than that familiar danger is yet another one — the danger of the whole ordinary world itself.

Tom and Judy die because they courageously dare to try to make the truck an instrument of escape, but they die also because Judy gets caught in the truck, and, as Tom tries to free her, the truck explodes. They die, in other words, because accidents do happen and because gas does explode when touched by fire. The living dead die again because the ordinary world may be turned into such an effective weapon. An innocent farmhouse becomes a quite formidable engine of war. Not only do knives and guns exercise a dangerous role in the film, but gasoline and old bottles and rags do as well, as do table legs and hammers, a garden trowel, and even a stuffed chair used as a flaming torch. Either by the action of accident or by that of human purposiveness, the ordinary, everyday world may become dangerous and deadly. Barbara jumps in fright when she sees the stuffed animal heads, and then she and the audience relax as they realize there is no danger in these inanimate things. But by the end of the film, not only have all of the human beings in it become dangerous to each other, but the familiar household objects around them have become as dangerous. The traditional fear of the dead sensitizes the audience to fear at the beginning of the film, but by its end, that audience has been exposed to a much deeper and more powerful fear — the fear of life itself.

Night of the Living Dead establishes the fear of the ordinary and of life itself with great skill, but even that does not give the film its special quality. For, after all, that fear has been expressed and examined and resolved countless times before. It is Søren Kierkegaard's sickness unto death or Edgar Allan Poe's fever called living or Jean-Paul Sartre's nausea pressed to its extreme; ways, both religious and secular, have been devised for its cure, and much of the greatest art of our culture has been an expression of that fear and of its vital resolution. The essential nature of *Night of the Living Dead* may be found in the way it resolves that fear which it has called up, in the textural and structural mode of the resolution — which proves to be finally less a resolution than a surrender to (and even a celebration of) the fear itself.

The film is primarily one of ceaseless and unremitting struggle, a struggle for survival. Its structural design is one of closing in; its plot is built upon that design, and its texture fills out that narrative and structural form.

The plot is really a simple one. Because of an accidental introduction of harmful radiation into the earth's atmosphere, the recent and unburied dead become activated into a semblance of life (albeit unconscious and unindividuated), and they attack the living for food. A group of people (three men, three women, and a child) seek shelter in an isolated farmhouse. There they struggle for their lives. Some of them respond to the challenge rationally and bravely. One of them responds with hysteria and cowardice. One retreats from the fight into a state of shock. All of them are killed, either by the living dead or by each other, except for one; he is killed by the posse who assume him to be one of the living dead. Within that simple plot line, the characters exhibit traditional virtues and vices, but the good and the bad, the innocent and the guilty, all suffer the same fate: they all lose. In fact, those virtues that have been the mainstay of our civilized history seem to lead to defeat in this film even more surely than the traditional vices. Helen Cooper dies because her mother's love for her daughter renders her incapable of defending herself against the child's ghoulish attack. Tom and Judy die because they have the courage to try to help the whole group escape and because they love each other. Barbara dies because she snaps out of her moral lethargy and goes to the aid of Helen Cooper at the door; there she sees her brother, Johnny, now one of the living dead, and is carried away to her death by him. Ben, whose strength and reason keep the group functioning as long as possible, sees all of his ideas fail and prove destructive, finds himself driven by rage to kill one of his fellow living men, and ends by retreating into the very cellar that his reason had earlier branded "a death trap." His death at the hands of the posse is only the final blow of a long series that have been slowly draining the life from him throughout the film.

The plot is, then, one of simple negation, an orchestrated descent to death in which all efforts toward life fail. The texture of the film fills out that negative narrative form. Stein has pointed out how the film is "a symphony of psychotic hands—the house is surrounded by endless rows of ghastly grasping insatiable claws which poke through boarded windows and seize victims whose own hands are munched like hand-burghers." The hand, that most active and productive physical extension of the human mind, is rendered perversely in this film; its values are inverted. At first, Ben is given to the viewer very much in terms of his hands—he rebuilds the house with them, he strikes Barbara to end her hysteria with his hand, he drags the body of the old lady away with his hands, he kills the first of the living dead to enter the house by hand, he covers Barbara's feet with shoes he has found for her (shielding their vulnerable bareness and offering her at least the appearance of the normal, of rational control). But as the film progresses, the futility of his manual efforts becomes increasingly apparent; the hand loses practical and symbolic power. His slapping of Barbara snaps her out of her hysteria but into a near coma. He is forced to turn to the rifle rather than the hand as the emblem of his power and the extension of his will. When the first ghoul's hand bursts through his handiwork (the boarded window), it signals the beginning of the end, the descent into Stein's "symphony of psychotic hands," the inexorable movement away from reason and value into mindless terror and loss of meaning. The eating of Judy's hand marks the final defeat of the hand as an effective emblem of rational and moral behavior.

The structural system of closing in is formed of three elements. The simplest of these is the visually textural and traditionally symbolic use of light. The film's movement is a traditional one in Western narrative and especially in horror films; it moves from waning daylight through a night of horror to a new dawn — the familiar structure of "Night on Bald Mountain," or, for that matter, St. John of the Cross's dark night of the soul. But *Night of the Living Dead* transforms that pattern by imposing fire into it. The movement from daylight into night is clear enough; dusk and the first of the living dead arrive at the same time. Electric light and fire cooperate during the early part of the night as tools of the human struggle for survival, but the electric light finally fails, and the fire takes on a dangerous force out of human control. Tom and Judy die by fire, and, by the light of the new day, Ben's body is thrown finally on a pyre and burned.

The geographical structure of the film is, like *Frankenstein,* vertical, but with a radical simplicity completely different from that film's structural ambiguity and complexity. The movement of the film is down and in. It opens on a car climbing a hill to a cemetery in the daylight. As the light fails and the living dead appear, it moves downhill with Barbara as she flees to the house. There, in the surrounded house, Ben fights against a further descent and for traditional human values. When Harry Cooper insists that "the cellar is the strongest place," Ben replies that "the cellar is a death trap." "You can be boss down there," he continues, "I'm boss up here." But Ben's conviction that "they can't get in here" depends upon strict communal cooperation, and when that cooperation fails, Ben himself descends into the cellar where he is ironically as safe as Cooper insisted he would be. But he descends even deeper than the cellar; he descends into the neurotic depths of himself, into a dark and primitive past without reason or light, only fear and hopelessness. After killing Harry Cooper once again (this time as one of the living dead, trying to rise again with the bloody stump of his arm waving feebly in the air — a grotesque parody of the promise of Christian resurrection), Ben, the articulate man, becomes completely silent; he upsets a table, turns around the room moving things aimlessly, and finally crouches with his gun in the dark corner of the cellar — hopelessly and permanently gone to earth.

There is, of course, a final ascent for Ben, but it is no more a counter-action of the descending structure of the film than is the dawn's light an effective counter to the fire's power. He climbs upstairs, still silent, his gun at the ready, and stares blankly at the posse crossing the field. But he is not the Ben who struggled so bravely through the night; that Ben was lost forever in the lightless cellar. His ascent ends only in his death, and the sheriff is symbolically accurate when he defines Ben simply as "that's another one for the fire." He has lost even the struggle for simple identity that Lawrence Talbot at least won by his death. Ben is carried with his head hanging down to the makeshift funeral pyre and burned, and this marks the end of his personal physical descent from a man on his feet throughout most of the film to the crouching figure of fear in the cellar to this limp and lifeless sprawl in the flames.

The third parallel structural element is the film's editing. Romero, who also cut the film, did not make George Waggner's mistake of underestimating the positive force of the moving medium of cinema. The editing throughout is fully supportive and expressive of the film's thematic, textural, and structural design. The film opens with a long shot of the car moving through the Pennsylvania countryside, a lyrical shot were it not for the bareness of the black and white image. The cutting is simple and conventional, even during the struggle with and flight from the first of the living dead, although the use of the neo-Whale angles begins to appear. After the shock cuts when Barbara enters the house and starts at the animal heads, the film moves into its longest speech (Ben's account of his experiences), which Romero keeps alive by supporting Ben's articulate account with a smoothly and rationally edited sequence of shots of Ben using his hands (and head, figuratively) to barricade the house. After the discovery of the Coopers, Judy, and Tom in the cellar, the film's cutting becomes increasingly nervous and agitated, easing off occasionally but never losing its increasing speed. After the deaths of Tom and Judy, the film's pacing becomes as frenetic as its action, subsiding only as Ben retreats into the cellar as the living dead stumble aimlessly about overhead.

The coming of dawn and the posse is handled very smoothly and simply; the editing supports the symbolic use of the dawn light—both indicate the reestablishment of human and rational order in the chaotic situation. But Romero undercuts the steady motion of the film just as he does the light. After Ben's death, he abruptly shatters the film's smooth forward motion. The account of the burning of Ben is composed of very grainy still shots with high-level voice overs, connected still to the narrative flow, but disjointedly and in fragments. After shattering the naturally vital force of the medium with these devices, Romero moves one step further, perverting its motion by forcing it to serve the negative symbolic force of the fire. The film moves one last time out of those grainy stills into clarity and motion, but that last moving image in the film is of the fire, devouring the hero's body and imposing its destructive light on the living light of the day.

Richard McGuinness suggests that "studded throughout the comic book dread and brought to its service are many situational motifs from Hitchcock movies and several bits of well-integrated Hitchcock technique." But he adds that "the Hitchcock aspects are shorn of their evasive, level-hopping, metaphysic-implying obfuscations and work simply to increase dread." Romero does use Hitchcock's devices "simply to increase dread," but that use itself expresses a metaphysical position. Despite its similarities to *The Last Man on Earth* and *Invisible Invaders,* the artistic antecedent for *Night of the Living Dead* is most clearly Hitchcock's *The Birds.* In both films, a group of people are besieged by an apparently harmless and ordinary world gone berserk, struggle to defend themselves against the danger, and struggle to maintain their rationality and their values at the same time. The similarities are interesting, but the differences are more revealing.

Hitchcock's colorful and highly artificial (in the fullest artistic sense) film is a parable of human existence in the face of a dangerous and, more important, inexplicable and mysterious world. In it, the characters are saved from that menace because of their rational efforts, but also because the world stops trying to kill them for the moment. Romero's consciously real and ordinary world is just as dangerous, but it is neither inexplicable nor mysterious. Its menace has a rational explanation (the radiation) that Hitchcock's birds do not, and its characters die because they are inhabitants of a world of blind and deadly chance. This world of chance may be meaningless, but its meaninglessness is its own explanation. The end of *The Birds* opens out (as does the last shot) to a sunlit world that is dangerous and inexplicable, but at the same time beautiful and awesome; *Night of the Living Dead* closes in to death and fire, both rendered in black and white, both implying a finality that is neither beautiful nor awesome, but merely ugly and cheap.

Even if Hitchcock had closed his film differently and used the static and closed shot, which he claims to have "toyed with" (a shot of the principal characters' arrival in San Francisco, the scene of safety, "lap-dissolving on them in the car, looking, and there is the Golden Gate Bridge — covered in birds"),[7] *The Birds* would still have been radically different from *Night of the Living Dead,* because its values would still have been ongoing. Its central characters develop and change for the better in its course; they maintain their values to the end, as exemplified by the young girl's taking of the love birds with her; they grow within themselves and in relation to each other. And the audience would still have been left, not with a fear of the ordinary and of life, but with a fearful sense of its largeness and its unfathomable mystery. Hitchcock's rich and positive use of the medium and all of its artifices simply would not have produced the ending and the values of *Night of the Living Dead.*

Romero's film is much closer to the nihilistic strain in the films of Roman Polanski; its ending repeats in its own terms and in dead seriousness the comically anarchistic ending of *The Fearless Vampire Killers,* and Ivan Butler's description of the horrific aspects of *Rosemary's Baby* (a film of which Polanski himself does not approve) could well be applied to *Night of the Living Dead:* "the menace of the everyday, above all the hidden, deeprooted fears in all of us, the unfaced awful possibilities we all 'know' could become reality — the nerve-ends themselves are touched with a cold finger"[8] But in fact, *Rosemary's Baby,* in which the devil is born into the world incarnate, has more magnitude and possibility than *Night of the Living Dead.* It at least expresses a belief in and a sense of something powerfully larger than a meaningless world of chance, even if that something is the embodiment of supernatural evil; the existence of Satan does imply the existence of God, and the tawdry silliness of the devil's disciples, despite their immediate success, does offer at least the hope of further opposition to evil. *Night of the Living Dead,* however, expresses only human smallness and ineffectuality. The posse at the end, with its lack of feeling ("Somebody's had a cookout here, Vince," the sheriff says when he finds the burned out truck in which Tom and Judy died) — that posse and its random killing of Ben diminish life and all of human possibility and value as much as the birth of Satan's son and more than any of the trick reverse endings of the new wave of horror films (*House of Dark Shadows, The Return of Count Yorga, The Velvet Vampire*), because it reduces life and its values to a nearly absolute minimum.

The real horror of *Night of the Living Dead* is not, then, a result of its inspiring a fear of the dead or even a fear of the ordinary world. It lies rather in its refusal to resolve those fears in any way that does not sacrifice human dignity and human value. The deaths in the film are all to no purpose; they do not finally serve the practical cause of survival, nor do they act to the enhancement of larger human value. When someone dies, his values die with him. The audience may feel at the film's end a certain sympathy for Ben, because of his attempts to maintain his values, but that sympathy lingers from the audience's preconceptions and not from the film proper. Ben loses his moral struggle as well as his practical one for survival; he surrenders to the darkness in himself and to that around him. Unlike Lawrence Talbot, he has no silver cane to pass on, for he has no values left.

The film as a whole undercuts most of the cherished values of our whole civilization, what William Faulkner called "the eternal verities." It ridicules government in the scenes in Washington, which seem to be left over from a Marx brothers movie, but more seriously it casts the whole rule of law into doubt with the territorial disputes inside the house and their final resolution in violence with the death of Harry Cooper. Courage is shown throughout to lead only to death. The idea of the family is perhaps more harshly assaulted than any other in the film. The Coopers snarl at each other, and their daughter finally kills her mother and partially devours her father. Family ties actually become dangerous in the film — Helen does not even try to save herself from her daughter because the idea of familial love was so deeply ingrained in her, and Barbara allows herself to be taken out by Johnny and the other ghouls because of the same idea and the shock of having it shattered. Love itself comes to nothing but a fiery end, as Tom and Judy's experience shows. Even the value of individual identity collapses as it reveals itself to be weak in the face of disaster, even weaker in one respect than the body, which is able to walk on without the guidance of individual consciousness.

Reason itself is negated, the traditional quality that separates man from the rest of nature. "Kill the brain," the television announcers advise, "and you kill the ghoul." The head becomes the primary target of violence in the film — for your own protection, kill the brain! McGuinness comes closest to realizing the full implications of the film when he describes the acting in it: "The actors' frenzies (of panicked flailing running, arduous pushing, fiendish clutching) are of an enthusiasm rarely seen in films but here look simply like reasonable responses to the circumstances." This frenzy does come to be the only reasonable act in the film, and at the end, with all brains killed among the central characters, only violence and the fire remain.

"It's not like just a wind that's passing through," Tom tells Judy before they go out to the truck. "We've got to do something fast." It is not just a wind that's passing through; it is the ordinary world revealed for what it dangerously is. And the real horror of *Night of the Living Dead* is that there is nothing we can do that will make any difference at all. Whether that horror is the result of a cynicism with an eye to commercial gain or (as Lewis suggests) a deliberate put-on or a genuine nihilistic vision, its depth and the thoroughness of its unrelenting expression make the film what it is. It is in the bad, Wallace Stevens suggested, that "we reach / The last purity of the good." *Night of the Living Dead* presents the bad with great force, but what good we reach in it is small and frail indeed.

NOTES

1. As quoted in Elliott Stein, "The Night of the Living Dead," *Sight and Sound* 38 (Spring 1970):105.

2. Ibid. Hereafter all references to Stein are to the same article and the same page and will be clear in the text.

3. Richard McGuinness, "Film: The Night of the Living Dead," *The Village Voice,* Dec. 25, 1969, 54. Hereafter all references to McGuinness are to this article and the same page and will be clear in the text.

4. Anthony Masters, *The Natural History of the Vampire* (New York: Putnam, 1972), 12. Many of these rituals are still performed in the mountains of western Virginia, and Masters might well have added the covering of mirrors so that the spirit will not see its terrible condition.

5. Joseph Lewis, "A Bloody Laugh," *The Point,* Feb. 26, 1970, 14. Hereafter all references to Lewis will be to this article and this page and will be clear in the text.

6. Calvin T. Beck, "Night of the Living Dead," *Castle of Frankenstein* 5 (1972):30.

7. As quoted in Peter Bogdanovich, *The Cinema of Alfred Hitchcock* (New York: Museum of Modern Art Film Library, 1963), 44.

8. Ivan Butler, *Horror in the Cinema* (New York: Warner Books, 1970), 218-29.

2

The Trauma of Infancy in Roman Polanski's *Rosemary's Baby*

Virginia Wright Wexman

Drawing on material included in her 1985 book, Roman Polanski, *Virginia Wright Wexman situates* Rosemary's Baby *in the context of Polanski's career, particularly his other horror films, which take as their principal concern not simply the "other"—a time-honored motif in the genre—but "otherness" itself. Wexman argues that by presenting insanity, regression, physical alienation, and female sexual dis-ease against a realistic backdrop,* Rosemary's Baby *and Polanski's other horror films evoke the sort of ambiguity that Tzvetan Todorov finds to be characteristic of the "fantastic." Unlike Dillard, Wexman devotes considerable attention to the textual positioning of the film viewer and thus raises fundamental questions about our role in and response to horror films.*

Wexman teaches in the department of English at the University of Illinois at Chicago and is the editor of Cinema Journal.

Roman Polanski's career encompasses both high art and popular entertainment. While some of his films, such as *Knife in the Water, Cul-de-Sac,* and *What?,* grow out of the absurdist tradition of the modern Polish theater in which he grew up, others, like *Repulsion, Dance of the Vampires, Rosemary's Baby,* and *The Tenant,* are variations on the popular horror formula. While Polanski's absurdist projects represent, by and large, uncompromising modernist statements, his horror films have been created to appeal to a mass audience. *Repulsion* was conceived as a potboiler that could make financing available for *Cul-de Sac; Rosemary's Baby* represented a chance to conquer Hollywood by filming a best-selling novel. In a medium that involves vast sums of money, such strategies have insured Polanski's position as a good financial risk. But commercial films have also expanded the resources of his art. His most mature, accomplished efforts—*Macbeth, Chinatown,* and *Tess*—show an assured sense of the interactions between art and culture that Polanski gained while coming to terms with the issues posed by the popular conventions represented by making his horror films.

"I love the clichés," Polanski has said. "Practically every film I make starts with one. I just try to update them, give them an acceptable shape."[1] The way he "updates" clichés — typically by tearing them out of their expected context and turning them against his audience — implicitly forces us to confront the ways in which we use the institutions of popular genres to express and disguise the structures of power underlying social interaction.

"Among other things," Laura Mulvey has hypothesized, "the position of the spectators in cinema is blatantly one of repression of their exhibitionism and projection of the repressed desire onto the performer."[2] In horror stories, this process typically operates through the creation of a monstrous *other,* which, as Robin Wood has noted, represents "what is repressed (but never destroyed) in the self and projected outward in order to be hated and disowned."[3] Many such stories feature villains who are identified as social outsiders. Polanski's tales of terror complicate this dynamic by making their protagonists outsiders, people trying to make their way in alien worlds. In *Repulsion* Carol Ledoux is a Belgian, yet she lives in London; in *Dance of the Vampires* Alfred is a German visiting Transylvania for the first time; in *Rosemary's Baby* a young, newly married woman from the Midwest moves into a strange old New York City apartment building; in *The Tenant* Trelkovsky, a Pole, tries desperately to survive in the hostile surroundings of Paris. Such a focus on protagonists who are themselves "others" arouses complex reactions that mix sympathy with xenophobic contempt for people who do not conform to accepted social standards.

But if Polanski's horror films deal with outsiders *to* the worlds they portray, they are even more centrally concerned with the outsiders who invariably exist *within* these worlds: women. The presence of women in such stories raises cultural anxieties not only about social status but also about sexual identity.[4] Terrifying tales of female victimage have their roots in the Gothic fiction that flourished in later eighteenth-century Britain with works such as *The Castle of Otranto, The Monk,* and *The Mysteries of Udolpho.* Such tales continue today in the form of pulp novels by writers in the tradition of Daphne du Maurier and as popular movies such as *Halloween.* Most often, these stories have centered on "a shy, nervous, retiring heroine, who was nevertheless usually possessed of a remarkable ability to survive hideously dangerous situations."[5] No matter what happened, she never acted to direct events. Pursued by unspeakable horrors, she was the object of desire and reward.[6] The hero was likely to be a powerfully masculine figure who, nevertheless, succumbed to the heroine's charms, thereby allowing the plot to be harmoniously concluded with a marriage. Such a narrative pattern displaces, and ultimately denies, female sexuality by surreptitiously encoding "perceptions about the subjugation of women and the covert social purposes of marriage and marital fidelity."[7]

In Polanski's horror films, women often become subjects rather than objects; consequently, their own sexuality is much more at issue. Both Carol Ledoux and Rosemary Woodhouse are plagued by demons inextricably connected with their femininity, Carol by her beauty and desirability to men, Rosemary by her pregnancy. And though *Dance of the Vampires* and *The Tenant* feature male rather than female protagonists, their uncertain sense of gender identity becomes a major source of sexual conflict for them.

Unlike classic paradigms of the genre such as *Dracula* and *Frankenstein,* which usually take place in remote locales, Polanski's horror films (with the exception of *Dance of the Vampires,* which parodies the genre's traditional iconography) are set in modern urban environments. In contrast to the spare and bizarre locations of the modernist films, these settings include a wealth of plausible social and physical detail, which encourages us to see the protagonists' problems within a believable context.

The protagonists of Polanski's horror films are oppressed both by a bigoted society and by a malevolent nature. *Repulsion* depicts a sexually grotesque culture in scenes set in the beauty parlor where the heroine works and in the pub where her boyfriend passes the time. *The Tenant* perceives society in terms of sadomasochistic interactions between bullying French landlords and victimized foreign tenants. *Rosemary's Baby* uses its realistic mise-en-scène to suggest the ways in which an ordinary setting may gradually begin to appear menacing and portentous, even to an ostensibly normal heroine. Paradoxically, this increased emphasis on a realistic social and psychological environment allows Polanski to explore individual psychology more intensely and completely than he could in the abstracted settings of the modernist films.

By focusing in these films on a single, fully developed individual within a recognizable setting, Polanski invokes many of the expectations of filmic realism. At the same time, however, the horror genre also poses an implicit challenge to realism, for it places the realist vision of plausible social interaction against a more primitive worldview that understands the universe in terms of magic and supernatural forces. Tzvetan Todorov's description of "the fantastic" as an effect growing out of the ambiguous tension between the uncanny — in which the protagonist is insane — and the marvelous — in which the supernatural reigns supreme — is well expressed in Polanski's films.[8] *Repulsion* and *The Tenant* feature protagonists who are insane, while *Rosemary's Baby* offers a supernatural explanation for the bizarre situations it depicts. In each case, however, tension is built by playing on the ambiguous interactions between realism and fantasy.

The confusion between inner and outer reality engendered by "the fantastic" reflects modes of experience that are psychologically infantile, recalling a narcissistic period of development in which the individual was unable to distinguish itself from the world around it.[9] Polanski's horror films achieve their effect by reproducing such infantile states both in their protagonists and in their audiences. Due to his early interest in the surrealists, who experimented with the artistic depiction of unconscious thought processes, Polanski commands an impressive arsenal of resources with which he is able to express such confusion.[10]

Though all of Polanski's films are about insanity, in the horror films insanity is expressed in story lines that are more linear and complex than those of the modernist films. If the modernist films reproduce narcissistic anomie through stylized technique and caricatures of sexual obsession, the horror films, through their protagonists, trace the development of regressive modes of relating inner and outer reality that lead to such states. Some of the modernist films hint at such narrative "development." The old woman in *When Angels Fall* harbors increasingly disturbed fantasies. The male protagonists of *Knife in the Water* and *Cul-de-Sac* turn from attempts at developing sexual relationships with their wives to more violent encounters with other men and finally to schizoid passivity as the action progresses. The horror films, however, develop this motif more fully. Carol Ledoux's tentative courtship in *Repulsion* gradually deteriorates into violence and catatonia. Alfred's romantic aspirations in *Dance of the Vampires* are eventually rewarded by having his beloved suck his body dry of blood. Rosemary Woodhouse's adoration of her handsome husband turns into a feeling of dread centered on the alien being that is growing inside her. Trelkovsky feels himself first an unwelcome tenant in his apartment building, his adopted country, and then eventually within his own body. The heroes' frustrated attempts to achieve mature sexual fulfillment drive them back into a world of violence and rage that ultimately expresses itself in terms of fragmented body images and aberrant perceptions of the universe.

In the modernist works the hero's ultimate powerlessness is normally expressed through static and objectified images. We watch from outside as George crouches fetally on a rock at the end of *Cul-de-Sac* and as Andrzej sits immobilized at the wheel of his car in *Knife in the Water*. In the horror films, however, Polanski exploits surrealistic techniques to express his heroes' conflicts subjectively, to encourage us to see the world in the distorted and fantastic vision of the protagonists. Though we may perceive the threatening quality of this world as the product of madness, it is nonetheless a madness we come to share intimately. Many shots show the protagonists in profile at the side of the frame, watching the action along with the spectators. Moreover, tracking shots accommodate to their movements more sympathetically than the coldly objective still camera setups Polanski favors in the modernist films.

In *Repulsion* our terror at the sight of the catatonic Carol lying under the bed at the movie's conclusion is experienced in the context of our sympathetic understanding of her sexual disgust earlier in the film: we can participate in her anguish. Though Rosemary Woodhouse's paranoid sense of a conspiracy is ultimately validated, we are still moved by the way the specter of witchcraft forces her to look and behave more and more like an infant until at last she meekly submits her adult will to the authoritarian control of a group of Satanists. By contrast, we ultimately judge Trelkovsky insane in *The Tenant;* yet his early efforts at ingratiating himself with his callous neighbors and co-workers evoke our empathy. As T. J. Ross has noted, "The films place us in such relation to the inner circumstances of their wild protagonists as to open up for us perspectives on the everyday scene of an eerie acuity and intransigence."[11] As a result, we feel intimately involved in the fates of these characters. In contrast to the modernist films, which begin with images of the absurd and grotesque, anomalies emerge only gradually in the horror films. Initially, everything appears natural; we — and the protagonists — are drawn into a more regressive mode.

Whether "sane" or "insane," all of the protagonists of the horror films are marked by a sense of disassociation between self and body. This sense is closely related to their feelings of sexual dis-ease. Polanski has developed ingenious methods of expressing this dis-ease while staying within popular realist conventions. In such regressed states, everything becomes an extension of the traumatic schism between body and self. Hence, images of fragmented or mutilated bodies abound. Many of the scenes in *Repulsion* open with extreme close-ups of body parts taken from unfamiliar angles. Frozen bodies reappear throughout *Dance of the Vampires*. Rosemary Woodhouse's body is misshapen by pregnancy. Trelkovsky disguises his body by creating a new one, which is flamboyantly female.

This discomforting sense of physical alienation is also projected outward onto the environment. Accordingly, what often appears superficially as a natural mise-en-scène is revealed as a subjective expression of the protagonist's disturbed perception. The anthropomorphized apartments in which these characters live, with their dilating rooms and womblike corridors, update salient features of the large, looming castles in which horror stories have traditionally been enacted. In addition, images of rotting food and of repulsively wrinkled old people present the world as a terrifyingly real portrayal of psychotic perception.

When the environment is not perceived as an extension of a devalued body image, it is likely to be seen by these insecure characters as a threat to that image. The heroes of the horror films are obsessed with fantasies of "plots" against them, and Polanski's cinematography encourages similar fears in the spectator. The mise-en-scène often seems to be harboring hidden, portentous points of view. In one scene from *Dance of the Vampires* we watch a "horrifying" incident that features Alfred and Abronsius driving a stake into a vampire's heart. Their actions are, however, presented in silhouette as they move about behind a sheet. Though the camera soon reveals its joke (the two are actually rehearsing with a pillow), the message to the audience is clear: we may also be victimized by our partial vision of the action, which the director may "plot" in such a way as to punish us with shocking outbreaks of horror and violence.

The ambiguous nature of Polanski's realistic mise-en-scène surfaces dramatically at the moments when the films achieve the effect of deep space by means of extremely wide fish-eye lenses. Realistic depiction then gives way to a distorted vision that imposes menacingly on the spectator by reflecting the paranoid projections of disturbed sensibilities. In *Repulsion* Carol looks at her face reflected in a kettle and later watches the living room of her apartment yawn cavernously before her (an effect achieved, in this case, by the use of specially built sets as well as special lenses). The apartments of Rosemary Woodhouse and Trelkovsky take on similarly ominous dimensions as their inhabitants grow increasingly anxious, and the faces of others, too, degenerate into misshapen leers. Even Alfred in *Dance of the Vampires* is terrorized by the distorted features of Herbert, the lecherous homosexual vampire who has designs on him.

Such distorted images may also express the protagonists' distorted sexual desires. These characters often look out through peepholes or peek out of windows, attempting to see others without being seen by them. The director includes the audience in this descent into voyeuristic passivity by presenting his characters themselves as objects of exhibitionistic display. These films all end with portraits within the cinematic text of audiences who coldly and sadistically view the protagonists as grotesque spectacles. In *Repulsion* several neighbors gather to gape at Carol's rigidly catatonic form. In *Dance of the Vampires* the guests at the ball "catch out" the three main characters by isolating the images of their bodies in a mirror. In *Rosemary's Baby* the members of the coven gathered in the Castevets' apartment quietly observe Rosemary as she wields a carving knife in a last, wildly extravagant attempt to save her baby. And *The Tenant* concludes by transforming the courtyard of Trelkovsky's building into a theater where the neighbors gather to applaud and jeer at the hero's suicide attempt.

These audiences mirror the response of the film's audience itself, which is increasingly encouraged to react to the protagonists in just this way, as alien and objectified "others," projections of forbidden impulses within ourselves. Polanski's horror films do not simply illustrate cultural processes that victimize and warp the powerless; they ask us to recapitulate our own participation in such processes, and they expose social and psychological structures of domination that popular conventions naturalize. In these films the subject is not "others," but "otherness" itself. This, apparently, is the kind of thing the director has in mind when he speaks of "updating" the clichés.

Rosemary's Baby has been the most popular of all Polanski's horror films. To him it represented a chance to prove himself in Hollywood, "the place that belonged more to my dreams than to my reality, at the threshold of where everything would be handed to me."[12] His name was put forward for the project by Robert Evans, then an executive at Paramount, who had been impressed by *Repulsion.* Hollywood producer Willam Castle, who owned the rights to Ira Levin's best-selling novel and had originally wanted to use it for his own directing debut, agreed to let Polanski do the project after the young Polish filmmaker enthusiastically pledged to adapt the book with a minimum number of changes. Polanski wrote the screenplay himself with some assistance from the film's designer, Richard Sylbert. The project was a great success, both critically and commercially, making over $30 million and spawning a whole genre of enormously popular Devil-child pictures such as *The Exorcist* and *The Omen.*[13] As a consequence, Polanski became a highly bankable commodity in the world's film capital. And though the director was later to comment that the film was "less personal because it didn't start as my project,"[14] he found ways of incorporating his own concerns into the finished work.

Levin's 1967 book describes a young, newly married woman who is impregnated by the Devil shortly after moving into the Bramford, a strange old apartment building inhabited by witches. The story encouraged Polanski to focus on the psychology of a complex individual who exists within a coherent social and physical environment. The fears aroused by his adaptation ultimately take the form of infantile terrors centering on bodily integrity. The film turns the conventional cinematic clichés of "innocent" childish experience back on themselves to reveal a world in which the psychological and the factual are terrifyingly indistinguishable, evoking the fantastic effect Todorov describes. The novel, by contrast, displaces this psychological issue onto the physical universe. In the book Rosemary's problem is not that she has the "pre-partum crazies," as her actor-husband

Guy suggests, but that there is an actual plot against her instigated by the Devil himself. By being encouraged to attribute the mysterious phenomena she encounters to the workings of supernatural powers, we are reassured about the disturbing connotations of Rosemary's emotional state.

Though Polanski's screenplay stays close to Levin's original story, the movie maximizes the ambiguity between paranoid projection and real events that the novel repeatedly strives to resolve. Among Polanski's films *Rosemary's Baby* is most similar to *Repulsion,* from which it borrows much of its iconography, most especially its anthropomorphized depiction of the Woodhouses' apartment. Here, however, in place of the insane heroine of *Repulsion,* a diabolical universe is ultimately exposed. But in both cases the audience's growing uncertainty about the nature of the reality that is being presented creates suspense and involvement. Though Polanski initially takes pains to establish a strong sense of verisimilitude, as his stories proceed, this initially credible facade increasingly polarizes into two divergent strands: perverse projection or diabolical plot.

In *Rosemary's Baby* the audience leaves the theater with a strong sense that the narrative has validated the heroine's vision of a "plot," which has led many critics to comment that the film actually diminishes the ambiguity of the novel.[15] And at a certain level, this is true. The world Polanski has created is filled with paranoid images. He often shoots his characters flanked by the strong verticals of the apartment's doorways, which visually constrict them. Near the end, we feel Rosemary's entrapment even more powerfully because of the film's imagery of imprisonment. When the evidence seems overwhelmingly to point to the Castevets' guilt, Rosemary appears in a gray and white striped dress and is put to nap by Dr. Hill on a similarly striped couch while the barlike shadows of the venetian blinds fall across her face. Though such images present the heroine as clearly and unambiguously trapped, we may overlook the question of *what* is trapping her.

The film offers a good deal of evidence that the trap exists within Rosemary herself. Polanski makes her psychological vulnerability more plausible by isolating her from family and from any benign neighbors, both of whom provide her with a certain security in the novel. But the triggering mechanism of her breakdown is her pregnancy. Later, when her baby is born, the source of her anxiety shifts from terror that part of her objectified body could be appropriated by others to an ambivalent hatred/affection toward the part of her body that is no longer hers, a response Ellen Moers has called "the motif of revulsion against newborn life."[16] Accordingly, she sees her baby first as endangered, then as diabolical.

To Rosemary, pregnancy represents the public avowal of her sexuality.[17] The viewer is alerted to the issue of sexual repression early in the film when Guy playfully caresses his wife's back in the elevator on their way up to view the apartment. Polanski follows the gesture with a close-up of the elevator attendant looking at them ominously. Shortly afterward, when her husband kisses her in the kitchen of their prospective home, Mr. Niklas, the building superintendent, comments from the next room, "No, no, no, no, not in the apartment!" Though he is referring to an earlier question about where the previous tenant had died, the timing of his exclamation suggests the embarrassment connected with open displays of sexual passion. Later, the heroine's dreams of her Catholic girlhood include the figure of a disapproving nun. When she is first told of her pregnancy, she herself wears a nunlike white-collared black dress, as she had done when she defended the pope on her first visit to her sinister neighbors, the Castevets.

Yet, though Rosemary is anxious about sexuality, she also has erotic desires. To resolve her dilemma, she conjures up an image of power and violence that is both erotic and punitive: a diabolical rapist. As Ernest Jones has formulated such a situation: "Sometimes voluptuous feelings are coupled with those of *angst;* especially with women, who often believe that the night fiend has copulated with them."[18] While being raped by what she imagines as the Devil, Rosemary is aware that her reaction is observed by the nude coven, which is pictured through a wide angle distortion suggesting grotesque fantasy. Following her dream of sadistic and guilty eroticism, we see Rosemary in bed while her husband is sleeping, as if to emphasize her emotional and physical isolation from him.

After confirming that she is indeed pregnant, Rosemary finds her body strange and repulsive. She begins to feed it disgusting foods: raw meat and an unpalatable-looking drink made for her by Minnie Castevet. Soon she tries to deny her sexuality by assuming the pose of a presexual child: to avoid facing the fact that she is having a baby, she becomes a baby. The winsome, ingenuous presence of Mia Farrow is used to good effect to help make this transition credible. As her body grows more distended, she has her hair cut to a babyish length by Vidal Sassoon.

As the heroine's figure changes, idealized representations of bodies begin to intrude in the mise-en-scène, suggesting Rosemary's increasing estrangement from her own body. A slim, long-legged nude statue occupies an important position in the frame when Rosemary is feeling unwell on the first day of her period, and we see the statue again as she sits in front of the television set doubled over in pain, watching women dancers moving in perfect synchronization. Polanski associates a second, limbless statue with Guy, who rehearses for a new role on crutches, a visual symbol of impotence. "I'm in love with no-one, especially not your fat wife," he says. "I'm a hopeless cripple." Rosemary, who arrives home from Vidal Sassoon in time to hear this speech, later adopts more childish clothing and loses weight. Her more immediate response, however, is to announce that she is in pain. At this moment the camera moves to focus in on the gracefully thin, long-limbed nude statue. The limbless statue appears behind Guy again when his newly pregnant wife confronts him about "not looking at me," and it is also shown when he hesitates to touch Rosemary's stomach after she jubilantly announces, "It's alive!"

The fears of sexuality and pregnancy that Guy may also harbor are in keeping with generalized social attitudes. Once Rosemary becomes pregnant, everyone begins to treat her strangely. The exaggerated fussing of the Castevets and of her friends at the party she gives is complemented by her husband's attitude of fear and avoidance. All convince her that her body has become an object of special consideration, for she is treated more as a pregnancy than as a person. Such a response contains components of sexual inhibition similar to those embedded in the solicitous cluckings of Minnie and Laura-Louise when Rosemary earlier announces that she is menstruating. These attitudes form the background of her paranoia, and the audience responds to them as unremarkable because we are part of the same culture.

Yet social attitudes per se are not at issue here so much as the more global world view implied by religious conviction. Polanski's *Rosemary's Baby* speaks to the ludicrous nature of all religious beliefs, for all religions grant the world an unambiguous meaning that the film wants to deny. The book, by contrast, unambiguously accepts the reality of devils—and of God.

The most striking difference between the film and the novel is the way in which the supernatural motif is handled. While Levin's story ultimately takes the question of the existence of God and the Devil seriously, Polanski relentlessly satirizes religion throughout the film, by equating good with evil. Rosemary's uneasy agnosticism, an important theme in the book, is glossed over in the film, which includes a shot of a *Time* magazine cover announcing "God Is Dead." As several critics have noted, the movie's final scene, with Rosemary in madonnalike attire receiving a foreigner bringing gifts, explicitly parodies the birth of Christ.[19] Earlier, during the dinner Rosemary and Guy share with their friend Hutch, Polanski adds a ghoulish joke about the Agnus Dei of Christian mythology. "They cooked and ate several young children, including a niece," observes Hutch, describing the activities of the infamous Trench sisters who formerly occupied the Bramford. Meanwhile, he serves the lamb he has just taken from the oven while his guests sip wine. The witches' cannibalism is thereby casually equated with Christian ritual. The conversation continues with Hutch's comment, "In 1959 a dead infant was found wrapped in a newspaper in the basement." To which Guy responds, "Mmm — you really rouse my appetite." "Drink your wine," Hutch replies. Such equations of orthodox religion with profane sects suggests that all religious beliefs are characterized by the projection of dark impulses that exist within their devotees.

If such dark impulses may motivate Rosemary's growing "faith" in a cult, they may also motivate the audience's desire to reach a similar point of certainty within the slippery world of the film. For Polanski calls all belief into question by continually playing tricks with the film's illusion of reality.[20] On the one hand, he repeatedly flaunts its verisimilitude. It is clear, for instance, that Mia Farrow actually has blood drawn from her arm in the scene in which Rosemary first visits the obstetrician, Dr. Hill. At the same time, however, the meaning of the most naturalistic images is continually called into question. Half-open doorways suggest a hidden reality by the partial views they offer of what is happening behind them, for people and actions are often only half seen. Rosemary's actor husband Guy clearly shows her both of his shoulders as in the novel to prove he has not been marked by the witches. But Rosemary looks dissatisfied at this revelation and does not respond "all right," as she does in the book. By thus problematizing what the film shows us, Polanski leaves the audience with no conclusive sense of the nature of the reality he is depicting.

Similar ambiguities are invoked by the casting of minor parts. The seemingly trustworthy Dr. Hill is played by Charles Grodin, whose too-even voice and manner would type him in later roles as a duplicitous opportunist. Elisha Cook, familiar to moviegoers as a small-time hood, has here been transformed into Mr. Niklas, a prim building superintendent. Conversely, Ralph Bellamy, long known for portrayals of bland but honest businessmen, has become a sinister, bearded Jewish physician. Though all of these performers play their roles creditably, the audience remains vaguely uneasy about them.[21]

Sound gradually becomes ambiguous as well. An unexplained crashing sound interrupts Rosemary's conversation with her neighbor in the building's laundry room. As in the book, the heroine ascribes sinister overtones to the event. Earlier, during Rosemary and Guy's first evening together in their new living quarters, the expected sound of the traffic and of a plane overhead are interrupted by another more inexplicable sound of chanting. Guy's joking remark, "Shhh . . . I think I hear the Trench sisters chewing," relegates the strange noises in the old building to supernatural causes, lightly invoking a level of explanation that Rosemary will take more seriously as she becomes more and more obsessed with the peculiar sounds she hears from the Castevets' apartment.

The meaning of words can also be treacherous. Mr. Nicklas's protest, "No, no, no, no, not in the apartment!" is a case in point. And later, when

Rosemary's friend Hutch remarks that World War II brought tenants back to the notorious Bramford, Rosemary's subsequent exclamation "Terrific!" prompts him to inquire "What? The house?" To which she responds, "No, the lamb." Such misunderstandings suggest the difficulty of interpreting language. Similar ambiguities arise as Rosemary later tries to use a Scrabble set to decipher the anagram that holds the key to the diabolical plot against her.

Polanski's camera lingers over such ambiguities to emphasize their inherently irresolvable nature. Hence, until Rosemary finally draws an irrevocable conclusion about her surroundings, the pacing is slow.[22] At moments of great stress, such as when the coven enters the apartment, and when she wakes after having given birth, we even hear clocks ticking.

What may finally be accepted as plausible may, in fact, be only what serves the interests of the psyche. Accordingly, changes in the environment echo the stages of Rosemary's regression. As her sense of security ebbs away, the filmic effects increasingly emphasize a threatened and polarized vision of the world. The paternal intimacy of Hutch's apartment gives way to a childishly rendered *Alice in Wonderland* vastness when Rosemary and Guy are in their own apartment, due to the wide angle perspectives viewed from camera positions near the floor. The distorting and intimidating effect of wide angle photography is even more pronounced near the end of the film when a hand-held camera precedes the fleeing Rosemary down the cavernous passages to the safety of her apartment. Similarly, the sweet harmonies of the film's opening lullaby are eventually replaced by dissonances that dramatize both Rosemary's pain and the diabolical machinations that she perceives around her. And the film's color at first contrasts the foreboding darkness of the apartments belonging to Hutch and to the elderly Mrs. Gardinia with the bright primary hues of the youthful Rosemary and Guy. Soon, however, this transformation leads to the garish discordances of the Castevets and ultimately to the devastating conflagrations depicted in their painting of a burning church.

The film's conclusion, in which the coven is revealed as an actuality, allows the audience to escape confronting these disturbing intimations of infantile psychological states. In a deeper way, however, Polanski decisively implicates us in such states through his naturalized portrayal of a fantastic world. For it is finally that dimension of the film that frightens us. By involving us with a seemingly normal character in a seemingly normal world, *Rosemary's Baby* gradually takes not only its heroine but also its audience back to a time of powerlessness and of traumatic confusion between fantasy and reality. Though we never see Rosemary's baby, the last image of Rosemary herself superimposes its unnatural eyes over her own; for the alien forces that terrorize her ultimately arise from within herself. The spectator's involvement with her is an involvement with these internal forces. To leave Polanski's film confident of its outcome is thus to deny the nature of our participation in it. For the horror generated by *Rosemary's Baby* is finally a horror of the helpless infancy we all once suffered.

NOTES

1. Paul D. Zimmerman, "Blood and Water," *Newsweek,* July 1, 1974, 94.

2. "Visual Pleasure and Narrative Cinema," *Screen* 16 (Autumn 1975):9.

3. "An Introduction to the American Horror Film," in Robin Wood and Richard Lippe, eds., *American Nightmare: Essays on the Horror Film* (Toronto: Festival of Festivals, 1979), 9.

4. The classic essay relating popular horror legends to psychological disturbances is Sigmund Freud's "The Uncanny," *The Complete Psychological Works of Sigmund Freud* (London: Hogarth Press, 1964), 17:217-52. This essay inspired other such studies, most importantly Ernest Jones's *On the Nightmare* (New York: Liveright, 1971), and Otto Rank's *The Double,* trans. Harry Tucker (Chapel Hill: University of North Carolina Press, 1971).

5. David Punter, *The Literature of Terror* (London: Longman, 1980), 419. Other useful recent discussions of the genre include Norman Holland and Leona Sherman, "Gothic Possibilities," *New Literary History* 8 (1976-77):279-94; Ellen Moers, *Literary Women* (Garden City, N.Y.: Doubleday, 1977); Phyllis A. Whitney, "Gothic Mysteries," in John Ball, ed., *The Mystery Story* (New York: Penguin, 1976); Elizabeth MacAndrew, *The Gothic Tradition in Fiction* (New York: Columbia University Press, 1979); and Judith Wilt, *Ghosts of the Gothic* (Princeton, N.J.: Princeton University Press, 1981).

6. See Gerard Lenne, "Monster and Victim: Women in the Horror Film," trans. Elayne Donenberg and Thomas Agabite, in Patricia Erens, ed., *Sexual Strategems* (New York: Horizon, 1979), 31-40, for a discussion of the ways in which Polanski's horror films manipulate this convention.

7. Punter, *Literature of Terrors,* 95.

8. Tzvetan Todorov, *The Fantastic: A Structural Approach to a Literary Genre,* trans. Richard Howard (Ithaca, N.Y.: Cornell University Press, 1975).

9. Such regressed modes have become the focus of considerable interest within the psychoanalytic community in recent years. Useful discussions can be found in Heinz Kohut, *The Analysis of the Self* (New York: International University Press, 1971), and his *The Restoration of the Self* (New York: International University Press, 1977); Otto Kernberg, *Borderline Conditions and Pathological Narcissism* (New York: Aronson, 1975); R. D. Laing, *The Divided Self* (New York: Penguin, 1969); and Jacques Lacan, "The Mirror Stage as Formative of the Function of the I as Revealed in Psychoanalytic Experience," *Ecrits,* trans. Alan Sheridan (New York: W. W. Norton, 1977), 93-100. Lacan is particularly relevant here because of his early ties with the surrealist group. For a discussion of this relationship, see Linda Williams, *Figures of Desire: A Theory and Analysis of Surrealist Film* (Urbana: University of Illinois Press, 1981), 43-45.

10. For a discussion of the way techniques of the horror film reproduce unconscious wishes, see Dennis L. White, "The Poetics of Horror: More than Meets the Eye," *Cinema Journal* 10 (Spring 1971):1–18.

11. Ross, *"Repulsion* and the New Mythology," *Film Heritage* 4 (Winter 1968–69):9. A similar point is made by Susan Sontag, who comments on the use of insanity among contemporary artists as a means of opening up the dramatic representation "to levels of experience which are more heroic, more rich in fantasy, more philosophical." *Against Interpretation* (New York: Delta, 1966), 169.

12. Larry Dubois, "The Playboy Interview: Roman Polanski," *Playboy,* Dec. 1971, 108.

13. For a fuller discussion of this phenomenon, see Charles Derry, *Dark Dreams* (Cranbury, N.J.: A. S. Barnes, 1977), 92–97.

14. Harrison Engle, "Polanski in New York," *Film Comment* 5 (Fall 1968):5.

15. See especially Ivan Butler, *The Cinema of Roman Polanski* (New York: A. S. Barnes, 1970), 160; and Robert Chappetta, *"Rosemary's Baby," Film Quarterly* 22 (Spring 1969):35–38.

16. Moers, *Literary Women,* 142.

17. Reviewers who commented on the importance of this aspect of the film include Andrew Sarris, *"Rosemary's Baby," The Village Voice,* July 25, 1968, 37; Henry Hart, *"Rosemary's Baby," Films in Review* 19 (Aug.–Sept. 1968):456–57; and Penelope Gilliatt, "The Chaos of Cool," *The New Yorker,* June 15, 1968, 87–89.

18. Jones, *On the Nightmare,* 46. A similar observation has been made by Todorov in *The Fantastic:* "Desire, as a sensual temptation, finds its incarnation in several of the most common figures of the supernatural world, and most especially in the form of the Devil" (127).

19. See Chappetta, *"Rosemary's Baby"*; Stanley Solomon, *Beyond Formula* (New York: Harcourt Brace Jovanovich, 1976), 149–52; and Marsha Kinder and Beverle Houston, *"Rosemary's Baby," Sight and Sound* 38 (Winter 1978):17, 26.

20. Many of the techniques by which this effect is achieved are analyzed in Kinder and Houston's essay on the film.

21. Polanski was less successful in the casting of Guy. Though he wanted the wholesome-looking Robert Redford, circumstances were such that the more diabolical-looking John Cassevetes played the part. Thus Guy's shallow egocentrism appears more unambiguously sinister than might be desirable. For further information about Polanski's feelings about the making of the film, see his autobiography *Roman* (New York: William Morrow, 1983).

22. Some reviewers complained about this aspect of the film. See especially Philip Hartung, *"Rosemary's Baby," Commonweal,* June 14, 1968, 384–85.

3

Seeing Is Believing: *The Exorcist* and *Don't Look Now*

Marsha Kinder and Beverle Houston

Marsha Kinder and Beverle Houston's comparative study of The Exorcist *and* Don't Look Now *is an edited but not updated version of an essay that first appeared in 1974 in* Cinema *(34). Relying on close textual analysis of narrative structure and visual style, Kinder and Houston argue that both* The Exorcist *and* Don't Look Now *foreground "the problem of interpretation," though these two films differ in their depiction of "metaphysical values" and "spiritual reality." We can now see that the necessity of interpretation (by characters and spectators alike) and the precise means of representing the supernatural and paranormal would prove to be of central importance in the many post-1974 films of demonic possession (*Carrie *and* Demon*) and psychic horror (*The Changeling *and* The Dead Zone*).*

Kinder and Houston are co-authors of Close-Up: A Critical Perspective on Film *and* Self and Cinema. *Houston is director of Critical Studies in the School of Cinema-Television, University of Southern California, Los Angeles, and is co-editor of the* Quarterly Review of Film Studies. *Her most recent publications include articles on television spectatorship and cinema melodrama. Kinder is professor of Critical Studies in the School of Cinema-Television, University of Southern California. She is a founding editor of* Dreamworks *and is on the editorial board of* Film Quarterly *and other film journals.*

Audiences have abandoned Watergate realism to follow movies into other worlds. In Los Angeles and New York huge crowds wait to see William Friedkin's *The Exorcist,* a big-budget Hollywood shocker. Britain's Nicolas Roeg may have his first U.S. commercial success with the occult *Don't Look Now,* while his earlier intriguing works, *Performance* (1970) and *Walkabout* (1971), remain only cult favorites. The popularity of these films suggests that new kinds of belief and morality may be rushing in to replace the almost intolerable decadence, corruption, and cynicism that currently mark our national experience. In a spirit of self-protection, it behooves us to see what is being offered.

Both *Don't Look Now* and *The Exorcist* reject the assumptions of most other recent horror films. They deny psychological explanations of the supernatural and accept the metaphysical nature of good and evil. Their most important precursor is Roman Polanski's *Rosemary's Baby* (1968).[1] Despite its playful self-reflexiveness (Rosemary's corrupted husband is an actor and his demonic cohorts look like characters from old horror films), Polanski's devil *is* an external force, a reality in the metaphysical organization of the universe, who cannot be explained away. As in *Don't Look Now,* the silliness of the demonic killers in no way lessens their capacity for evil. The visual style of *Rosemary's Baby* also draws attention to the objects, colors, textures, and surfaces of the environment rather than leading to symbolic interpretations. The concrete nature of the data raises questions about belief. What kind of empirical evidence is necessary to validate an expanded view of reality or to prove the existence of the devil? As in *The Exorcist,* the devil is presented in a fully Christian context involving Christ and organized religion, but with one important difference. The birth of Rosemary's devil child parodies the birth of Christ, an ironic complication that obscures the clear antagonism between good and evil. In *The Exorcist* there is no such confusion; Christ is the enemy of the devil and the only opponent capable of vanquishing the evil one.

Don't Look Now acknowledges that there is an external power that is dangerous and unknowable and possibly responsible for modern ambiguity and complexity. Though the world is in a desperate situation, the film suggests that the only fruitful attitude is to keep in touch with what is valuable in the past, while remaining open to new modes for the future, especially the possibility of expanded consciousness and perception. Roeg infuses the film with a radical chic of the late 1960s and early 1970s — a perspective rarely seen in horror films.

In contrast, *The Exorcist* denies the complexity and desperation by externalizing the evil and locating it handily in one mythic figure — the Christian devil, who is presented as vulgar, limited, and preoccupied with sex. Offered as a reactionary social corrective, he becomes in the film responsible for all modern evil. Once we recognize this and call on the church (and traditional morality), we can cast him out and make everything good again. Perhaps the ease of this solution lies at the heart of the film's popularity.

The Exorcist (1973)

As a special effects movie, *The Exorcist* is extremely successful. Its power to terrify is largely based on makeup and sound effects. You see before your own eyes a twelve-year-old child transformed into a yellow-eyed, thick-lipped, scarred and growling monster, who spews out jets of bright green bile. Plastic molds were made of Linda Blair's body to increase the authenticity of one of the devil's (and Friedkin's) best tricks — he turns the child's head around 360 degrees on her neck. The sound track is extremely loud, providing a cacophony of noises that keeps the audience tense and edgy: the devil's poundings; the clanging hammers of the archaeological dig; the city noises; the loud thud of punching bag and tennis balls; the roaring subway train; the intolerable screech of the medical instruments. But most astonishing of all, the child's mouth opens and, through the wonders of modern technology, out comes a string of voices from Mercedes McCambridge's gutteral devil through the whining accents of the priest's mother, a series of languages including Greek, Latin, French, and gibberish, and, with terrifying effect, the wheezing and roaring growls of some huge monster beast. The power of these effects lies in the fact that we see and hear for ourselves, which is precisely dramatized in the confrontation between the mother, Chris MacNeil (played by Ellen Burstyn), and the doctors. In controlled voices of reason, they try to diagnose these terrifying phenomena as "pathological states" and "accelerated motor performance." Refusing to have her perceptions invalidated, the distraught mother cuts through their jargon, screaming, "What're you talking about? Jesus Christ! . . . Did you see? Did you see?" Later, when a battery of doctors finally has to suggest exorcism, they try to lessen their discomfort with "rational" explanation: "It works only because the patient believes he's possessed . . . purely by force of suggestion." Again Chris cuts through the verbal screen: "You're telling me that I should take my daughter to a witch doctor, is that it?"

The language of the film contrasts with the powerful visual and sound effects that confront us directly. Like the doctors, William Blatty and Friedkin use language to attempt a symbolic inflation. Most of the characters' names have obvious associations: Regan (Lear's daughter, the ungrateful child "sharper than a serpent's tooth"); Chris(t) MacNeil; Father Damien Karras (who is charitable like his namesake Saint Damian, but who ends up possessed by the demon); Burke ("to murder by suffocating, to suppress quietly"), who is murdered by Regan; Father Merrin (preserving ancient orthodoxy and ritual like the Maronite Catholics); Sharon (referred to as "Shar," who shares the horror); Lt. Kinderman (protector of children and childlike man); Father Dyer (who is dying inside, reborn through Damien's sacrifice). As Father Dyer walks down the street in the final scene, a sign reading "Prospect Avenue" appears over his shoulder. The gratuitous allusions to *Body and Soul* and *Othello* (as well as the name of the inner movie, *Crash Course*) are equally heavy-handed; they are probably introduced as "allegory" or because self-reflexiveness is currently chic. Blatty's script is full of banalities ("Mrs. MacNeil, the problem with your daughter is not her bed, it's her brain").

In developing the film's antilanguage position, director and screenwriter fail to solve an admittedly difficult problem — how to develop this negative attitude in language that does not also fail aesthetically. In contrast to these other techniques, they succeed with Father Merrin's silence. In the archaeological dig in northern Iraq, Father Merrin is the dominant figure and there is practically no dialogue. He's the archetypal silent man; we recognize him from genres like the western, frequently starring Gary Cooper, Clint Eastwood, or Steve McQueen. Instead of talking, he acts. As Merrin says in the last line of the opening sequence: "There's something I must do." He is contrasted with Father Karras, whose wit and intellectuality manifest the devil's wicked tongue, which Karras has developed at "Harvard, Bellevue, Johns Hopkins, places like that." Chris MacNeil is even more blatantly linked to the devil through her incessant cursing and blaspheming ("Circumstances, my ass. He doesn't give a shit. . . . I've been on this fucking line for twenty minutes! Jesus Christ!"). During the exorcism sequence, Father Merrin will not listen to Karras's "background" of the case, and he warns Damien to "avoid conversations with the demon . . . the devil is a liar." Indeed, throughout the film, language is the devil's instrument, and Friedkin and Blatty succeed in developing his verbal prowess.

As the film denies the explanatory power of language, so are the conventional sources of emotional identification denied in character development. Pauline Kael points out: "We in the audience don't feel bad when the saintly Father Merrin dies; we don't even feel a pang of sympathy when the words 'Help Me' appear on Regan's body. . . . There is no indication that Blatty or Friedkin has any feeling for the little girl's helplessness and suffering, or her mother's." The basic situation and the tone of psychological realism provide the potential for strong sympathy, but Blatty and Friedkin choose not to develop it. They present us with data for a psychological interpretation (divorce, Regan's jealousy of Burke, the father's rejection of Regan, her forthcoming thirteenth birthday, unusual physical contact between mother and daughter); then they reject it in favor of a phenomenological devil. We don't care about Regan's terrible decline; our only reactions are curiosity and a delicious terror, for which we are carefully trained. Every time the camera goes upstairs and looks at Regan's doorway, we get turned on, anticipating the expensive horrors that will follow.

The basic structure of the film is designed to draw us into the exorcism. Divided into three parts, the film's organization itself suggests a ritual pattern. (These segments roughly parallel three of Northrop Frye's phases of symbolism and modes of power, to be developed later.) The opening segment, set in northern Iraq, presents us with phenomena that evade rational explanation, but are powerfully effective at another level. Framed by the opening and closing images of a sun glowing over an empty landscape, the events at the archaeological dig create an ominous tension, primarily through the way they are presented. The emphasis is on movement. The camera pans, zooms in and out, assumes odd positions, tracks with or against the movements of people; the film cuts abruptly between interior and exterior, close-up and long shot, light and dark; on the site and in the marketplace, the workers dig and hammer in a kind of unison, creating incantory rhythms. The sound track is dominated by a strange combination of powerful sounds that, despite their highly rhythmical quality, create a sense of confusion: religious chanting, the banging of the tools, the murmur of voices, the loud ticking clock, the rattling of the carriage, the snarling of the dogs, and, intermittently throughout, the strange electronic music. The sense of mystery is heightened by the sparse dialogue in a foreign language. The few fragments that we can understand take on a greater significance, which is inexplicable till later in the film: "Strange — not of the same period"; "Evil against evil"; "There is something I must do." We have a similar response to many of the visual images. Though at this point in the film, we do not yet understand their symbolic meaning, they still have the power to make us uneasy: eyes, both blind and staring; the circle images of the sun; the woman looking down menacingly from above; the strange amulet from another period; the demonic statue; the growling, fighting animals; Father Merrin's pillbox; and his near-death from the carriage. Finally, the development of mysterious significance grows more self-conscious at the end of this opening segment. With great purposefulness, Father Merrin returns to the dig. After a moment of danger before the Arab guards identify him, he climbs up to a high point where the huge demonic statue stands out in sharp relief against the orange sky. The camera examines its face and pulls back to a longer shot of the hilltop and strange things happen — the wind begins to blow and becomes the weird electronic music, rocks roll down the hill behind him, a mysterious old Arab watches intently, and suddenly two dogs begin a horrible growling fight. Finally the camera reveals Father Merrin positioned opposite the demonic statue with the great orange sun between them, foreshadowing their adversary relationship that is to dominate part three of the film.

Whereas the opening segment was developed through a phenomenological mode, emphasizing perception without interpretation, the second part shifts to a more familiar kind of melodrama that combines psychological realism and Gothic horror (this mixture goes all the way back to *Caligari* and *Nosferatu*). In Frye's terms, the shift is from the ironic mode, where images are presented directly through simple juxtaposition, to the mimetic mode, where they function as similes or analogies. This is the part of the film where we are teased with psychology, but the facile explanations characteristic of this mode are ultimately rejected. We are frightened not through direct apprehension of unexplained phenomena but through conscious manipulation of conventions from the horror film. Every film buff knows that noises in the attic and candles that blow out mysteriously cannot be explained by rats. As in most films of this genre, we are most surprised by our first look at the monster — our hero or heroine transformed by inspired makeup. Like the dreams in *Caligari* and *Rosemary's Baby,* Damien's dream develops two dimensions: the psychological realism of his guilt about his mother, and his supernatural awareness of images from the first segment — the amulet, the black dog, and the time piece. When Regan is subjected to the spinal tap and X rays, the huge clanking, flashing equipment is strongly reminiscent of Frankenstein's laboratory and various Gothic torture instruments. In the same sequence, a needle inserted in her neck brings forth a stream of blood that must excite both Dracula and his fans.

This attack on science is part of a larger condemnation of sophisticated, decadent, bourgeoise culture (which we also remember from *Rosemary's Baby*). The second section begins with a dissolve from the powerful, primitive image at the dig to a bridge in the big city, establishing the context in which all the intractable modern evils are to be mechanically catalogued: poverty in the New York slums; sordid subways; overcrowded hospitals and asylums; loneliness of the old; casual acceptance of swearing, liquor, drugs, and divorce; campus violence and the media that exploit it; a leftover "Nazi butchering pig" in Chris's kitchen. And at the center of the film lie the faithlessness and decadence of the "enlightened" clergy. Even Father Damien ("the best we have") has lost faith and wants to leave the Order. The decadence is epitomized by Father Dyer's vision of the heavenly city: "A solid white nightclub with me as headliner for all eternity, and they *love me.*"

This modern world is explored by intercutting between two parallel plots. Chris MacNeil, a rich, famous movie star, is having troubles with her two-faced daughter. Poor Father Damien is torn between loyalties to two mothers — the church, and his earthly mother who is dying in poverty. The MacNeils' materialism and his spiritualism are both beset by soullessness and mental illness.

The last sequence creates a transition between parts two and three. Whereas part two has formerly cut between the MacNeils and Father Damien (who are not united until part three), this final sequence crosscuts between Lt. Kinderman and Chris MacNeil as they make parallel discoveries (e.g., she discovers the cross under Regan's pillow; he finds Regan's clay sculpture at the foot of the stairs) and unites them as they both tell lies (he pretends the autograph is for his daughter; she lies to prevent him from seeing Regan). In the end they move toward the same conclusion. Friedkin complicates the inevitability with a bit of heavy-handed irony: the "facts" force Kinderman to conclude that Burke Dennings was killed by "a very powerful man," while we in the audience watch Chris catching up with what we already know about Regan's guilt. Like Father Merrin and the demonic statue at the end of the first part, Kinderman and MacNeil are established as adversaries; in the secular urban context, good versus evil has become cop versus suspect. When Kinderman leaves, Chris runs to her daughter's room to find objects flying through the air, and Regan masturbating (or mutilating herself) with a bloody cross. Forcing Chris's head down between her legs, she screams: "Lick me, lick me!" When Regan turns her head around 360 degrees for the first time and sends the bureau after her mother, this is the turning point. We know, beyond the shadow of a doubt, that a psychological explanation is no longer possible.

Part three focuses on the exorcism. The shift from part two to three is not as abrupt as the move from northern Iraq to Georgetown. We are not confronted with different characters in a new setting with a shift in style. Rather, we gain a different perspective on the same phenomena. In place of the psychological explanation from the mimetic part two, we now see through the eyes of Christian mythology. In Frye's terms, we have entered the mythic mode or anagogic phase, where symbols represent identity and action takes the form of ritual. But instead of moving directly from irony to myth, which Frye describes as the characteristic pattern in twentieth-century art, the film regresses backward through the mimetic mode to express its reactionary vision. Regan is no longer acting like a devil; she *is* the devil. When Father Damien takes Communion, the traditional water is not to be interpreted as a symbol for Christ; it *is* Christ's body and wine *is* his blood. As viewers, we believe in the devil (and, by implication, in Christ) because of what we see and hear (for example, Regan's bed floats several feet above the ground). But, paradoxically, true faith requires rejection of our senses, as Father Merrin warns Karras that the devil lies and creates illusions. The exorcism also brings together all the plot strands and creates apparent complexity for the sake of full resolution. Details of the first two parts (Merrin versus the statue, the ominous carriage, the pills, the fighting dogs, the devil's tricks, the social corruption, etc.) develop their full meaning as they are shown to be part of the basic metaphysical dichotomy between good and evil, Christ and the devil.

Part three opens as Chris and Father Karras meet on a bridge (the same transitional image that opened part two). As she involves him in exorcising Regan, we realize that his plot line from part two (developing his guilt about his mother) provides him with a psychological handicap that makes him vulnerable to the devil. He is contrasted with Father Merrin, whose weakness is physical (old age, heart trouble). And with Father Merrin comes clarification of many ideas and images from part one. Into his wooded retreat comes a young priest (like the boy who carries the message at the dig) with a letter that Merrin simply puts in his pocket, as if he knows its contents full well. We begin to suspect that he left Iraq because he knew the devil was waiting for their next confrontation. Bringing back another technique not used since part one, the film dissolves from Father Merrin in the woods to the new face of his old adversary. Regan's distorted image takes over the whole screen in a huge close-up and defines Merrin's task. Her face dissolves into a classic Gothic image—carrying a small black case, a black-clad stranger (Father Merrin) descends from a cab in the foggy night.

Even though it is clearly suggested that the church has the power to unify all aspects of the experience and give them meaning, there is still a conflict between the old and new within the Order. Merrin relies on church ritual, whereas Father Karras's power lies in human interaction. Though we see him move toward renewal of faith during the exorcism, his psychological weaknesses do not allow him to use the traditional weapons. But when Chris asks him, "Is she gonna die?" he gains new determination, draws the devil to himself, and saves Regan through personal sacrifice. In this way, like Caligari, he takes on the triple identity of priest, psychiatrist, and demon.

The film's final shift takes place in the brief epilogue after the devil has been and gone. It opens with a cut to the stairs where Father Karras died. They are now empty, silent, revealing no trace of what has happened. As she prepares to drive away with her mother, Regan, who is said to remember nothing, suddenly stares at Father Dyer's collar and reaches up to kiss him, showing that her unconscious knows for all time whence her help cometh. As he walks away, the camera pulls back for a "prospect" shot, suggesting that life will begin again with new knowledge of the devil, as earlier transitions foreshadowed events to come.

As Regan's bruises heal, we have a moment to reflect on the nature of this devil who is making so much money on the comeback trail. First of all, his powers are extremely limited, confined mostly to simple acts of levitation and teleportation. When he magically slides a drawer in and out of the bed-table, Karras tempts him to repeat his trick. He replies, in a parody of Christ at Gethsemane, that this would be "a vulgar display of power." But the point is, the devil cannot transform the world through his own power, whereas Christ could but would not. Instead, the devil must rely on his victims' weaknesses (Dennings drank too much, Karras had psychological problems, Merrin was physically weak, and Regan had the vulnerability of the child, complicated by her incipient adolescence). The incident on which the novel is said to be based actually involved a boy, but the sex change also introduces the dimension of woman as the weaker vessel. (Genesis teaches that Satan gets to men through their emotional sympathies for the weaker sex; Regan, Chris, and Mother Karras all make demands on Damien and increase his vulnerability to the devil.) With his real power so limited, the devil must be frustrated. Stripped of all his glamour, he is extremely noisy, disgustingly messy, and unwholesomely concerned with sex. But even here, he is provincial. Far more limited than the Marquis de Sade or William Burroughs, the worst insult he can fling at the priests is that they or their relatives commit acts of oral and anal sex. But the film grants him wide domain, implying that the Christian interpretation of the cosmic order is universally true. This devil has reared his head in Iraq, in Africa (where Father Merrin performed an exorcism some years ago), and in Washington, D.C. He is real for Catholics (all the priests), atheists (Chris and family), and Jews (Lt. Kinderman). He also provides excellent grounds for anti-intellectuality in the Babel that characterizes science and the arts in this film (confirming the belief of many that this stuff is, indeed, the devil's work). He is presented as the cause of all the social ills catalogued earlier in the film. We do not have to solve (or even worry about) urban poverty, spiritual death, or corruption in the highest places. Instead, we are taught to fear all irreverence, unconventionality, rebellion, and complex sexuality.

Don't Look Now (1973)

Don't Look Now takes a radical view of the supernatural. Instead of retreating to a Manichean vision of good and evil like *The Exorcist,* it challenges the basic polarities defined by our rational, dualistic culture: life/death, present/future, sacred/profane, ordinary/bizarre, good/evil, true/false, real/imagined, normal/crazy. Like R. D. Laing, Carlos Casteneda, Norman O. Brown, and Doris Lessing, in this film Roeg accepts expanded consciousness and the powers of telepathy, suggesting (as in *Performance*) that "nothing is true. Everything is permitted." In *Don't Look Now* the hero finally accepts his second sight, but the delay insures misinterpretation, and he forfeits his life. Roeg's style makes a similar demand on the audience to expand their vision, providing an implicit affirmation of nonordinary reality as a source of power.

Based on the story by Daphne du Maurier, the film follows a modern couple, John (Donald Sutherland) and Laura Baxter (Julie Christie) to Venice after the death of their little daughter. In Venice they meet two middle-aged Scottish sisters, Wendy (Celia Matania), who is dumpy and ordinary, and Heather (Hilary Mason), who is blind and psychic. These two women convey contradictory qualities that are held in tension throughout many aspects of the film; they appear mundane and ordinary, like the familiar British women who travel the continent, but, like the "weird sisters" in *Macbeth,* at the same time they convey a sense of ominous mystery, which is enhanced through multiple mirror images in our first encounter with them and strengthened later through a sudden cut to the two sisters laughing wickedly. Heather claims to have established contact with the Baxters' dead daughter, Christine, who is trying to warn her parents to leave Venice. She also affirms that John, too, has second sight.

John and Laura react very differently to their encounter with expanded reality. She is established in the opening scene as a seeker of new knowledge as she consults a book, *Beyond the Fragile Geometry of Space,* to answer her daughter's question: "If the world is round, why is the frozen pond flat?" John, who is about to have a clairvoyant flash, answers with the aphorism: "Nothing is what it seems." A few minutes later, in a slide of the interior of a cathedral that John is examining, a patch of red appears, which grows into a shape like a bloodstain. If we (and John) look closely, we can discern that this stain is growing out of a red, hooded cape worn by a small figure seated in the cathedral (who, at the end of the film, will become John's murderer). But John interprets only one aspect of the warning correctly; growing suddenly frightened, he rushes outside to find that his daughter, wearing her red mackintosh, has drowned in the pond. After the first encounter with the two sisters, Laura, who does not have second sight, is convinced that Heather has actually made contact with Christine's spirit and is restored to health and vitality by this knowledge. Not yet having recognized his own powers, John is skeptical; yet he is impressed by Laura's improvement, which he can perceive in her face and voice. He offers a second aphorism, "Seeing is believing," which apparently contradicts his earlier assertion that "nothing is what it seems." Later, when John and Laura get lost in the alleys of Venice, John has another clairvoyant experience in which he sees the red-coated figure and he hears a sigh and a scream. Laura sees nothing, but is frightened, though still dominated by curiosity: "What on earth was that?" John, the seer, denies his vision, claiming it is "a cat or a rat . . . maybe it was only my imagination." Leading her back to the main street, he reassures her: "It's okay. I found the real world." Thus John again ignores the foreshadowings of his own death (the site and the murderer), interpreting his perceptions as unreal.

In the next encounter with the sisters, while Laura is eagerly trying to make contact with Christine, Heather tells her that John "has the gift. That's why the child is trying to talk to him. Even if he doesn't know it.

Even if he's rejecting it. It's a curse as well as a gift" (another important paradox in the film). As they are talking, the film cuts to John, who almost falls while unveiling a gargoyle high on the church facade. The sequence evokes the previous church where the Baxters narrowly missed running into the sisters and foreshadows John's fall in the cathedral, which is to occur soon after. After the seance, John and Laura again argue. She is convinced that the sisters are right in warning John that there is danger while they remain in Venice. John (who has been drinking) suddenly gets sick and must throw up. Ironically, upon his return, he tries to convince Laura that *she* is sick and should resume taking her pills. Verbally, she accepts, and then hides the pills. When a phone call comes and they learn that their son has had an accident at his school, Laura interprets this as a validation of the prophecy: "This is it. They were right. You see." John facilitates her departure without accepting the supernatural interpretation.

But his skepticism begins to waver soon after when his scaffold breaks and he almost falls to his death in the cathedral. Afterward, the bishop remarks: "My father was killed in a fall," and John, badly shaken, replies: "It's unbelievable. My wife warned that I was in danger." The bishop confirms: "I wish I didn't have to believe in prophecy, but I do." The irony intensifies here as John moves toward belief, but grasps at this event as the whole truth, still denying that it is one more link in the chain connecting him with the red-hooded figure and death in Venice. John is presented with these linking visions in the very next scene, where he chances upon the body of a murdered victim being raised from the canal against an out-of-focus red background. He immediately flashes back to his own fall and to the image of his daughter rising out of the pond. John now intends to leave Venice, but is prevented by his next clairvoyant experience. Laura, dressed in black, and the two sisters pass by on a hearse boat with a casket, moving slowly down the Grand Canal. Again, as in the opening, he recognizes the danger, but interprets it partially, responding to its immediate shock, while failing to recognize that it is a vision of the future. Concluding that Laura (who is supposed to be in England with their son) has been kidnapped by the two sisters, he goes to the police. When he finally calls and finds that Laura is indeed safe in England, he and Laura reverse positions. He tries to explain his vision, while she is totally involved in the ordinary and mundane, confirming that he must meet her at the airport. Confronted with the fact that there is no "natural" explanation for his vision, he still refuses to acknowledge his second sight or the danger it implies. Instead, he shifts his attention to the sisters, focusing on his guilt over Heather's arrest.

These feelings lead directly to his death. When he finally encounters the red-hooded figure in the dark Venice streets, he interprets her as a child in need, and moves in to help her, calling: "I'm a friend. I won't hurt you." Not until the dwarf turns on him and cuts his throat does he accept his second sight, which is revealed through the chain of images that passes before his eyes. This belated acceptance is made quite explicit in the Du Maurier story: "And he saw the vaporetto with Laura and the two sisters . . . and he knew why they were together and for what sad purpose they had come . . . and, 'Oh God,' he thought, 'what a bloody silly way to die.'"

Roeg adds a final scene emphasizing the contrast between John's resistance and Laura's acceptance. Recreating John's vision, the hearse vaporetto passes down the canal as Laura stands with a calm smile on her face, her eyes blank like Heather's; somehow her openness to another reality has given her the strength to accept John's death at least with resignation.

This contrast between Laura and John is important in establishing the film's attitude toward nonordinary experience. Throughout, Laura has focused on concrete perceptions rather than abstractions or attitudes defined by the culture. For example, when asked whether she's a Christian, she replies: "I don't know. I'm kind to animals and children." She is open to explanations that contradict normal perceptions and beliefs. This helps her to accept the deaths of loved ones because in the world of the spirit, there is no rigid distinction between life and death.

Don't Look Now develops another important ambiguity concerning the nature of "the gift." Even if John had been able to accept his second sight, could he have escaped his death, which seems to have been ordained by fate? Does clairvoyance involve warnings of events that might not happen? Roeg intensifies this ambiguity by an emphasis on accidents that is not present in Du Maurier's story, where Christine dies of meningitis rather than drowning, and Johnny is endangered by appendicitis rather than an injury in a game. Roeg invents the opening sequence of the drowning and the immediate reactions of the parents, enabling us to see in a concrete manner that this accident evokes clairvoyant foreshadowings (Du Maurier begins the story in the Venice restaurant). He also adds the parallel slow-motion falls of Laura in the restaurant and John in the cathedral. While hers can be explained in terms of her psychological condition and reaction to Heather's psychic powers, his remains unexplained except as the workings of fate. Both accidents raise doubts about John and Laura's safety, yet it is John's that provides the true foreshadowing—the more ominous because without apparent cause. The accidents make the universe more dangerous and suggest a pattern of events that is inexorable, but only partially perceptible. In the restaurant before her fall, Laura says to John: "It's incredible. You can't change your course." If this is true, what is the value of the warnings? The film never resolves this question:

it remains one of the many paradoxes that are offered in the place of the logical, either/or thinking of Western culture.

Another of Roeg's significant additions is the development of John's occupation. In the story, the couple goes to Venice for a holiday, while in the film, their visit is motivated by John's restoration work. While Du Maurier also emphasizes the decadence of the Venice environment, her focus is on the physical decay: "Venice is sinking. The whole city is dying." Robberies and murders are increasing. There are many gluttonous eating scenes that make the decadence worldly and material. The psychic moments are comically deflated when juxtaposed with the eating of spaghetti. But Roeg's treatment is entirely serious. As signs tell us throughout the film, "Venice is in peril." It seems a perfect visual metaphor for mysterious patterns of danger moving from the past into the future. After John's clairvoyant vision as the body is raised from the canal, he crosses the Ponte de Miracolo (Bridge of Miracles). Later, as he searches for the pensione, the camera reveals another sign, reading Ponte de Vivante (Bridge of the Living). The names suddenly attain symbolic significance, implying that the ancient city itself has supernatural powers that emerge at fated moments. Venice is not threatening to those who cannot read the signs. As Heather tells John: "One of the things I love about Venice is that it's so safe for me to walk. The sounds. . . . My sister hates it. She says it's like a city in aspic after a dinner party, and all the guests are dead. It frightens her . . . Milton loved this city."

Though sighted and aware of material dangers not perceived by blind prophets like Heather and Milton, John ignores the signs. His concern with restoring cathedrals allows Roeg to extend the decadence to art and religion — the world of the spirit — both of which are more closely connected with the supernatural. It also develops John's character by presenting his attachment to the traditional in art as well as in perception.

As in *The Exorcist,* the urban environment is important in developing themes of good and evil, energy and weakness, health and corruption, order and chaos. But Friedkin uses the modern city simply as a vehicle for mechanical enumeration of social and moral evils. In *Don't Look Now* the bishop and the police inspector, both representatives of institutions that sanctify order, are developed with considerable ambiguity. Both are immediately sensitive to John's extraordinary, disturbed state of mind, almost to the point of telepathic awareness. The police inspector probes insistently to discover John's hidden fear; during their conversation, the inspector glances casually out the window at the moment when the two sisters happen to walk by; as John talks on, the inspector doodles on the eyes in the police drawing of Heather, making it look more like her. The bishop awakens suddenly at the moment of John's death. The connection between these public figures and the chain of supernatural events is also strengthened visually. The display of ecclesiastical costumes in the bishop's chamber is set against a red background; the map of Venice in the inspector's office is shaped very much like the red stain on the slide in the opening sequence. Yet at the same time, these characters are subtly undermined. The police inspector holds weird theories about visual correspondences: "Age causes women to look more like each other . . . men grow quite distinct, but women seem to converge . . . the purpose of the police artist is to make the living appear dead." When Laura informs him that the drawing does not look like Heather, he replies: "It doesn't matter." The worldly bishop makes Laura "feel uneasy." John explains: "It's because he makes God seem less than immaculate." After discussing mosaic tiles with the bishop, John concludes: "He doesn't give an ecclesiastical fuck about churches." Thus, the police inspector's rationality is suspect, and we must question the breadth and purity of the bishop's spiritual commitment.

The film's visual style confirms the existence of second sight. In contrast to *The Exorcist,* where ordinary and nonordinary experience are presented in the same mode, making it easy for anyone to perceive them without struggle, *Don't Look Now* forces us to see in new ways and confront the problems of interpretation. Hence the audience is placed in the same situation as the characters. Visual and auditory images work phenomenologically, as in part one of *The Exorcist.* When image fragments constantly reappear, we look for the key in patterns and repetitions. We are confronted with photographs, drawings, portraits, slides, statues, and modern replicas of ancient mosaics; we are led into tracing their resemblances to each other and to the originals on which they are based. Thus, we acquire the habit of acute perception (which we may take out of the theater), since interpreting nonordinary reality within the film is a matter of life and death.

The editing style destroys the linear structure of the literary source. The montage of quick shots juxtaposes present with past and future. The opening sequence has predictive value for the whole film. The first shot is of rain on the pond where Christine is soon to drown, establishing water imagery that is to permeate the film as it does the city of Venice. This image is used with verbal irony when the wife of the headmaster reassures John that his son is "right as rain." The second image is unrecognizable, but later when we see it in context — the Venice hotel room — we learn that it is light coming through a lattice window screen. In a series of quick cuts, several images become contaminated by association with Christine's death: her red mackintosh and red and white ball, fire imagery (to be repeated in the church candles), piano music (which recurs when John is looking for the pensione of the weird sisters), and John's howl and Laura's

scream (which are associated with the screeching drill that follows immediately, the ambiguous sounds at the sisters' hotel that could be a baby
crying or a cat howling, and with the strange whimperings of the dwarf).
The image of breaking glass appears at least twice during this sequence
and recurs later in Laura's and John's falls. In the cathedral a piece of
wood smashes through the flimsy glass (reminding us of the book title,
Beyond the Fragile Geometry of Space); like the unbroken surfaces of
the bar window, the whiskey bottles and glasses, the mirrors, and the slide,
this glass functions as a screen, a metaphor for the illusions that must
be shattered to confront supernatural experience ("nothing is what it
seems"). The images in the slide establish the hooded dwarf, the cathedral, the color red, and the shape of the stain as signs of danger. At the
end of the sequence, John rushes out to reclaim Christine's body from
the pond while Laura (behind the window) and Johnny (his finger bloodied
by broken glass) look on. The visual pairings of characters predict that
the next victim will be John despite the apparent threats to Laura and
Johnny. The film is framed with the deaths of Christine and John, ful-
filling the prophecy of the opening: at the funeral, Laura and Johnny are
reunited as spectators.

Frequently, when ordinary reality is transcended, a loop style is used
to merge past, present, and future. In the ladies' room at the restaurant,
we experience Heather's powers for the first time. The group of images
is framed by close-ups of Heather's vacant blue eyes, which look like water.
The next shot is of John's blue eyes, suggesting that he, too, has second
sight. Then we see sparkling water, railings on a bridge, a close-up of Laura
driving away from the house in the rain with a sad look on her face (is
this a flash backward to Christine's death, or forward to John's?). Next
the camera pulls in to a shot of rain on watery ground before cutting back
to Heather's eyes. Second sight provides Heather with a series of images
just as Roeg provides them for us. She has to interpret what she sees, to
realize the connections within the montage as we do. The first time we
see the film, it is difficult to recognize the autonomy of this vision because
rapid cutting characterizes the whole film; but the repetition of Heather's
eyes becomes the key. As John lies dying, he sees a vision that integrates
all the images from Heather's vision, some from the opening, and from
other, nonlinear sequences such as the love-making scene and the raising
of the body from the canal. The convention of the dying man's life flashing before his eyes is given new significance through its association with
clairvoyance and the supernatural.

John's vision of the vaporetto is unique. Presented in longer takes with
little cutting, it creates a more conventional visual reality. Paradoxically,
this clarity is confusing; we, like John, are tempted to interpret this as

the present. Yet we have seen the pattern of the three women grouped together before, and usually juxtaposed with a child or an inanimate figure (this time, John's corpse). Thus we are taught to look for patterns, not only in the editing, but also in visual and verbal elements within a single shot. In the church scene, as Laura describes Christine's death to the two sisters, we see the three women in the background with a statue in the foreground, before cutting to John struggling with a gargoyle whose face reminds us of the grotesque dwarf. In the next scene, when Laura goes to visit the sisters for a seance, Roeg intercuts between John seated before three bottles and the three women seated in the room, their heads in a row, as they try to contact the dead child. Over the mantle is a painting of three women with the Christ child. Later, when John discovers their pensione for the police, the camera dwells on this portrait, as if it is a key to the mystery. This pattern establishes Laura's identification with the two sisters, invalidating John's kidnap theory; potentially, it also could have predicted his own danger. His misinterpretation is compounded because he has cut himself off from the incidents in which this pattern has previously appeared.

The love-making sequence rearranges linear reality, not to confound, but to affirm the experiential value of merging past, present, and future. At first, it seems that the love-making is the film's present and is being intercut with flashes forward to dressing (Laura's black pants and silver top). Then as more time is spent on the later images, it seems that the dressing sequences are the present reality, intercut with flashes *back* to the love-making. We gradually learn that Roeg has controlled time to show the value of obscuring distinctions and to emphasize the flow, as John and Laura's bodies move together in the love-making. In this sequence the content is part of everyday reality rather than the extremes of death or second sight. The banal and the extraordinary are also merged as the action is initiated by the most mundane of details. Laura says: "You have toothpaste on your mouth," and John replies: "Eat it off." The intense love-making (characterized by energy, creative variety, and full, active commitment by both Laura and John) is intercut with shots of them sharing the bathroom as they get dressed. Laura puts on mascara; John winds his watch and fixes a drink. The cutting suggests that it is possible to go from the most intense to the most mundane smoothly and without emotional loss. Some of the images stress the carryover of warmth as Laura looks in the mirror admiring her own sensuality and repeating the gestures she used in making love. As they walk through the hotel lobby, glamourously dressed for the evening, Laura puts her hand on John's arm and leans her head on his shoulder affectionately. Their glowing vitality contrasts with the sterility of the shrouded hotel furniture, which signals that Venice is about to close down for the winter. In contrast to *The Exorcist,* which treats sex as a manifestation of decadence and evil, Roeg's film elevates it to an act of regeneration. It is a rite of passage signaling the end of the couple's mourning for their daughter and Laura's return to full participation in life.

The success of this sequence grows out of the fact that content and style are combined with an equal power that is unusual for the film. Generally speaking, *Don't Look Now* succeeds primarily at the perceptual level; its emotional impact is considerably weaker. This limitation is most apparent in John's murder. Despite the vivid horror of the blood and the twitching, the seriousness of Roeg's tone is undermined by the fact that John's been done in by a killer dwarf ("What a bloody silly way to die"). Despite all the visual preparation, the instrument of his death appears like a *deus ex machina.* In some ways, of course, the dwarf is associated with Christine, primarily through size, shape, and color. However, this association only heightens the abstraction with which the child's death is handled. As in *The Exorcist,* Christine and the demon become polarities of good and evil, victim and killer, but here the emphasis is on fusion, which obscures the traditional distinction. Though our perceptual skills are advanced and we may become more open intellectually to nonordinary experience, *Don't Look Now,* unlike *Performance* and *Walkabout,* does not touch our deepest fantasies and needs. Further, the supernatural experiences of the film are not linked to growth toward positive ends, but to acceptance of a declining world and sudden death.

In *Don't Look Now* death is absurd. Laura's acceptance provides only the ability to bear her loss. Shifting from the visionary and symbolic modes of Roeg's earlier films, which both lead to profound reevaluation of symbolic experience, *Don't Look Now* offers a low-mimetic realism that is far more commercially accessible. It enables Roeg to use competent professionals like Sutherland and Christie, who are credible and appealing, but who lack the magic of rock star Mick Jagger in *Performance* and authentic aborigine Gulpilil in *Walkabout.*[2] The fascination of the surface is *Don't Look Now*'s primary source of value. Involvement in human experience focuses on exploration of formal patterns that may, indeed, be unchangeable, no matter how much is known about them.

Both *The Exorcist* and *Don't Look Now,* in trying to affirm a basic metaphysical value and expand our spiritual reality in a world dominated by corruption and despair, draw our attention to the richness of the phenomenological surface but remain unconvincing at the deeper levels of conceptualization and emotional power.

NOTES

1. We have written at length on *Rosemary's Baby* in *Close-Up* (New York: Harcourt Brace Jovanovich, 1972).

2. We have written at much greater length on the relationship among these films (and also *The Man Who Fell to Earth*) in "Cultural and Cinematic Codes in *The Man Who Fell to Earth* (1976) and *Walkabout* (1971): Insiders and Outsiders in the Films of Nicolas Roeg," chapter 6 of *Self and Cinema* (South Salem, N.Y.: Redgrave Publishing, 1980).

4

Eyes of Laura Mars: A Binocular Critique

Lucy Fischer and Marcia Landy

Much more explicitly than the first three essays in this collection, Lucy Fischer and Marcia Landy's "binocular critique" of Eyes of Laura Mars *(reprinted from* Screen *23 [Sept.–Oct. 1982]) is the demonstration of a critical method that utilizes insights gleaned from contemporary work in feminist, ideological, and psychoanalytic film criticism and theory. Accordingly, Fischer and Landy's focus is not simply on the representation of women in* Eyes of Laura Mars, *but also on this film's "ideology of vision" and its treatment of "spectatorship." Is the self-reflexivity of this film, Fischer and Landy ask, a means of directing us toward an informed, progressive view of sexual politics? Or is it merely one more eclectic, seductive strategy that trades on "the female body, violence, and aggressive vision"? Given that modern horror has become increasingly self-reflexive and preoccupied with the violent victimization of women, the two alternate readings of* Eyes of Laura Mars *offered by Fischer and Landy have important implications for our understanding of the course the genre has taken since the late 1970s.*

Fischer and Landy are both professors in the Film Studies Program at the University of Pittsburgh. Fischer's articles on film have appeared in such journals as Film Quarterly, Cinema Journal, Millennium, *and* Wide Angle. *In addition to her recent book,* Fascism and Film: The Italian Commercial Cinema, 1930–1943, *Landy has published articles on film in* New German Critique, Cine-tracts, Film Criticism, Jump Cut, *and other journals.*

In recent years the criticism on women and film has surfaced strategies for identifying the nature and presence of male-dominated vision in cinematic discourse. Psychoanalysis, in particular, has provided a method and language for reading texts and locating their patriarchal ideology. Such readings, however, have limited their scope to the text and have not taken into account the film's impact on audience or the stylistic devices through which the text is materialized. Furthermore, they do not place their analyses within a broader consideration of the film's existence as a product in the marketplace, its relationship to film traditions and genres, and its interaction with other cultural practices.

To raise questions about the incompleteness of such readings, we are proposing a two-part essay in which these critical issues are addressed. Part I offers a serious reading of a film that remains within the boundaries of the text. In particular, the reading will entertain a psychoanalytic examination of the narrative as a way of identifying the sexual politics of the film. Part II places that reading in dialogue with a consideration of the film's mode of production, its stylistic strategies, and its cultural allusions and thereby tests the adequacy of the reading for deciphering the position of women. Through structuring our essay in this manner, we address the question of how to read a film so as to avoid treating it as a static, hermetic object and, rather, to view it as a dynamic system in interaction with its own multiple codes and with other cultural articulations.

We have chosen, specifically, to examine *Eyes of Laura Mars* (1978), directed by Irvin Kershner, because the film openly raises certain relevant issues concerning the representation of women in film: the relationship between sexual oppression, violence, and pornography and the role of film, television, advertising, and photography in producing and reproducing patriarchal ideology. Furthermore, *Laura Mars* seems to be capable of generating controversy because it can provide diametrically opposing reactions. When we recently taught the film, for example, the students in the class were divided as to whether the film was unmitigated pornography because of its unrelieved fusion of sex, aggression, and spectacle, or a subtle exposure of sexual politics, surfacing connections between female subordination and the media's exploitation of ways of seeing women.

How can a film be considered by some viewers as critically progressive and by others as ideologically suspect? The answer to this question may be located in the problematics of the text, or it may reside in the critical methods brought to bear on it. This essay seeks to address these issues.

I.

> Narrative does not show, does not imitate; the passion which may excite us in reading a novel is not that of a "vision." . . . Rather, it is that of *meaning,* that of a higher order relation which also has its emotions, *its hopes, its dangers, its triumphs.*
> — Roland Barthes
> "Structural Analysis of Narratives"

As Roland Barthes has noted in an essay on literature, one of the motivating forces that propels us through narrative is the desire to ascribe meaning to stories, to fathom their significance. Some narratives are openly resistant to such a process, subverting the reader's urge to comprehend. Others seem to invite the enterprise, conveniently providing the reader with the resonant details and clues.

Eyes of Laura Mars is a work in the latter category. Though on one level it presents itself as merely a transparent genre piece of the thriller/ horror variety, on another plane it poses as a work of some self-consciousness that seems to perform the metacritical act of commenting on its own mode of being and address. Thus, *Laura Mars* encourages the viewer not only to naively follow the narrative action, but also to peruse it for deeper implications. As Roland Barthes has remarked, such an interpretive process has its "hopes," but also its apparent "dangers."

But the question arises as to why *Laura Mars* invites the viewer to undertake such a reading, and, furthermore, what kind of a reading it ultimately engenders. It is the very subject matter of the work that initially intimates a degree of self-reflexivity, since the film suggestively concerns a woman photographer whose associates are killed by a madman and whose vision becomes progressively associated with that of the murderer himself. Given this emphasis on photography and sight in a voyeuristic mad-slasher movie, the spectator is invited to assume a certain self-consciousness on the part of the filmmakers, and to wonder whether the work might perform an autocritique. If the viewer accepts such an invitation, what kind of a reading might he or she formulate? And what are its "hopes" and its "dangers"?

To begin such an analysis, it is useful to return to the title of the film which emphasizes the *eyes* of Laura Mars — her sight, her vision. This, of course, refers to her narrative status as a photographer and also to her role as a psychic "seer" of the murderer's villainous acts. Furthermore, throughout the film her "look" is stressed through an optical eye/iconography of close-ups of her eyeballs, poised in gaping horror. But beyond the issue of her literal sight lies the more intriguing question of her "vision" as a photographer. What kind of a vision is it, and what are its implications within the narrative discourse?

Laura Mars is a high-fashion photographer whose work has an original cast to it. Her poses involve mostly female models in postures of stylized violence. In many of the pictures they seem to be victims: in one a woman in garters lies draped across a bed, as though she had been murdered. In other photographs the models seem disturbingly aggressive, as in the image of a woman holding a gun over a dead man in a pool. In yet other pictures the women seem engaged in a lesbian struggle. In a sequence Laura shoots at Columbus Circle, two models in underwear and fur coats enact a hairpulling "girlie fight" while posed against the background of a burning car. The sadomasochistic thrust of her photography is clear, with women placed either in the role of mutilated victims or Amazonian assailants. In both situations women's bodies are fetishized and the connection made between female sexuality and violence.

Clearly we recognize in the images created by Laura Mars an iconography oppressive to women, a vision that is decidedly patriarchal. Whether her models are portrayed as passive objects of brutality or perpetrators of violence themselves, they function not as females but as the sign of male sexual fears. In their aggressive postures they enact a threat to man, and in their stance as victims they are "punished" for it. In this respect, the high-fashion photography of Laura Mars shares much with the mise-en-scène of pornography, which, as critics have noted, shapes "female sexuality in the image of male sexual fantasies."[1]

Thus Laura Mars has what we might term "male vision"—a way of seeing that reflects the dominant sexist ideology. Perhaps that is why the décor of her apartment favors mirrors that constantly barrage her with the sight of the female image. Within this context, even her name seems filled with significance, since Mars was a Roman war god and his astrological sign has been used as the symbol of masculinity. Even the narrative action of the film raises this issue quite explicitly when a reporter at Laura's gallery opening asks her to respond to charges that her work is "offensive to women."

In the sense we have used the term thus far, "male vision" has been meant metaphorically, to suggest that Laura sees "like" a man. But what is interesting about the film is that it articulates this notion on a literal level. Whereas Laura tells us that years ago she saw artistic flashes of violence that inspired her work, now she experiences literal visions in which she sees through the eyes of a male killer. What is intriguing about this narrative configuration is not Laura's status as a psychic, which seems a mere narrative ploy. Rather, what stands out is the connection implied between Laura's work as a photographer and the act of homicide, her artistic vision and the murderer's point of view. Significantly, the victims are all associated with Laura or her work and include her editor, her models, her manager, and her husband. Furthermore, her moments of second sight are linked to her photographic practice. After her first episode (which comes as a kind of nightmare), she immediately goes to her light box and examines a series of pictures, while playing nervously with a pair of scissors. At another point, a psychic vision hits her while she is developing prints and then while she is in the middle of a photographic session. Even the dialogue seems to emphasize the ties between her photographic enterprise and murder: "Kill the shoot!" her manager, Donald, screams as Laura finds herself unable to continue work. Finally, when she is brought to the police station for questioning about the murders, a detective, John Neville, points out the parallels between her fashion compositions and unpublished crime snapshots.

Thus through its particular choice of narrative actions, the film literalizes the notion of Laura's "male vision." Her work is not only influenced by a patriarchal point of view, but also her sight is literally taken over by that of a man. At the moments of her psychic inspiration, her own female vision is blinded — and she stumbles around her environment, bumping into walls. In this respect the film seems to operate as a kind of cautionary tale for the male-oriented woman who, in adopting patriarchal attitudes, cannot fail but to oppress her own sex, to engage symbolically in their murder. By the end of the film, Laura has even taken in hand the killer's gun — an object she has consistently refused to recognize as an extension of her photographic lens. Laura's "confusion" regarding gender identification seems encapsulated in a particular image of her manager, Donald, who dresses up in her clothes one night to help throw police bodyguards off her trail.

There is yet another aspect of the narrative and stylistic construction of *Laura Mars* that makes it suggestive as a discourse on male/female vision and it has to do with the moments in which Laura herself is pursued. At these times, since she sees through the eyes of the killer, she views herself in the third person, from behind, stalked from some hidden vantage point. The first such occurrence takes place in her dockside studio, when the killer chases her down a hall. As she runs into Donald's arms for safety, she cries: "I saw him looking at me." The final instance of this trope occurs at the end of the film when the killer is revealed to be the policeman, John Neville.

Again, what is provocative about this narrative/stylistic device is the way it can be read to literalize an issue in the ideology of vision. In an often-quoted section of *Ways of Seeing,* John Berger states: "*Men act and women appear.* Men look at women. Women watch themselves being looked at. . . . The surveyor of woman in herself is male: the surveyed female. Thus she turns herself into an object — and most particularly an object of vision: a sight."[2]

It is precisely this split consciousness of the male-oriented woman that is dramatized in the vision of Laura Mars. When her sight is dominated by the killer, she literally sees herself as an object, and her consciousness functions both as the "surveyor" and the "surveyed." Within the narrative, this can be read as the logical extension of her photographic work in which she generates images of women designed to satisfy the male gaze.

Even the fact that Laura is symbolically "punished" for her work seems contained within a patriarchal ideology. In the same text Berger talks of how female nude models were often posed holding a mirror. He remarks:

"You painted a naked woman because you enjoyed looking at her, you put a mirror in her hand and you called the painting *Vanity,* thus morally condemning the woman whose nakedness you had depicted for your own pleasure."[3] In *Laura Mars,* of course, the mirror has been augmented by a camera, but she, too, stands chastised for treating women as men have trained her—as an object of sight.

There is a final way in which the film literalizes certain notions concerning male vision and, in this regard, has particular relevance to film. In her article "Visual Pleasure and Narrative Cinema," Laura Mulvey discusses how dramatic movies are structured according to the male gaze. Through the figure of a central hero, the audience is led to identify with a masculine perspective. As she writes: "The male protagonist is free to command the stage, a stage of spatial illusions in which he articulates the look and creates the action."[4] Thus, though women may be present in the film, it is the male characters (and, by extension, the male audience) who are the "active controllers of the look," and who, therefore, dominate the narrative trajectory.[5]

Though in most classical films this dynamic is masked by codes of seamless editing, in *Laura Mars* the control of the male gaze is brought to the surface, as part of the actual plot. In an article on "Myths of Women in the Cinema," Claire Johnston terms women the "pseudocenter of the filmic discourse" because they function only as signs of male consciousness.[6] Again, in *Laura Mars* this concept is literalized in the figure of a photographer whose mind and body seem almost "inhabited" by a male double.

While emphasizing male vision, the film also seems to enact a prohibition against female vision, another feature of sexist ideology. While man is traditionally posited as the ideal spectator and woman positioned as the object of his surveillance, she is never accorded an equal scopic stance. Rather her vision must be entirely muted and passive, and she must never actively return the look. Again, the plot of *Laura Mars* articulates this repression. In the beginning of the film, Laura instructs her male beauticians to highlight the models' eyes, to make them "pop out." But once the murderer begins stabbing his victims' eyes, she instructs her makeup artists to tone them down, to hide them with waves of hair. Thus, within the film, women are symbolically warned against looking, and their vision regarded as a clear and present threat to man. It is as though the female look had the power to arouse some deep-seated male anxiety and to trigger some violent retaliatory response. In this regard one thinks of the shocking image of the eye being slashed in Luis Buñuel's *Un Chien Andalou,* and of Jean Vigo's critical question: "When we flinch from the screen image of a woman's eye sliced in half by a razor, is it more dreadful than the spectacle of a cloud veiling a full moon?"[7]

But on what is this apparent dread of woman based? And, moreover,

what is its relevance to *Eyes of Laura Mars?* Once again, it is the very
narrative of the film that invites us to examine the issue. For when the
identity of the murderer is revealed, the killer is portrayed as a psychopath who offers us a tendentious monologue to "explain" the roots of his
crime. Neville stands there before Laura and begins talking in the third
person, as though the biography he recounts pertains to Laura's chauffeur, Tommy, on whom he is trying to pin the heinous deeds. He talks
of how "his" mother was a hysterical woman, a hooker, who left him in
dirty diapers for days at a time, while "she sold her ass in the streets of
the nation's capital." Laura interrupts on several occasions, bewildered,
objecting: "No, that's not Tommy's story." Gradually, Neville's monologue
shifts to the first person as he tells her how one day a man (who may have
been the child's father) appeared and slit the prostitute's throat as punishment for her maternal negligence. Neville goes on: "*I* sat there and watched
the blood dry on her face until it was just about the color of your hair."
"Neville, you said 'I,' " Laura gasps. This confusion in person continues
later on as Neville puts a gun in Laura's hands and, in a gesture of suicide,
tries to force her to shoot him. He tells her: "If you love *me,* kill *him.*"

Other narrative/stylistic details of this sequence seem loaded with significance and encourage the spectator's decoding. For example, the final
confrontation scene takes place against a background of mirrors, with
Neville's and Laura's reflections frequently divided into a triptych. And
at the crucial moment when Neville finally breaks down, he takes his icepick and stabs his reflection three times in the eye.

This smorgasbord of Freudian symbolism is difficult for the viewer of
healthy semantic appetite to resist. Unlike the end of *Psycho,* where a
psychiatric explanation is offered dryly as a kind of closing convention,
in *Laura Mars* the scene addresses the audience with high drama and pathos
and solicits their complicity. But what does the scene mean? And can it
be read to display any intelligence on the part of the filmmakers concerning psychosexual dynamics? On a certain level it can, for what the scene
tends to dramatize is the classical male fear of woman as linked to the
maternal figure. Furthermore, it posits that fear as a pathology and views
it as the potential cause of violence toward women.

In an insightful article on pornography, Susan Lurie sees male brutality
toward women (be it physical or symbolic) as an exorcism of infantile castration fears. As she writes: "The torture, rape, mutilation of women . . .
reverses the death threat associated with the castration men fear from
women."[8] But wherein does this danger lie?

In her explanation of this phenomenon, Lurie differs somewhat from
Freud. Whereas he sees male anxieties as stemming from the perception
of the female "lack" — her disturbing absence of a penis — Lurie sees male

fears as derived from a sense of what females possess — of their power. While desiring bodily and spiritual reunion with the mother, the male child suspects that this will mean castration. As Lurie remarks: "He fantasizes that *union with Mother is to be what she is, not what he is.* That is he fantasizes that this union is one in which Mother's superior will presides to so great an extent that he is formed in her likeness. And while this seems to have been a satisfactory, indeed delightful, arrangement during infancy, his present individual/sexual self, symbolized in his penis, clearly could not survive such an arrangement."[9]

Thus Lurie emphasizes the notion of female *power* rather than that of female *lack*. She sees the man's view of woman as "castrated" as arising only as a second-order configuration, and not the primary source of his fear. As she states: "The concept of the 'mutilated creature' is a wish-fulfillment fantasy intended to combat the early imagined dread of what his mother's intentional power . . . might have in store for him."[10] Lurie also implicitly critiques Freud's notion of identifying the threat of castration with the father. Rather, she sees the male fear as tied to anxieties regarding the maternal force.

Clearly, as Neville recounts his autobiographical history in *Laura Mars,* many elements of Lurie's analysis of male-female psychodynamics are present. His infantile fear of the mother (and her prostitute's sexual powers) have obviously been transformed into hostility. And in his image of her slit throat, we see a version of Lurie's fantasy of the "mutilated creature," or what Mulvey has elsewhere termed "the bearer of the bleeding wound."[11] Finally, in Neville's forcing the gun into Laura's reluctant hand and squeezing the trigger into his belly, we find dramatized the male fear of woman as appropriator of the phallus through some violent destructive act.

Given this context, it comes as no surprise when Neville ultimately stabs himself in the eye, as though a symbolic punishment for viewing his mother as object of dread and desire. As various feminist critics have pointed out, the sexual implications of a man robbed of his sight go far beyond the Oedipal tale.[12] In a different Greek myth the seer, Tiresias, is blinded by Hera after he has declared female sexuality more pleasurable than male. And in another legend, Peeping Tom is blinded for looking at the nude body of Lady Godiva.

Neville's confession also hints at Oedipal conflicts, though (contrary to Freud) it casts the father more in the role of savior than aggressor. Still the Oedipal triangle seems clearly implied in the plethora of triadic mirror images that flood the final sequence. Furthermore, Laura is portrayed in the closing sections of the film in a maternal stance — at one point wearing a madonnalike scarf. Even her characterization as psychically potent can be seen as a transposition of the notion of Mother as a magical force.

Finally, as Neville's monologue veers toward incomprehensibility, he speaks to Laura as though he had a rival for her affections. "I don't know what you see in that guy," he complains incoherently. "I'm the one you want." His persona in this speech (which shifts fluidly among that of his father, his mother, and Laura) parallels his earlier split between first and third person, as though he were the psychic battlefield for some struggle of identity and identification.

What this discussion of *Laura Mars* has sought to demonstrate is the kind of reading that the film readily occasions. It presents itself to the viewer as more than a simple thriller or horror movie—a story of crime and its resolution. Rather, its dense and allusive surface proposes it as a veritable discourse on the issues of violence toward women and the psychosexual dynamics of sight. It does so by suggestively taking as its subject the figure of a photographer, one who exploits women in her work. Then, quite fittingly, it casts the photographer as "possessed" by the vision of a deranged male sex killer, whose homicidal point of view becomes identified with her art. The film even hints at the roots of such misogyny in its characterization of the murderer as a psychopath whose savage acts are clearly compensatory for his fear of women. The film then goes on to associate his hatred of females with the dynamics of vision: with the dread of viewing the "castrated" female body, and the voyeuristic pleasure of seeing women sexually abused. Moreover, through its choice of the killer's particular crime, the film alludes to man's horror of the woman, who reverses the dynamics of vision, who dares to look back.

Read in this fashion, *Eyes of Laura Mars* appears to document a psychosexual problem that afflicts the cinema as a scopic medium, and especially the sensational horror/thriller genre. To borrow Roland Barthes's language from the opening quote, we might say that such an interpretation can, at least, raise such "hopes" for the text. But following Barthes's line of thought a bit further, we might question whether such a generous exegesis is truly exhaustive or whether it might mask certain critical "dangers." It is for this reason that we have chosen not to take just a monocular view of *Eyes of Laura Mars,* but rather to see it in dual focus as a gesture of binocular critical vision.

II.

During the last few years, an overlay of erstwhile mythic significance has become a valuable selling tool (or so many producers and directors think) and the result has been that a number of very small films have been invested with a grandiose importance the weight of which they can hardly bear. Irvin Kershner's *Eyes of Laura Mars*

(1978) is a perfect example of this ploy. At the center of the film is a very short, rather silly plot upon which is hung great gobs of would-be significance. Semioticians speak of a sign of communication composed of two equal halves: the "signifier" and the "signified." A film like *Laura Mars* is all signifiers that never connect with the signifieds. Or to put it more poetically, full of sound and fury.

— James Monaco, *American Film Now*

It is interesting that James Monaco singles out *Laura Mars* to exemplify the banality and seductiveness of many contemporary Hollywood films. Apparently he selects it because it is a film capable of generating misreadings. Yet the film deserves more than Monaco's hasty dismissal. As the discussion above has shown, the film does connect its signifiers and signifieds. The problem is not, as Monaco indicates, that the film says nothing but that it says everything. This section will examine *Laura Mars* as an eclectic film that, in its eclecticism, subverts its own ostensible intentions. Our previous discussion reveals how the film documents the classic paradigm of female oppression, but if we place that reading within the dynamics of a larger filmic discourse, the question arises as to whether *Laura Mars* exposes the phenomenon of male-dominated vision and the cultural hostility toward women, or merely exploits its audience in the name of these issues, or does both at the same time. A second analysis of the film is therefore necessary.

Laura Mars belongs to the Hollywood "new wave" of films identified with independent producers, featuring prestigious directors such as Francis Ford Coppola, John Frankenheimer, Arthur Penn, Martin Scorsese, Woody Allen, and others. This generation of producers and directors is reputed to have a larger measure of control over their works in contrast to the forms of production characteristic of the old studio system. Great involvement in financing has enabled directors to have more influence over subject matter and treatment of films, enabling them to entertain a broad array of issues in ostensibly more direct fashion. The 1968 lifting of the censorship code and the institution of a rating system in the United States have further encouraged the representation of formerly taboo subjects as divorce, adultery, sexual relations, social deviance, and violence in more explicit ways.

Yet a closer examination of the economic structures governing these films exposes the illusory nature of independent production. Most particularly, the tendency toward conglomeration in the 1970s has made the movie industry more dependent than ever on immediate and large-scale profits and especially on the control of outside investors. The nature of conglomeration is such that the production of film is only one aspect of a network of merged but diversified industries. For example, Monaco describes how MCA, "one of the first film conglomerates to take shape . . . own several record companies, Spencer Gift stores, a train manufacturer, a savings and loan association in Colorado, a computer service company, and three publishers: G. P. Putnam's Sons, Coward, MacCann, and Geohegan; and Berkley; as well as *New Times* magazine."[13]

The effects of conglomeration have been mixed. Studios in danger of disappearance have been salvaged by the new system. The "new corporation men," according to Michael Pye and Lynda Myles, "lacked the technical knowledge that past producers shared. Their ignorance now distances them from the film-makers. But it also makes them dependent on the film-makers, on being offered ideas from directors, writers, and producers who are younger, who know the art and craft of film, and who know a world outside the studio machine and have some instinctive sympathy with the new cine-literate generation that comprises the majority of film audiences."[14] But, as Monaco has also suggested, today film has become more of a business than an industry with an emphasis on profit first, the product second. The product can be as "disparate as film and insurance, records and sugar cane,"[15] and loss in one area can be compensated for in another; however, the commitment to film is considerably lessened under this system of financing and management.

Changes in Hollywood modes of production can be documented in the diminished number of films produced, in the consequent emphasis on creating "blockbusters," in the high-powered advertising strategies developed for ferreting out audience response, in particular, the use of consumer-research methods similar to the hard-sell tactics in other areas of advertising, in the influx of "outsiders" into the film industry from television, and in the incorporation of eclectic strategies within the films for attracting the broadest possible audiences.

Thus, the process of economic diversification is paralleled in the forms and treatments of these films that draw on different strata of the public. *Laura Mars,* for example, makes an attempt to appeal simultaneously to intellectuals, pop culture fans, horror film buffs, film aesthetes, high-fashion consumers, viewers of pornography, and the budding moral majority. The film also tries to make contact with the earlier genre film production, altering it to suit contemporary audiences. The thriller/horror film, in particular, continues to enjoy a rebirth, though it incorporates more sophisticated strategies to suit its urbane audiences. As with other genre films that continue to be produced, the use of self-reflexive techniques, psychoanalysis, allusions to political events or movements, a capitalizing on social decadence, and a foregrounding and use of high technology and other media characterize the eclecticism of *Laura Mars* in its treatment of genre. This eclecticism applies to the film's style, system of references, narrative strategies, and also to its point of view, which seems, at the same time, straightforward and parodic.

Above all, an analysis of many of these films of the 1970s and 1980s reveals them to be especially self-conscious in their strategies for wooing spectators, "poised," as one critic has suggested, "between mockery and indulgence of the audience."[16] It would seem, therefore, that a fruitful method for interrogating the ideology of these films would reside in an analysis of their uses of the means and ends of self-reflexivity and spectatorship particularly as these interact with the mode of production described above.

The sound track of *Laura Mars* is heavily dependent on pop music. From the first moment of the film to its conclusion, the lyrics and music serve to identify the film's connection to the world of commercialized pop culture. The introductory and concluding song, in particular, performed by a woman, emphasizing imprisonment, psychic pain, and oneiric experience merges with the film's situating of the woman as the focus of vision and of verbal aggression and physical assault. But the music, independent of the narrative, also fuses with the other uses of media in the film to create an autonomous and gratuitous experience for the audience, akin to the self-absorption associated with listening to pop music. The audience can appreciate the music in and of itself, independent of its role in developing the film's thematics. For example, during the scene of the models dressing for a photographic session, a song is heavily overlaid on the sound track, turning the sequence into a disco number. Furthermore, the songs "Let's All Chant" and "The Eyes of Laura Mars" (sung by Barbra Streisand) were released well in advance of the film, the former song having occupied a place for a time among the top-ten list of hits. Thus, the film was able to tap other resources for arousing audience expectations as well as to capitalize on other avenues of profit.

At the same time that the film woos its pop culture constituency, it also appeals to intellectuals. For example, early in the film, in a shot of one of the victim's apartments, we see books on Talleyrand and Russia and one by Studs Terkel, which provide further clues to the film's eclecticism. The intellectual allusions are thus fused with the pop culture elements, thereby inviting a diverse audience to view the film. The foregrounding of the book, *Eyes of Laura Mars,* identified with the film's title, connects the subject matter and style of the book to the film, indicating the circularity and self-enclosed nature of the filmic text, that it is in dialogue with itself.

Laura Mars's attempts at self-reflexivity can further be documented in the film's absorption of still other media. Beyond the uses of pop music, books, and photography, the film calls attention to television, television technology, newscasting, newspaper reporting, celebrity interviewing, and high-fashion modeling. Moreover, the playing with onstage, backstage, and off-stage settings, in the sequences involving costuming, makeup, directing, and photographing as well as in the casual scenes at home, acts to suppress differences between performance and life, to fuse media spectacle and private experience. The question raised throughout the film, exemplified particularly in the comments of the newscaster at the exhibition of Laura Mars's work is: What is the connection between media practices, sexual exploitation, violence, and profit-making? In his words, "Is this all a hype?" A woman reporter asserts that the photographs of nude and semi-clothed women are offensive to women, and one of the models comments that the "world you see is violent" and that the photographs merely mirror that violence for the spectator. Thus, *Laura Mars,* in its self-reflexive gargantuanism, even anticipates and coopts the potential responses of the external audience.

The element of spectatorship linked to the film's self-referential ploys also reveals a self-conscious taxonomic treatment of ways of seeing, but, like the reiterative use of the split mirrors replicating the image of Laura Mars, the ostensibly different forms of looking merge to reproduce one form of gaze, namely, of aggressive and voyeuristic spectatorship. The first image of the film confronts the external viewer with the close-up image of an eye. A long take forces prolonged viewing of a positive image of Laura Mars, which is transformed into a negative image. These shots are repeated at the film's conclusion. The particular object of focus that the audience confronts—the object of mutilation—is the right eye and the instrument of attack is an icepick. The violence that the spectator is forced to observe is therefore associated with vision and particularly with the monocular vision of the camera eye. Though the murderer is not a photographer, his act of vengeance is merged with the photographer's vision. One scene in the film particularly dramatizes this dynamic. When Laura tries to explain to Neville the nature of her second sight, she uses the video cameras and monitors for her demonstration.

Furthermore, the external spectator's gaze is identified with the killer's (and with the camera eye). The spectator is positioned in the empty space behind the moving camera, which approaches the victim. In these shots, particularly, the identification of the audience with the psychotic and violent criminal is unambiguous. The voyeurism of which Laura is accused by Neville when he first meets her is thus attributed to the external audience as it occupies a privileged space in the scrutiny of mutilation.

Aggressive spectatorship is not limited to the male solely but is also attributed to women in the film. Laura as photographer and particularly as a photographer of female victims shares with the killer a complicit look at the violent destruction of other females. Not only does the film, therefore, reinforce the connection among photography, violence, and the victimization of women but it also implicates both sexes in the process. Moreover, the film's self-referentiality serves also to implicate the film itself in reproducing these connections.

Laura Mars also identifies other spectators. For example, when Laura arrives at the gallery, the camera focuses on the street crowd of celebrity seekers who observe her as she emerges from the car. She is subject to the same scrutiny as her models. Her physical appearance is calculated to arouse sexual curiosity. Though her torso is completely covered, a shot of the lower part of her body reveals a deep slit in her skirt as the camera focuses in close up on her exposed thigh and leg. She wears a similar costume in the scenes where she photographs models on the street and, again, the camera focuses on her exposed legs.

During the photographing session, still more spectators are identified. Tommy, the chauffeur, a prime murder suspect, is portrayed suspiciously as a voyeur. Laura's view of the models through the lens is shared with the audience as the scene shows the women fighting with one another and the image of a burning car. The sequence also captures passers-by on the street who become part of the film. While obviously not scripted, they nonetheless assume a role in the film's incorporation of different spectators. The orchestration of male and female, fictional and "real" spectators, threatening and random surveillance are concentric, all leading to the same object of regard, the focus on the female and on scenes of violence, creating a bond of complicity between the internal and external spectators to the film.

The dual structure of narrative and self-referentiality work, therefore, to blur rather than distinguish between filmic and actual events. The reflexivity not only assimilates the audience into the narrative but also creates a sense in which the audience is implicated vicariously or actively in the act of looking at and of experiencing a world where there is no escape from media manipulation, psychopathology, and aggression. Like the thriller/horror film to which it is related, *Laura Mars* attempts to exploit a highly stylized and choreographed use of the camera and editing to unsettle and involve the viewer. The positioning of the victims under surveillance and attack is predictable. They are shown in undefended, vulnerable positions, cornered and unable to escape. The audience, however, does not occupy their position but remains in the aggressive position of the voyeur and demented killer. Unlike Michael Powell's *Peeping Tom* (1960), where the audience shares the places of aggressor and victim, the spectator in *Laura Mars* is rarely, if at all, in the position of the victims.

Moreover, in *Peeping Tom,* we are aware from the outset of the killer's identity, whereas *Laura Mars* adds, among its other affect-arousing strategies, elements of suspense and uncertainty, suggesting further that Kershner is less interested in an analysis of the killer's psychopathology than in the generating of audience involvement.

With the exception of the scenes following the death of two of Laura's models, where Laura and John are walking in the woods and the following scenes where they make love, the film does not provide any safe or tranquil vantage points, any alternative vision of an outlet from the urban-media nightmare. Alone in their homes, women are shown, as in the classic thriller/horror film, as potential targets of male aggression and murder. Furthermore, in Tommy's apartment house, as he ascends to meet Neville, the sounds of marital discord and squabbles over money can be heard in the hall, further contributing to the film's atmosphere of antagonism and discord.

If *Laura Mars* is contrasted with *Peeping Tom,* a film that is also self-reflexive, involving filmmaking and the equation between spectatorship and aggression, the sexual problematics of Kershner's film can be identified more clearly. In *Peeping Tom,* Powell uses the self-referential elements to distance rather than implicate the audience. Also, the acts of looking and violence are concentrated in the male whose erotic desire is sublimated in the camera eye. The film does not fetishize the female body nor highlight gratuitous scenes of sexual deviance. The killer is identified specifically with his father, the person responsible for warping the son's vision, and the son, in his desire to fuse with the dreaded father, enacts the crime of killing the mother. Thus, the father, not the mother, is the source of conflict. The psychological emphasis in *Laura Mars,* on the other hand, is disappointment with the mother. The "explanation" for Neville's aggression, reserved for the final moments of the film, is over-identification with and revenge against the mother.

Throughout the film, the portrayals of men reveal the men to be weak and impotent, and their weakness seems traceable to fantasies of female dominance. One of the policemen comments that "the city is full of creeps." Donald, a homosexual, is a victim of the killer's assault. Tommy is an ex-criminal and a voyeur. A gratuitous image of a male dwarf appears early in the film. The police are presented as unsympathetic, lecherous, and trigger-happy, and the murderer himself is a policeman. Michael, Laura's former husband, presents himself as a total failure and an exploiter of women. His impotence and rage against females is most clearly demonstrated in his accusations that Laura's career is to blame for his writer's block.

That Laura Mars's photography corresponds to the police photographs provides further evidence of the film's reductive treatment of the relationship between art and society, which sees art merely as a reflection of social decadence, the mirror replication of sexuality and violence without mediation. The film invites the audience to confirm the notion that individuals and institutions are the creation of a "sick" society, suffering from the absence of family stability and proper male and female roles. Furthermore, the film's fusion of male and female vision does not lead toward a critique of phallocentrism but in an opposite direction, toward an attack on shifting sexual relations, identified as a major source of pathology. The male killer and the female photographer proclaim themselves to be "old-fashioned" and moral, and both are presented as stunted by their perverse environment in their capacity for a "natural" life. Thus in the final analysis, the film veers toward nostalgia and traditional sexual attitudes. In effect, Laura Mars's costume provides a clue to the film's operations. Like the severe, old-fashioned outfits she wears, the film maintains a conventional moral view, but it has an ideological "slit" that invites prurience and undercuts this point of view. In this way *Laura Mars* sustains diverse and contradictory attitudes.

Finally, it is in the film's eclecticism that it most reveals the way it produces ideology. Not only does an analysis of the content confirm the reproduction of familiar sexual attitudes but also an analysis of the form, the film's system of references, and, especially, its treatment of audience reveals the film's cynicism and its complicity with exploitative modes for generating cinematic involvement. In spite of the film's uses of self-reflexivity, the distancing devices associated with such a practice are absent, and the treatment of spectatorship seems to corroborate that the film reproduces the ways of seeing it purports to question, specifically in its exploitation of voyeurism toward the ends of profit. The film's treatment of ostensibly different modes of spectatorship have culminated in a familiar gaze, the gaze that fixes on the helpless victims — independent females, homosexuals, or social deviants, all figures of marginality. The film's concern with marginality functions in the now-familiar ideological terrain where society is viewed as being threatened by socially aberrant behavior. The film points an accusing finger at these social "misfits" as the products and producers of conflict and commercial exploitation. Capitalizing on pop music, on the glamour and increasing prestige of high-fashion photography, the screen presence of a star like Faye Dunaway, and the appeals of high and low culture commodities, *Laura Mars* combines hard-sell advertising techniques with traditional content. Moreover, not only is the audience asked to experience the threat of an unstable world, but it is also coerced to share the responsibility for that world, even to view itself as the producer of the images it consumes.

Thus, it would seem that the film's combination of self-referentiality and studied spectatorship, its inclusion of the issues of homosexuality, psychopathology, and abuse of women are mere strategies for seducing the broadest possible audience by means of the most diverse techniques. In the final analysis, this diversity is transformed into the unitary objective of profit-making, and the medium of exchange is, as always, the female body, violence, and aggressive vision.

NOTES

1. Susan Lurie, "Pornography and the Dread of Women: The Male Sexual Dilemma," in *Take Back the Night,* ed. Laura Lederer (New York: William Morrow, 1980), 159. Lurie's remarks on the male fear of female power are reminiscent of the earlier theories of Karen Horney. See Karen Horney, "The Dread of Women," in *Feminine Psychology,* ed. Harold Kelman (New York: W. W. Norton, 1967).

2. John Berger, *Ways of Seeing* (New York: Penguin, 1977), 47.

3. Ibid., 51.

4. Laura Mulvey, "Visual Pleasure and Narrative Cinema," *Screen* 16 (Autumn 1975):13.

5. Ibid.

6. Claire Johnston, "Myths of Women in the Cinema," in *Women and the Cinema,* ed. Karyn Kay and Gerald Peary (New York: E. P. Dutton, 1977), 411.

7. Jean Vigo, "On Un Chien Andalou," in *L'age D'or and Un Chien Andalou,* ed. Luis Buñuel and trans. Marianne Alexandre (New York: Simon and Schuster, 1968), 75.

8. Lurie, "Pornography and the Dread of Women," 172.

9. Ibid., 162–63.

10. Ibid., 165.

11. Mulvey, "Visual Pleasure and Narrative Cinema," 7.

12. See Lurie, "Pornography and the Dread of Women," and Lucy Fischer, "The Image of Woman as Image: The Optical Politics of Dames," in *Genre: The Musical,* ed. Rick Altman (London: Routledge & Kegan Paul, 1981), 70–84.

13. James Monaco, *American Film Now* (New York: New American Library, 1979), 34.

14. Michael Pye and Linda Myles, *The Movie Brats* (New York: Holt, Rinehart, and Winston, 1979), 47.

15. Monaco, *American Film Now,* 32.

16. Richard Combs, "The Eyes of Laura Mars," *Monthly Film Bulletin* 45, no. 538 (Nov. 1978):219.

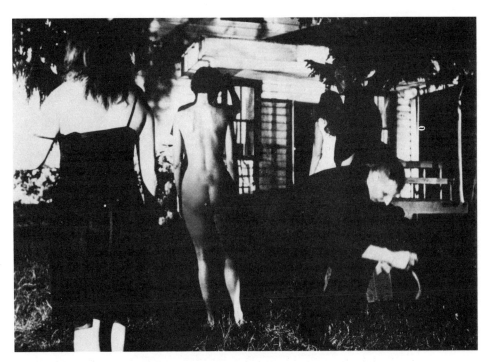

Situating horror in the everyday world of contemporary America: ordinary people become flesh-eating undead creatures in *Night of the Living Dead* (1968) and unlikely Satanists in *Rosemary's Baby* (1968).

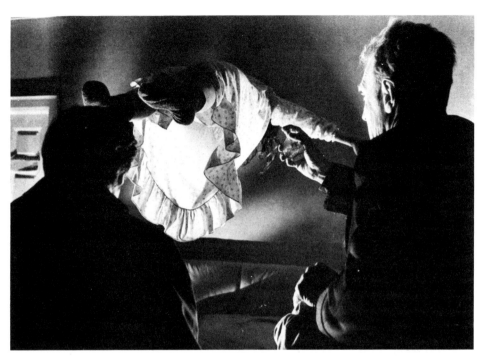

Restating cultural myths: uncommon "masculine" valor and the ritualistic challenge to Evil in *The Exorcist* (1973); all-too-common female victimization and the struggle for survival in *He Knows You're Alone* (1980).

Retelling and commenting on classic monster movies: the modern werewolf cum Big Bad Wolf in *The Howling* (1981); the pathetic creature, whose familiar mask covers his monstrous deformity, confronts his father in *The Funhouse* (1981).

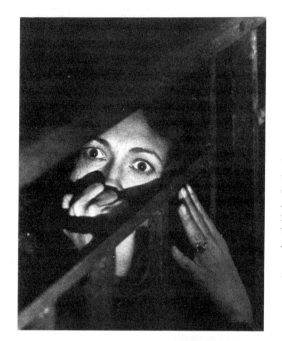

Violence and (and against) women: the terrorized seer in *Eyes of Laura Mars* (1978); the "innocent" object of desire in *Jaws* (1975); the "guilty" object of punishment in *Dressed to Kill* (1980); and the would-be victim armed for self-defense in *Eyes of a Stranger* (1981).

The singular threat as commanding, aristocratic vampire in *Dracula* (1979), psychopathic slasher in *Night School* (1980), and malevolent semi in *Duel* (1971).

The multiple threat as natural pests in *Frogs* (1972) and technocratic conspiracy in *Scanners* (1981).

5

Returning the Look:
Eyes of a Stranger

Robin Wood

*Like Lucy Fischer and Marcia Landy, Robin Wood in this essay
(which originally appeared as "Beauty Bests the Beast" and is reprinted
with permission from* American Film *[Sept. 1983],* © *1983, The American
Film Institute) takes up two related questions: the manipulation of the
"look" in modern horror and the ideological import of the representation
of violence against women. Writing after the stream of so-called slice-and-
dice movies had saturated the market in the wake of* Halloween *(1978)
and* Friday the 13th *(1980), Wood discusses this cycle as a phenomenon
that in its emphasis on the sadistic terrorization of women and the seemingly endless butchery of promiscuous teenagers speaks to certain "needs"
of our capitalist, consumer culture. Wood parts company from the
standard critique of these films by insisting that we pay attention to "different uses of the same generic material," so we can differentiate between
the "reactionary" and the potentially "subversive" examples of the cycle.*

*"Returning the Look" shares the same basic method and set of critical
assumptions with Wood's often-reprinted essay, "Return of the Repressed"
(*Film Comment *[July–Aug. 1978]), which in expanded form appears in
a 1979 anthology he co-edited,* American Nightmare: Essays on the Horror
Film. *Among his many books are* Hitchcock's Films *and* Hollywood from
Vietnam to Reagan. *Wood teaches film studies at York University, Toronto, and is a member of the editorial collective of* CineAction!

Confronted over the past few years with the proliferation of esca-
latingly violent and gruesome low-budget horror movies centered on
psychopathic killers, one may take away the impression of one undiffer-
entiated stream of massacre, mutilation, and terrorization, a single inter-
minable chronicle of bloodletting called something like *When a Stranger
Calls After Night School on Halloween or Friday the Thirteenth, Don't
Answer the Phone and Don't Go into the House Because He Knows You're
Alone and Is Dressed to Kill.* In fact, the films are distinguishable both

in function and in quality, and however one may shrink from systematic exposure to them, however one may deplore the social phenomena and ideological mutations they reflect, their popularity (especially — indeed, almost exclusively — with youth audiences) suggests that even if they were uniformly execrable they should not be ignored; an attempt both to understand the phenomena and discriminate among the films seems valid and timely.

The films can be seen to fall into two partially distinguishable categories, answering to two partially distinguishable cultural "needs": the "violence-against-women" movie (of which Brian De Palma's *Dressed to Kill* is the most controversial — as well as the most ambitiously "classy" — example) and what has been succinctly dubbed the "teenie-kill pic" (of which the purest — if that is the word — examples are the three *Friday the 13th* movies). The distinction is never clear-cut. The two cycles have common sources in Tobe Hooper's *The Texas Chain Saw Massacre* and John Carpenter's *Halloween* (which in turn have a common source in *Psycho*); the survivor in the teenie-kill movies — endurer of the ultimate ordeals, terrors, and agonies — is invariably female; the victims in the violence-against-women films are predominantly young. But the motivation for the slaughter, on both the dramatic and ideological levels, is somewhat different: in general, the teenagers are punished for promiscuity and the women are punished for being women.

Both cycles represent a sinister and disturbing inversion of the significance of the traditional horror film: there the monster was in general a "creature from the id," not merely a product of repression but a protest against it, whereas in the current cycles the monster, while still "produced by" repression, has become essentially a superego figure, avenging itself on liberated female sexuality or the sexual freedom of the young. What has not changed (making the social implications even more sinister) is the genre's basic commercial premise: that the customers continue to pay, as they always did, to enjoy the eruptions and depredations of the monster. But where the traditional horror film invited — however ambiguously — an identification with the "return of the repressed," the contemporary horror film invites an identification (either sadistic or masochistic or both simultaneously) with punishment.

On the whole, the teenie-kill pic seems the more consistently popular of the two recent cycles, and one can interpret this as a logical consequence of a "permissive" (as opposed to liberated) society. The chief, indeed almost the *only,* characteristic of the film's teenagers (who are obviously meant to be attractive to the youth audience as identification figures) is a mindless hedonism made explicit by a character in Steve Miner's *Friday the 13th Part 3,* who remarks (without contradiction) that the only things worth living for are screwing and smoking dope. The films both endorse this and relentlessly punish it; they never suggest that other options might be available. (After all, what might it not lead to if young people began to *think?*) What is most stressed, but nowhere *explicitly* condemned, is promiscuity—the behavior that consumer capitalism in its present phase simultaneously "permits" and morally disapproves of.

The satisfaction that youth audiences get from these films is presumably twofold: they identify with the promiscuity as well as the grisly and excessive punishment for it. The original *Friday the 13th,* directed by Sean S. Cunningham, dramatizes this very clearly: most of the murders are closely associated with the young people having sex (a principle that reaches ludicrous systematization in the sequels, where one can safely predict that any character who shows sexual interest in another will be dead within minutes); the psychopathic killer turns out to be a woman whose son (Jason) drowned because the camp counselors who should have been supervising him were engaged in intercourse. In the sequels Jason himself returns as a vaguely defined mutant monster, virtually indistinguishable from Michael of the *Halloween* films, introducing another indispensable component of the cycle, the monster's unkillability: the sexual guilt that the characters are by definition incapable of analyzing, confronting, or understanding can never be exorcised.

The violence-against-women movies have generally been explained as a hysterical response to 1960s and 1970s feminism: the male spectator enjoys a sadistic revenge on women who refuse to slot neatly and obligingly into his patriarchally predetermined view of "the way things should naturally be." This interpretation is convincing so long as one sees it as accounting for the intensity, repetitiveness, and ritualistic insistence of these films, and not for the basic phenomenon itself. From *Caligari* to *Psycho* and beyond, women have always been the main focus of threat and assault in the horror film.

There are a number of variously plausible explanations for this. As women are regarded as weak and helpless, it is simply more frightening if the monster attacks *them;* the male spectator can presumably identify with the hero who finally kills the monster, the film thereby indulging his vanity as protector of the helpless female. That he may also, on another level, identify with the monster in no way contradicts this idea; it merely suggests its inadequacy as a *total* explanation. Second, as men in patriarchal society have set women up on (compensatory) pedestals and, thereby, constructed them as oppressive and restrictive figures, they have developed a strong desire to knock them down again.

As in every genre, the archetypal male-constructed opposition of wife-whore is operative. In the traditional horror film the women who got killed were usually whore-figures, punished for "bringing out the beast" in men; the heroine who was terrorized and perhaps abducted (but eventually rescued) was the present or future wife.

The ideological tensions involved here are still central to our culture. The films obliquely express what Alfred Hitchcock's films, for example, consistently dramatized: the anxiety of the heterosexual male confronted by the possibility of an autonomous female sexuality he cannot control and organize. But the key point is that in the traditional horror film, the threatened heroine was invariably associated with the values of monogamous marriage and the nuclear family (actual or potential): the eruption of the Frankenstein monster during the preparations for his creator's wedding in the 1931 James Whale movie was the locus classicus. What the monster really threatened was the repressive, ideologically constructed bourgeois "normality." Today, on the other hand, the women who are terrorized and slaughtered tend to be those who *resist* definition within the virgin-wife-mother framework. As with the teenie-kill movies, the implications of the violence-against-women films are extremely disturbing.

The dominant project of these overlapping, interlocking cycles is, then, depressingly reactionary, to say the least. However, as both can be shown to have their sources in contemporary ideological tension, confusion, and contradiction, both also carry within them the potential for subverting that project. There is, for example, no inherent reason why a filmmaker of some intelligence and awareness should not make a teenie-kill movie that, while following the general patterns of the genre, analyzes sexual guilt and opposes it: it would chiefly require characters who are not totally mindless, for whom both filmmaker and spectator could feel some respect. The recent *Hell Night,* directed by Tom De Simone, in which sorority pledges brave a haunted house, shows vestiges of such an ambition — it at least produces an active and resourceful heroine (Linda Blair) capable of doing more than screaming and falling over — but in general the apparently total complicity of the youth audience in these fantasies of their own destruction has licensed a corresponding mindlessness in the filmmakers.

Feminists (of both sexes) have, on the other hand, been quite vociferous on the subject of violence against women, and this can be credited with provoking various degrees of disturbance in recent specimens of the genre, ranging from vague uneasiness to an intelligent rethinking of the conventions. In *Dressed to Kill* the violence to women is consistently countered by a critique of male dominance and an exposure of male sexual insecurities; it is among the most complete expressions of De Palma's obsessive concern with castration, literal or symbolic. Armand Mastroianni's *He*

Knows You're Alone, in which a maniac stalks brides-to-be, is finally very confused, but makes a highly sophisticated attempt (through a very conscious, intermittently reflexive play with narrative) to analyze violence against women in terms of male possessiveness and the fear of female autonomy. It is certainly worth discriminating between it and Joseph Ellison's *Don't Go in the House,* which may be taken as representing the cycle at its most debased: the latter is a film in which the most disgusting violence (a pyromaniac flays his victims alive with a blowtorch) is significantly juxtaposed with some unusually strident dialogue about "faggots" in a way that can be seen as indicating, however inadvertently, some of the sexual tensions that motivate the cycle as a whole.

Ken Wiederhorn's *Eyes of a Stranger* strikes me as the most coherent attempt to rework the conventions of the violence-against-women cycle so far. Although the film doesn't escape contamination (the generic patterns are to some degree intractable), it does come closest to embodying a systematic critique of the dominant project. Disgracefully mishandled and thrown away by its distributors, it seems to have come and gone virtually unnoticed on both sides of the Atlantic (apart from some predictable abuse from journalist-critics incapable of distinguishing between different uses of the same generic material). The film follows the basic rules of the cycle faithfully, so the necessary synopsis can be brief. A psychopath is terrorizing women (obscene phone call, followed by rape and murder); a television news reporter (Lauren Tewes) comes — correctly — to suspect a man in the apartment opposite her own; she endangers her own life by searching his apartment for evidence while he is out; he discovers who is harassing him and, in the climactic scene, invades her apartment in return, assaulting her younger sister (Jennifer Jason Leigh), who is blind, mute, and deaf from the shock of being raped and beaten when she was a child. I shall restrict analysis to three aspects, representing the major components of the subgenre.

The psychopath, the "look." Much has been made of the strikingly insistent use (in both teenie-kill and violence-against-women movies) of the first-person camera to signify the approach of the killer, perceived by many critics as an invitation to sadistic indulgence on the part of the spectator. There is a simple alternative explanation for the device: the need to preserve the secret of the killer's identity for a final "surprise." The second motivation might be seen merely as supplying a plausible alibi for the first: the sense of indeterminate, unidentified, possibly supernatural or superhuman menace feeds the spectator's fantasy of power, facilitating a direct spectator-camera identification by keeping the intermediary character, while signified to be present, as vaguely defined as possible. In *Eyes of a Stranger* the psychopath's identity is revealed quite early in the film: a rather ordinary-looking, confused, ungainly, unattractive man who strongly evokes memories of Raymond Burr in *Rear Window*. The point-of-view shots of strippers, naked women, and so on (surprisingly infrequent for the genre) are always attached to an *identified* figure: so that if the male spectator identifies with the point of view, he is consistently shown precisely whose it is. Hence, although the film is posited on the terrorization of women (and, during its first half, certainly gets too much mileage out of that for its own good), this is never presented with simple relish, and the sadism can never be simply enjoyed. It is difficult to imagine audiences *cheering* the murders — a not uncommon phenomenon within this cycle — deprived as they are of all possible perverse "glamour."

The other male characters. The two "attractive" young men — potential hero figures, though one is murdered very early in the film — are both associated with the killer on their first appearances (a device also employed, though less strikingly, in *He Knows You're Alone*). The first frightens the first victim by appearing in her doorway wearing a grotesque mask that resembles the killer's face under its concealing stocking (meanwhile, the killer is already hiding in her apartment); the second (Tewes's lover, the film's *apparent* male lead) leaps on her violently in bed in a parody of sexual assault. Male aggression is thus generalized, presented as a phenomenon of our culture; the lover, significantly, is trying throughout the film to circumscribe Tewes within his values and his apartment. Consistently, the men in the film are either unhelpful or uncomprehending, or they are active impediments. The police refuse to investigate the first victim's reports of harassment in time to save her because Tewes's (fully justified) warning newscast has provoked an epidemic of obscene calls that turn out to be "jokes," like the lover's pretended assault. The lover refuses to accept Tewes's evidence (circumstantial but persuasive, and strongly supported by that "intuition" that men like to see as the prerogative of the female so that they can condescend to it) until it is too late, because of his commitment, as a lawyer, to one of the dominant institutions of patriarchy. Tewes's attempts to express her concern on television are met by her fellow newscaster with bland indifference; the film is very shrewd in pinpointing the tendency of television to cancel out and reassure, Tewes's warning to women being immediately followed by the determinedly comic antics of the (male) weather reporter.

The women. The film is consistently woman-centered. Our identification figures are exclusively female, and the temptation to produce a male hero who springs to the rescue at the last moment is resolutely resisted, the women handling everything themselves. Tewes and Jennifer Jason Leigh are both presented (in their different ways, and within the limitations of the generic conventions) as strong, resourceful, and intelligent. Here, too, comparison with *Rear Window* is interesting. In Hitchcock's film, Grace Kelly invades the murderer's apartment to demonstrate her courage to a man; Tewes's motivation, in the corresponding scene of *Eyes of a Stranger,* is a genuine and committed social concern. It is true that this is shown to have roots in personal psychology (her feeling for her younger sister and a largely irrational guilt about what happened to her), but the film strongly suggests that this has become generalized into a concern about the victimization of women in contemporary society. Crucial to the film is its reversal of the patterns of male domination: the turning point is the moment when Tewes phones the killer to persuade him to turn himself in, but also to let him know what it feels like to be on the receiving end of an anonymous phone call.

The conclusion of the film is particularly satisfying by virtue of its play on the "look," and the way in which it "answers" the beginning. The opening images show a man photographing marine life along the Florida coastline who suddenly finds himself photographing a woman's body: the "look," innocent enough on the personal level, is symbolically established as male, the "looked-at" as female (and passive). The psychosomatically blind sister's recovery of her sight during the murderer's assault — dramatically predictable and, if you like, "corny" (I find it, like many "obvious" moments in the cinema, very moving) — takes on corresponding symbolic significance in relation to this, and to the film's play on "looking" throughout (from its title onward).

Leigh's regaining of her sight, and her voice, can be read in terms of pop psychology (the reliving of a traumatic experience); the film also makes clear that she sees at the moment when she finally realizes that she has to fight for her life. The regaining of sight represents the renunciation of the passivity into which she had withdrawn: immediately, the power of the look is transferred to the power of the gun with which she shoots the murderer, the reappropriation of the phallus. In accordance with current convention, he is not really dead, and Tewes, returning just in time, has to shoot him again; unlike Michael and Jason, however, he is by no means signified as indestructible. The contemporary horror film has, typically, two possible endings (frequently combined): the "heroine"-survivor alive but apparently reduced to insanity; the suggestion that the monster is still alive. (Like so much else in these twin cycles, the endings were initiated by *The Texas Chain Saw Massacre* and *Halloween,* respectively). *Eyes of a Stranger* ends with the murderer, definitively dead, slumped ignominiously in the bathtub, his eyes closed, his glasses still perched incongruously on his nose: an unflattering reflection for any male who relished the sadistic assaults.

6

The Stalker Film, 1978–81

Vera Dika

Vera Dika's essay on the cycle of texts she dubs the stalker film covers Halloween *and several films discussed elsewhere in this collection by Lucy Fischer and Marcia Landy, Robin Wood, and J. P. Telotte. Although she, too, examines the role of point of view and the "masculine" controlling vision in these films, her primary intent is to determine systematically those elements that define the stalker film as a specific subgenre of modern horror: its recurring character types, cinematic techniques, and plot functions, as well as its organization of themes and values into a series of binary oppositions. Dika offers a structuralist analysis of narrative, modeled in part on Will Wright's application of Lévi-Straussean methods to the study of popular film in* Sixguns *and* Society.*

Dika has completed a book-length study of the stalker film. She holds a Ph.D. in Cinema Studies from New York University and is currently teaching at Rutgers University, New Brunswick, New Jersey.

During the years 1978–81 the American film market was flooded by the largest number of horror films in recent history. Many of these films exhibit an unprecedented level of explicit violence and so have commonly become designated as "splatter"[1] or "slasher" films. The latter term has been used specifically to define those films characterized by the presence of a psychotic killer usually involved in a multiplicity of murders.[2] This method of classification, however, is ultimately ineffectual because it allows for an overinclusion of works. Although a number of contemporary horror films depict the character and action described above, they nonetheless vary in other aspects of their characters, settings, plots, and cinematic conventions. In this essay I propose to define what I call stalker films. As a cohesive body of works, these films share a distinctive *combination* of narrative and cinematic elements. They are similar in their manner of production, their type of distribution, and in the makeup of their viewing audience. Unlike the more general body of low-budget, independently produced horror films, many of which achieve only limited distribution, the stalker film reached nationwide markets during this period.

The audience for the stalker film, as is typical of the horror genre, is over-whelmingly young: these R-rated films (no one under seventeen admitted without a parent or guardian) were frequented by adolescents between the ages of twelve and seventeen, and these films of excessive violence against women found an audience that was 55 percent female. What relationship do these various elements have on or to one another? In the following discussion I describe the distinguishing characteristic of the stalker formula and suggest some of the psychological and sociological relevance that this formula may have had for young Americans during the years 1978–81.

The beginning of the stalker cycle can be most effectively traced to the impressive success of John Carpenter's *Halloween* (1978). Made for a reported $325,000, it has since grossed over $80 million in worldwide sales, giving it one of the highest proportional returns of any film in history. The films that followed *Halloween* copied its narrative and cinematic struc-ture in the hope of replicating its success. The first was *Friday the 13th*. Also made on a low budget, *Friday the 13th* returned huge profits to its producers and has since spawned several sequels, each almost an exact copy of the original. The impetus toward a high level of replication is, in fact, a hallmark of the stalker film. Not only are the narrative elements of these films closely repeated from film to film, but so are their formal and visual elements.[3] Shot structures are often held in tact, as are framings, com-positions, situations, and even the explicit content of the image. This level of replication gives the films an "already seen" quality that is more exten-sively realized than in any other popular movie formula. The following is a list of films released between 1978 and 1981 that incorporate the greatest number of conventions from the formula for the stalker film.

> 1978: *Halloween*
> 1979: *Friday the 13th*
>   *Prom Night*
>   *Terror Train*
> 1980: *My Bloody Valentine*
>   *Night School*
>   *The Burning*
> 1981: *Friday the 13th Part 2*
>   *Graduation Day*
>   *Happy Birthday to Me*
>   *Hell Night*

On a narrative level, most of these films portray the struggle between a killer, who stalks and kills a group of young people, and a central char-acter, usually a woman, who emerges from this group to subdue him. The single most distinctive characteristic of these films, however, lies in their representation of the killer: he is either kept off-screen or masked for the greater part of the film. He is thus depersonalized in a literal sense, with his body and the more intricate workings of his consciousness hidden from the spectator. This characteristic distinguishes the stalker film not only from most contemporary horror films but especially from those that also depict a psychotic killer involved in multiple murders. In the latter, the killer may be identified on-screen and psychologized (as in *Maniac* [1981], *Fade to Black* [1980], or *When a Stranger Calls* [1979]), while in the stalker film the killer's presence is indicated primarily by the musical score and a series of distinctive shots. The most famous of these shots is the moving camera point-of-view shot, which stealthily approaches an unsuspecting victim. By failing to return to a reverse shot of the killer's face, the film's spectator is presented with only the victim's field of action. Less discussed but equally as conventionalized is a sequence of shots that signify the killer's presence but fail to confirm his exact position within the space. These shots tend to fragment the visual field by observing a potential victim from a variety of different focal lengths and angles. Some of these can be read as subjective shots because they suddenly approach the victim, are taken from behind doorways or partitions, or are merely held too long. But since they are rarely confirmed by a reverse shot, they cannot be clearly attributed to the killer's look or taken as an indication of his position in space. We know that the killer is there, but where? Through their repeated usage within each film and across the films of the cycle, these shots have become conventionalized and have established a set of expectations that involve the viewing audience in a guessing game: "Where is the killer?" "When will he strike?"

This manipulation of expectations has been known to elicit a voiced response from the audience. Viewers shout warnings to the film's victims, but, strangely, they do not seem to be overly concerned for the victims' welfare. Instead, the young spectators greet the gruesome events on screen with open enthusiasm, cheering and laughing, and dividing their support primarily between the heroine *and* the killer. Although the repetition of stock situations and characters tends to lower the sense of realism in the stalker film and so elicit a somewhat distanced response, it is the specific manipulation of the spectator's identification process that allows for the shifting of sympathies between the heroine and the killer. Since the spectator shares the killer's point-of-view shot so often during the course of the film, it might be assumed that he or she is made to identify with the killer. This, however, is only partially true. The structure of identification in the stalker film allows the viewer to identify with the killer's look, but not with his character. As noted, the killer's point-of-view shot is not followed by the traditional reverse shot, which not only would reveal his person but also give us access to his humanity. Without this reverse shot the spectator is left with an unattributed vision, which he or she can indulge in without identifying with the character who has generated it. Through the predictability of its usage, however, the spectator does know the intention behind this unclaimed stare. The characters presented by the point-of-view shot are the objects of sexual investigation and/or the intended victims of the killer. The spectator is allowed to participate in this kind of involvement, but, because of the structure of identification, is freed from sharing the emotional or moral implications of this act. The spectator's moral identification is instead reserved for the heroine of the film. As a good and valued character, the heroine is usually allotted a larger number of close-ups and reverse shots and is given more screen time than all other on-screen characters. As the spectator's point of narrative identification, she ultimately does battle with the killer and triumphs over evil. The sum of these techniques then allows for a shifting of identifications between the killer and the heroine, maximizing the spectator's involvement in the screened events while also allowing her or him to maintain a degree of moral distance.

Along with the characters of the killer and the heroine, the stalker film is comprised of a group of young people — the film's victims. They distinguish themselves from the heroine and the killer by their inability to see and to use violence and ultimately by their inability to generate the flow of narrative. Unlike the heroine, who is herself an essential member of this young community, they have no knowledge of the killer's threat or of the murder of their friends. They cannot cinematically return his gaze by having a point-of-view shot of his presence attributed to them and concomitantly they have no ability to use force against him. Instead, they are quickly dispatched, punished in terms of the film's formal logic not only because of their inability to see but also because they have allowed themselves to be seen. The young victims of the stalker film are often presented as sexual objects. Portrayed by attractive, energetic actors who radiate good health and normality, they engage in activities that facilitate the spectator's voyeuristic enjoyment. The soon-to-be victims may bathe, frolic, make love, or participate in sports, but they never perform narratively significant actions. Their activities are transitional, and, in terms of the narrative development, static. It is primarily the killer, and to a lesser extent, the heroine, who have the means to drive the narrative forward, for only these two characters can both see and use violence.

Although it may at first seem that the violence in these films is directed overwhelmingly against women, a closer look reveals a curious fact. While it is true that violence against women is highlighted in the stalker film —

either made more sensational or featured more predominantly—there seems to be a pronounced tendency across these films to be evenhanded. In *Halloween,* for example, the majority of victims are female. But in *Friday the 13th* and *Graduation Day* the victims are as often male as female; in *Happy Birthday to Me* all but one of the killer's victims are male. It is interesting to note, however, that within this widespread assumption about the victimization of women lies an intuitive understanding of one of the stalker film's basic dynamics. Although the killer may be represented as either male or female in the stalker film, the dominant and controlling vision can best be described as "masculine." In a way that complies with the feminist theoretical assumptions on the inherent dynamic of the classical narrative cinema, the killer as looker occupies a traditionally male position within these films.[4] As pure subject, he is rarely held as the object of another's gaze. Instead, he has that power over others and, with it, the ability to generate the flow of narrative. The victims, on the other hand, occupy a "feminine" position because their narrative and cinematic enfeeblement has rendered them functionally "castrated."[5] Caught by a relentless and controlling gaze, incapable of sight and narrative action, they are the helpless objects of the film. They are deemed guilty, sexually investigated, and then brutally punished, their wound, as the symbolic site of their castration, is meant to be manifestly seen.

This play of sexual tension is then literalized in the character of the heroine. Although this lead character is most often represented as a woman, there is usually a certain ambiguity to her sexual identity. Since she is both like the killer in her ability to see and to use violence, and like the victims in her civilized normality and in her initial inability to see, she is portrayed with both male and female characteristics. In *Hell Night,* for example, the heroine's name is "Marty," but she is dressed in a feminine dress of velvet and lace. Although plump and soft, she is also an auto mechanic (to put herself through school). In *Graduation Day* the heroine is a naval officer. Pretty and delicate, she nonetheless has military training and a mysterious position overseas to underline her power. And while the lead character in *The Burning* is male, this fact is counterbalanced by his representation as a deeply troubled character. The hero is short, unattractive, unpopular, and so, in a symbolic sense, castrated. But even as the enfeebled hero of the film, he still has the power of vision. It is then only with the help of a more perfect male (one who is tall, handsome, and in control) that he is able to triumph over evil and to fulfill the hero function of the film.

The heroine of the stalker film maintains her position as a privileged character by the sum of her narrative and cinematic attributes. Not only is she elevated from the rest of the young community because she can see and use violence, but also she is less extensively held as the sexual object of the killer's gaze. Since the heroine shares with the killer the ability to function as subject she is presented in a manner that complies with her more "masculine" status. She is less likely to disrobe to the point of nudity for the camera or to be involved in extensive on-screen sexual activity. Although she may be represented as a virgin (as in *Halloween*), or as having a greater sense of propriety and restraint (as in *Hell Night*), or as a sexually active person whose more private moments are simply not presented on screen (as in *Friday the 13th Part 2*), she does not necessarily have a greater morality than do the others. Instead, it is her position as a capable character, with a potential for awareness and for action, that restricts her representation as a sexual object. Moreover, this position makes her a more valuable character and distinguishes her from the rest of the young community, who are less aware and whose display of sexual activity is less circumscribed.

Even the low production values of these films help formulate the distinction between the heroine and the rest of the young community. Since the victims are played by unknown, often inexperienced actors, their acting ability and their lack of star quality tend to reduce their value as screen objects. By comparison the heroine is privileged, not only by her more selective casting, but also by the specific connotations brought to the role by the actress who plays her. Jamie Lee Curtis, the star of *three* stalker films, initially gained prestige in *Halloween* from her famous parents (particularly from Janet Leigh, who played Marion Crane in *Psycho*). Later her presence connoted strength and power gleaned from her own previous appearances in these films. *Hell Night* stars Linda Blair, who had proved her ability to survive not only in her well-known role in *The Exorcist* but also as the hostage in *Raid on Entebbe*. And, in reverse fashion, Melissa Sue Anderson's appearance as the perverse and potentially dangerous heroine in *Happy Birthday to Me* is an ironic comment on the sappy innocence she brings from her role on the television series "Little House on the Prairie."

The heroine, the killer, and the victims of the stalker film are depicted as being in conflict, but they are usually members of a single young community. In opposition to this insular group is an outgroup of older people —parents, teachers, psychiatrists, or policemen. In the stalker film, however, these traditional authority figures have lost their power: they are usually friendly and concerned about the welfare of the young community, but they have no power to alter the events of the film. Many are oblivious to the threat against the young people, while others, who may know of the danger, are incompetent, negligent, or ineffectual in warning the young community or in protecting its members from harm. In *Halloween,* for example, the psychiatrist talks incessantly of the killer's danger, but he has no power to protect the young community. He succeeds in stopping the killer only at the very last moment, saving the heroine's life but not those of the other young people. In *Prom Night* policemen withhold information of a psychotic killer's return to the community. That this individual is not the killer preying on the young community not only makes their act meaningless but also serves to underline their incompetence. In *Hell Night* the police dismiss a young person's frantic plea as a prank, while in *Friday the 13th* the young community ignores the warnings of an old man. So, regardless of its particular representation, the traditional community is always shown as being tangential to the young community and as consistently ineffectual in altering the major events of the film.

Unlike the complex characterizations of more individualistic works, the characters in the stalker film (and arguably of other genre products) form a distinctive set of binary oppositions that represent principles, concepts, or social types.[6] Based on our discussion thus far, we can qualify the nature of these oppositions and note the manner in which the interaction of the films' characters generates meaning within the texts. The heroine and the young community in the stalker film are separated by an opposition that can best be described as *valued/devalued.* The sum of the heroine's characteristics mark her as a privileged on-screen character, while those of the young community undermine their status and mark them as the eventual victims. The relationship between the heroine and the killer as opposed to the young community is *strong/weak,* since the two leading characters can see and use violence while the others cannot. The members of the old community are separated from the young community by the opposition *ingroup/outgroup.* This opposition is marked by the inability of these two groups to influence each other, and so it further delineates the young community as a singular, isolated entity. The whole of the young community is separated from the killer by the opposition *normal/abnormal.* The members of the young community are physically perfect, young, energetic, and depicted on-screen. The killer's abnormality is dramatized by physically excluding him as an on-screen presence and by his status as an archaic element. So, although the killer is presented as being part of the young community, or indigenous to the place they occupy, he is also significantly unlike them in the sum of his attributes. Finally, the opposition that separates the heroine from the killer is best described as *ego/id.* Although theirs is an essentially *controlled/uncontrolled* opposition, the heroine and the killer are usually represented as somehow linked: occasionally as opposing sides to a single self, but always as part of the same community or place. This battling of interior forces is then formally supported by the viewer's shifting identification with the two main characters, which splits our involvement between them. The choice of the psychoanalytic terminology is especially effective because it underlines the reading of the heroine and the killer as opposing sides to a single internal dynamic. In constant tension, theirs is a struggle for the dominance of restraint over violence.

Although the killer is presented as occupying a position in the young group, he is an archaic element, a relic from an earlier time that has now returned to disrupt the present stability of the young community. This reemergence is often depicted by the act of traveling: either the killer returns to a place or the members of the young community travel to where the killer lives. In *Halloween* and *The Burning,* for example, the killer returns to the site of the past crime, while in *Hell Night* and *Friday the 13th,* the young community travels to the place where they will ultimately encounter the killer. But even when this return is portrayed by the commemoration of an event that reactivates the killer's force, the entire action takes place in a single location. The setting is exclusionary, separating the young community from the rest of society: usually in a suburban or rural location, the stalker film may be set at a summer camp (*The Burning*), in and around a suburban school (*Graduation Day*), on a few semi-deserted streets (*Halloween*), or on a moving train (*Terror Train*). Once the community has arrived at that setting, however, there is little movement into or out of it. Moreover, the stalker film is almost always positioned in a middle-class American community, which fosters a degree of likeness to that of the viewing audience, or, at least, to their American ideal. But this setting is never identified as an existing geographical location: the destinations are fictional—"Camp Crystal Lake," "Haddonfield, Illinois," or merely unspecified. This generality gives them the ability to represent a place that is simultaneously everywhere and nowhere, but yet distinctly American.

Along with these character, setting, and cinematic conventions, the stalker film is typified by a particular sequence of plot functions. It is always presented with a two-part temporal structure. The first part (which may occur at the beginning of the film or in flashback) presents an event occurring years earlier: the killer is driven to madness or is seen as already mad because of an extreme trauma. This trauma is caused by his viewing of, knowledge of, or participation in a wrongful action that has often been directly or indirectly perpetrated by the members of the young community. The killer experiences a loss and responds with rage, either expressed immediately in an act of vengeance or withheld until the second part of the film. The plot functions that characterize the events may have fewer actions than the ones listed below, but never more:

Past Event
The members of a young community are guilty of a wrongful action.
The killer sees an injury, fault, or death.

> The killer experiences a loss.
> The killer kills the guilty members of the young community.

It is interesting to note that regardless of the specific narrative situation in the stalker film's opening sequence, i.e., whether the killer punishes his victims because of a previous crime (*Friday the 13th*), sees the murder of a loved one (*Prom Night*), or even experiences a loss of his self-esteem (*Terror Train*), the opening sequence *always* presents a woman's death and/or an image of her mutilated body. Moreover, this opening sequence often involves the representation of a kind of primal scene, as in *Halloween* or *Terror Train*, where the killer and the viewer watch a couple involved in a sexual activity. Even when this specific representation is eschewed, the killer is still presented as seeing the injury or death of a woman: in *Prom Night* the killer witnesses the murder of his sister; in *Hell Night* we are told a story in which the killer saw his father kill his mother and his sister; and in *The Burning* we watch from the killer's point of view as he murders a prostitute.

In the second, or present-day, section of the film, the killer returns to take vengeance on the guilty parties or on their symbolic substitutes. Occasionally, a "seer" warns the community of an impending danger, but the young people take no heed. The killer begins his bloody task, alternately observing the actions and the bodies of his young victims, and then killing them. A heroine emerges from the group of young people, sees the killer, and does battle with him. The heroine manages to subdue the killer or even to kill him, but she is not free. The following is a list of narrative functions that characterize the second section of the stalker film:

> **Present Event**
> An event commemorates the past action.
> The killer's destructive impulse is reactivated.
> A seer warns the young community.
> The young community takes no heed.
> The killer stalks the young community.
> The killer kills members of the young community.
> The heroine sees the murders.
> The heroine sees the killer.
> The heroine does battle with the killer.
> The heroine subdues the killer.
> The heroine survives but is not free.

The heroine has subdued the killer, but her triumph does not liberate her. On one level she is not free because she has come to a new stage of awareness. Through the course of the film she has come to face the reality of

The young community is usually portrayed by young, energetic actors who radiate good health and normalcy (*Friday the 13th* [1980]).

The heroine does battle with the killer and triumphs over evil (*Friday the 13th Part 2* [1981]).

The members of the old community are ultimately ineffectual in protecting the young community from the killer's threat (*Halloween* [1978]).

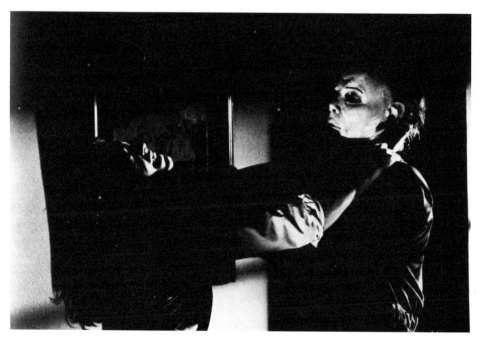

The heroine and the killer as opposing sides to a single internal dynamic: *Halloween* (1978).

death and violence. Gone are the illusions of everyday normality, for now she has to live with the memory of her murdered friends. In many stalker films, however, this lack of freedom is more directly represented. The heroine in *Prom Night,* for example, is not free because she has unintentionally killed her beloved brother, who was also the film's brutal killer. In *Halloween* and in both *Friday the 13th Part 1* and *Part 2* the heroine is not free because the killer is still alive and so threatens her with his return. And in *Happy Birthday to Me* the heroine is literally not free because the police assume she is the killer and all of the witnesses to the contrary are dead. Here the heroine is framed as the object of the policeman's sight, caught in his gaze, and so returned to a powerless position as object. As in all of the stalker films, the heroine's loss is literalized by the film's formal elements. If the killer is dead or subdued, the heroine loses her motivation for sight and for violence and so her ability to drive the narrative forward. With the death of the killer, the film ends. One of the last images of the stalker film is often that of the heroine, trapped within the confines of the frame and returned to her position as object. In *Friday the 13th* she is caught in a tight shot/counter shot with the doctor who attends her, and in *Halloween* as the object of the psychiatrist's gaze. Actually, in *Halloween* the film ends with an image of the house in which the heroine now finds herself. But this is not presented as an objective shot but is rather attributed to the killer's gaze: he is still alive and once again dominates the visual field. As a result of this reappropriation of the image, the heroine is returned to her feminine position, no longer capable of maintaining her role as subject. In a most literal fashion, she is not free because the threat against her continues.

Although the films listed here comply most closely with the combination of elements for the stalker formula, individual conventions occur, to a greater or lesser degree, in many other recent horror films. *When a Stranger Calls,* for example, incorporates a number of these elements, but ultimately fails to comply with the significant combination that characterizes the formula. The opening of *Stranger* is typical of a stalker film. It depicts a past event, and a young woman is taken as the object of the killer's gaze. The visual field is fragmented as she is framed from a variety of different angles, alerting the spectator to the killer's lurking presence but not to his exact position within the space. But *Stranger* makes a major divergence from the stalker formula when, in the second portion of the film, the killer is exposed, and his psychology and motivation are investigated. *Eyes of Laura Mars,* on the other hand, originally written by John Carpenter, is in most ways a stalker film. It maintains the two-part temporal structure (although the past event is only recounted and not shown) and adheres to the prescribed list of narrative functions. Moreover, the dominance of the male gaze and the feminine position as object are directly featured in this film that takes the issue of the representation of women in the media as its central topic. But since *Laura Mars* was made on a high budget, with major stars, and with a self-reflexive attitude, it lacks the described balance of elements found in the stalker formula. These films need their less-than-professional look, their devalued quality, and their lack of sophistication to reduce the realism of the screened events and to encourage a gaming response to the film. Moreover, *Laura Mars* does not have a youthful protagonist or community: it is set in New York City, and it depicts the high-fashion world of art and photography. It thus eschews the usual representation of youthful middle America, and so the connotation of the mainstream or the ordinary. In that *Laura Mars* purports to be an individualistic work it presents the specific, not the general, and stands outside the sequence of replication that tends to give the stalker film its characteristic already seen quality.

The stalker formula is then a combination of narrative and cinematic conventions that has proven to be most successful within a particular historical period and has been most capable of engendering copies. The films that best embody this formula make up a cohesive body because of their high level of violence, their single narrative component, and a distinctive combination of elements that are experienced as particularly satisfying by their audience. The unavoidable and perplexing question that now arises is, of course, why, and especially why at this particular time in history? For the answers to these questions we must once again look to the combination of satisfying conditions that the stalker film provides.

One answer might be found in the congruences between the heroine's basic struggle and the young spectator's stage of psychological and sociological development. The stalker film usually enacts the heroine's growth from childhood into an awareness of the harsh realities of the adult world. Many of the stalker films use rites of social passage to underline this point: *Prom Night, Graduation Day, Happy Birthday to Me,* and *Hell Night* even incorporate these events into their titles. But there are additional congruences between the films and the audience's particular stage of development that can be seen to resonate on a deeper psychological level. The two-part temporal structure of the stalker film first depicts an event long past, and then a resurgence of that event after a period of latency. The past event often takes place in childhood and usually involves the viewing of material that is either explicitly or implicitly sexual. *Halloween* presents a kind of primal scene, as does *Terror Train*. In both films a character watches a sexual couple and is unacknowledged by them. Both films also involve the viewing of violence inflicted on a woman's body. In *Halloween* the young woman is stabbed, and in *Terror Train* we see a female corpse with severed limbs. Even in films such as *Prom Night,* where the opening sequence involves no overtly sexual material, we are still presented with the humiliation and punishment of a young female, her wound made visible to the spectator. A psychoanalytic interpretation of this material would claim it to be a reenactment of a young boy's first viewing of the female genitalia.[7] According to this theory, the boy notes the female's absence of a penis and assumes an act of castration has occurred. The "bleeding wound" inspires fear and revulsion, but it also creates a compulsion to look at the female genitalia. The stalker film dramatizes this compulsion by the series of murders that are the symbolic reenactments of the fantasized act of castration. Since the stalker film presents material that theoretically parallels the individual's own psychosexual growth from childhood to adolescence, it can be particularly satisfying to an adolescent audience.

Not only does this conclusion disregard the psychology of the female members of the audience, but it also fails to address the constant nature of human psychology in the face of the rather brief popularity of the stalker film. If it can be argued that the inherent psychology of each successive group of adolescents remains unchanged, why did these films appeal so strongly at one time and not another? Even if one group were oversaturated with the run of these films, there should have been a subsequent group that would have embraced them anew. This, of course, has not happened. Although the *Friday the 13th* sequels proved commercially successful, there has been no widespread resurgence of newly made stalker films, nor a significant revival of the old films. And while it may be argued that the stalker film oversaturated the market and so extinguished the viability of its elements through overuse, it is crucial to investigate the cultural and political milieu that saw the rise of the stalker film. It is here that we can see how these films were very much a product of their time and also a comment on it.

The stalker formula achieved its greatest success at a transitional period in American history. After the humiliation, loss, and guilt of Vietnam, America found itself in an enfeebled world position, faced with a faltering economy. Moreover, the Carter administration, much assailed because of its incompetence in maintaining a position of strength for the United States, received its most crushing blow with the Iranian hostage crisis. In 1979, at a time paralleling the rise of the stalker film, American government personnel were held captive in Tehran for over a year. While the United States acted with restraint, the national mood was one of outrage and impotence. The desire for action often found expression on buttons, bumper stickers, or graffiti that read "Fuck Iran" or "Nuke Iran." The American hostages were finally released in 1980, on the day of Ronald

Reagan's inauguration. With the Reagan presidency came the finalization of an already ongoing process that tended to reverse the ideals, aspirations, and attitudes of the 1960s. America returned to traditional values — to family, home, and religion. "Do your own thing" was replaced by conservative personal conduct and a reassessment of career goals. The economy made it necessary for young people to think of making money and not to indulge in a variety of less-than-practical creative pursuits. Moreover, the radical style of the hippies was replaced by a new kind of radicalism. Punk fashion replaced the 1960s attitude of peace and love with a harsh, aggressive artificiality. Violence and sadism were featured prominently in punk music and performance style. Both forms, however, reused earlier elements from the music and fashion of the 1950s and early 1960s. The tendency to reuse images, words, music, sounds, movements, and styles from earlier works began to characterize the art of the 1980s. The radical aspiration, abstraction, and individualism of modernism were replaced by postmodernist practices characterized by the return to representation, the method of pastiche, and a blurring of the distinction between high and commercial art.[8]

As a cultural product of the late 1970s and early 1980s, the stalker film shares this dominant shift in attitude. It too uses material from earlier films, creating works almost entirely composed of previously seen narrative and cinematic elements. Moreover, like the greater body of horror films during this period, it presents a high level of violence and does so gleefully, irreverently, almost thumbing its nose at the outdated notion of pacifism. But it is the particular story structure of the stalker film that can be seen to explain the changing cultural attitudes to its viewing audience. The heroine is valued over the young community because she displays personal restraint not only in sexual matters but also in her family or professional relationships. This control gives her an incipient ability for sight and, ultimately, for violent action. The young community, on the other hand, are devalued because of their social behavior, which makes them weak, incapable either of assessing the threat against them or of protecting themselves against it. The killer comes out of the past and continues his vengeance against those guilty of wrongful actions. His behavior is dominated by a wild and uncontrollable force that is contrasted to that of the heroine. Because of her generally more powerful characteristics, which combine both restraint and violence, she is able to subdue the killer. But the killer's threat continues even in his banishment and makes the heroine's sustained awareness a necessity.

This configuration of elements can then be seen to explain how old attitudes are now ineffectual and how new attitudes are needed to survive. To the stalker film's young audiences, on the brink of adulthood and ready to formulate ideas on careers, politics, and family, these films demonstrate the inefficacy of sexual freedom, of casual, nongoal-oriented activity, and of a nonviolent attitude. In a recent article on *Halloween,* J. P. Telotte claims that this film functions as a morality play because it urges its audience to "watch out," to be vigilant against the evil that surrounds them.[9] My contention is that the stalker film not only provides an injunction to the spectator, but also presents an explanation of an ongoing cultural conflict. While it is true that the victims of these films are often too self-involved to assess the threat against them, it is also true that the heroine survives not only by her ability to see the evil, but also by her ability to use violence. In fact, the confrontation between the heroine and the killer is the culminating action of the film and is characterized by a long, protracted battle of wits and strength. The sum of the heroine's actions, ones defined as superior to those of the young community, are examples of a new adaptive attitude and demonstrate her ability to survive.

In that the killer rises from the community itself and comes into conflict with the members of that community, the stalker film dramatizes a struggle of interior forces, of opposing attitudes in a single society. Like the cowboy hero of the western, the heroine engages in a justifiable act of aggression. But unlike that hero, her actions are not justified by her desire to save the community. Hers is purely an act of self-defense, the young community having already perished as an example of the inefficacy of old ideas. Thus, the cheers at the end of these films are for an enfeebled but still strong America, one symbolized by a once weak female character who has now been fortified with a new set of ideals for survival. Read in this way the stalker film functions more like a modern-day myth than a morality play, since it is a system of communication that imparts to the members of its society an explanation for the ongoing conflicts within it.[10]

NOTES

1. In *Splatter Movies* (Albany, N.Y.: Fanta, 1981), John McCarty attempts the classification of a subgenre of the horror film based on its characteristic representation of violence. This approach yields an overinclusive body of works, grouping together films produced between 1963 and 1981 and including titles as varied as *Friday the 13th, Caligula, The Long Riders,* and *Eraserhead.*

2. Robin Wood in "Returning the Look: *Eyes of a Stranger,*" 79–85 herein, assumes that those films "centered on psychotic killers" compose a single group. He then proposes the existence of the "violence-against-women film" and the "teenie-kill pic" as two distinct types within this larger category. Acknowledging that these types are only slightly distinguishable from one another, he nonetheless defines the former as films representing violence against women who have not fulfilled their traditional woman's role, and the latter as representing violence

against teenagers who indulge in promiscuous sexuality. Wood then mentions several narrative and cinematic conventions for these films. In the teenie-kill pic the killer never dies, and the female teenager is left as the sole survivor. He also mentions the use of the first-person camera to signify the approach of the killer as distinctive of both the teenie-kill pic and the violence-against-women film. Although most of these characteristics are found in a number of recent horror films, they do not qualify as a set of distinguishing characteristics for a specific form. One has merely to test this group of elements against the films mentioned by Wood to note the difficulty in classification they pose. Is *When a Stranger Calls,* for example, a teenie-kill pic or a violence-against-women film? The young woman who is stalked at the beginning of the film is a teenager, but she is not involved in sexual activity. Moreover, as a somewhat older woman in the second portion of the film she is once again stalked; yet she is a dutiful wife and mother. What traditional woman's role has she broken? Or again, if *Prom Night* is a teenie-kill pic according to Wood's definition, why does the killer die in the film?

3. In "The Future of an Allusion: Hollywood in the Seventies (and Beyond)," *October* 20 (Spring 1980), Noel Carroll notes the tendency in much of 1970s and 1980s film to reuse material from earlier cinematic works. The difference between this wider practice and the stalker film is that the high level of replication in the latter is within a single prescribed formula. Moreover, the allusions within the successive stalker films have through repeated usage lost much of their reference to earlier sources (most specifically to *Psycho* on which *Halloween* is largely based) and refer, if anything, only to their own conventionality.

4. Laura Mulvey, "Visual Pleasure and Narrative Cinema," *Screen* 16 (Autumn 1975):6–18. For Mulvey, the pleasure derived from looking has been inscribed into the cinema in a manner that reflects the unconscious structures of the dominant patriarchal order. The erotic fascination children find in looking at others as objects (to assess sexual difference, to view the presence/absence of the penis, or to view the primal scene itself) and the narcissistic pleasure derived from identifying with the image seen form the basis of cinematic visual pleasure. Because of the dominance of patriarchy, however, the image of women has been encoded into the cinema as the object of visual fascination, both for the viewer and for the film's characters. But this pleasure is threatened by the possibility of unpleasure; her body connotes the absence of a penis and so produces anxiety by the threat of castration that it implies. This anxiety can be tempered either by making her image a fetish (a glorified object as is the image of the female Hollywood star) or by reenacting the original trauma (the realization of the female's lack of a penis), in which she becomes both the object of investigation and the object of devaluation and punishment.

5. This apparent compliance with feminist theory, however, is not altogether accidental. John Carpenter's *Eyes of Laura Mars* (a film for which he wrote the original screenplay) and *Halloween* deal quite specifically with the theoretical assumptions and the cinematic structures defined in this theory. As Lucy Fischer and Marcia Landy have noted in "*Eyes of Laura Mars:* A Binocular Critique," 62–78 herein, *Laura Mars* exploits the issue of the representation of women in

the media and the inherent voyeuristic structure of the cinema and then incorporates a psychoanalytic explanation for the fascination of looking at the female into the content of the film. *Halloween* also exploits the cinema's voyeuristic structure by its deliberate system of looking at women as sexual objects and as objects of aggression. Moreover, it presents a kind of primal scene in its opening sequence, thinly disguising the child's assessment of sexual differences and his fantasy of castration as he watches the events, and then uses this as an explanation for the killer's compulsion to sexually investigate, humiliate, and punish his female victims. It is interesting to note that the subsequent stalker films have shown a tendency toward a more liberal (although fatuous) attitude in the representation of women. They have attempted to present an equal number of male and female victims, but they have nonetheless maintained the overriding psychosexual content and structure derived from *Halloween*.

6. Will Wright, *Sixguns and Society* (Berkeley: University of California Press, 1975). Wright demonstrates that the characters in the western do not represent specific individuals but instead form a series of contrasting pairs from which their conceptual meaning is derived.

7. Sigmund Freud, "Three Essays on the Theory of Sexuality," *Standard Edition*, 7 (London: Hogarth, 1953).

8. Fredric Jameson, "Postmodernism and Consumer Society," in *The Anti-Aesthetic,* ed. Hal Foster (Port Townsend, Wash.: Bay Press, 1983), 111–25.

9. J. P. Telotte, "Through a Pumpkin's Eye: The Reflexive Nature of Horror," 114–128 herein.

10. In this analysis I have demonstrated that the stalker film complies with the mythological structure that Wright found operating in the western. It is structured by a set of binary oppositions and by a consistent list of plot functions. Moreover, the stalker film complies with Wright's definition of a myth as a system of communication that explains a cultural conflict and provides a model for social action.

7

The Funhouse and
The Howling

Bruce F. Kawin

*According to Bruce F. Kawin in this revised version of a review
that originally was published in* Film Quarterly *(Fall 1981; © 1981 and
is reprinted by permission of the Regents of the University of California),
not all horror films are "fantasies of victimization and destructive aggression." At its most successful the genre offers unsettling — even mythic — narratives concerned with the nature of vision and the possibility for integration of the repressed. In contrast to, for example, the stalker films Ver
Dika discusses, reflexive texts like* The Howling *carry on the best tradition of the genre and instruct us in the ways of reading horror. If Dika's
essay raises questions about the precise manner in which popular genres
spawn new, historically specific subgenres, Kawin's essay suggests that there
are significant ahistorical affinities between the classic horror of* The
Cabinet of Dr. Caligari *and* Nosferatu, A Symphony of Horror *and the
modern horror of* Don't Look Now, The Last Wave, *and* The Funhouse.*
Kawin, professor of English and Film at the University of Colorado
at Boulder, also develops his view of horror in "The Mummy's Pool,"*
Dreamworks *1 (1981). His books include* Telling It Again and Again: Repe-
tition in Literature and Film; Mindscreen: Bergman, Godard, and First-
Person Film; The Mind of the Novel: Reflexive Fiction and the Ineffable;
Faulkner's MGM Screenplays; *and* How Movies Work.

> When the eyes and ears are prevented from perceiving meaningful order,
> they can only react to the brutal signals of immediate satisfaction.
> —Rudolf Arnheim, *Film as Art*

Any genre has its highs and lows. Confronted with the current
glut of stupid, gory, sexist ripoffs of *Halloween* and *Jaws,* and before
them, of *The Exorcist* and *Carrie* — unredeemably bad films like *Blood
Beach, Zombie, The Boogey Man, Prom Night,* and *The Final Conflict,*
among others — it may be hard to remember that many of the masterpieces
of film history have been horror films. By the latter I include both those

with supernatural themes (*Nosferatu, Vampyr*) and those whose psychological involutions implicate their normal protagonists as the dreamers
of the nightmares of their worlds (*The Cabinet of Dr. Caligari, Vertigo,
The Lathe of Heaven*), as well as monster movies on the order of *King
Kong.* Although most people would resist the notion that *Vertigo* might
be a horror film — since it is clearly a mystery, has only the most tangential
relationship with the metaphysical problem of reincarnation, and has
nothing in it that could conventionally be considered a "monster" — it does
manipulate many of the recurring themes of the horror genre, notably
that of the problem of vision. In *Vertigo* Judy is killed by Scottie's insistence that she match the image of Madeleine, and in *Mad Love* — another
example of problematized vision — Dr. Gogol's insanity begins in mirrors
and ends in the delusion that his obsessive attention has brought a wax-
work to life. Horror films often present us with images that are painful,
grotesque, awful — horrible to look at — but they regularly imply that these
images somehow need to be looked at, that they will show us something
we might be more comfortable not to see but ought to see nonetheless.

But vision is not a simple process: what one sees may not go to the truth
of the situation, and what one envisions may not have anything to do with
the realities of the world. When a character in a horror film sees something that is utterly out of the ordinary, like a walking carnivorous plant
or a forty-foot tarantula, the problem of vision — of the reliability and
value of what has been seen and of the way it has been seen — becomes
urgent. Although many films achieve their resolutions by simply validating what may at first have appeared to be unreliable visions — for example,
by demonstrating a consensus that the monster exists — and confirming
also the ways the monster is seen, other films, however, raise questions
about vision and leave them unresolved. This accounts for much of the
difference between the horror film that is felt to be troubling (*The Last
Wave*) and the horror film that is felt to be escapist and uncomplicatedly
spectacular (*Friday the 13th*). Many of the greatest horror films turn out
to be of the troubling kind, the kind that make us wonder just what we
have seen, what we have learned about seeing, and why we have chosen
to have this particular — and often unpleasant — theatrical experience.
Caligari, Dead of Night, and *Vampyr* work in this manner, and, regardless
of whether one prefers to see *Vertigo* primarily as a mystery or as a horror
film, it is still a useful example of a psychological paradigm that regularly
informs this problematic genre. (The same could be said about *The Lathe
of Heaven,* which is as much a science fiction film as *Vertigo* is a mystery.)

The problem of the unreliability and validity of vision, addressed in
so many of the best horror films, is often related to the aesthetic and
political problem of reflexivity, which can most simply be thought of as

a gesture by which a work of art acknowledges and declares that it is a work of art and that it knows it is a work of art. Sometimes this awareness is *systemic,* i.e., the whole work reflects a degree of self-awareness as a limited artistic structure; sometimes the awareness is *authorial,* i.e., we are aware of the author's awareness of his or her status as the controller of the system and as someone working in a particular artistic tradition; sometimes the awareness is localized in a character within the system and may or may not go farther, into the systemic and authorial levels of self-consciousness. The two genres that deal most consistently and successfully with these problems are the horror film and the musical, though the send-up comedy (e.g., *Hellzapoppin*) is a close runner-up.

Vampyr, for example, addresses the problem of vision and reflexivity, for David Gray's dream of a windowed coffin-lid becomes an explicit metaphor for the "window" of the movie screen before which the audience is entombed in its own category of dreaming. I have argued elsewhere[1] that watching a film is often like having a dream and that some films deliberately model themselves on dreamlike structures; the legitimacy and even the primacy of the horror film is to be found in the analogy of the nightmare, which plays at one time or another in everyone's darkened theater. The best horror films are not sexist bloodbaths but unsettling confrontations with intuition (*The Last Wave, Don't Look Now*), repression (*The Wolf Man*), childhood trauma (*Bride of Frankenstein*), and the power of imagination (*The Curse of the Cat People*), though many of them use such confrontations as a base from which to make social and political observations (*Freaks, Bedlam, The Island of Lost Souls, Invasion of the Body Snatchers, Caligari*). A staple figure in the horror film is the intuitive seeker — often the "first victim" — who probes at his or her peril the mystery that presents itself as a calling (*Vampyr, The Last Wave*) and who often finds evidence in some kind of unconventional, suppressed, or unpublished text: Caligari's notebooks, the underground paintings in *The Last Wave,* the Scroll of Thoth in *The Mummy,* the *Necronomicon* in H. P. Lovecraft's fiction, and the *Book of the Vampire* in *Vampyr.* In *The Turn of the Screw* and comparable fictions, such a text may itself become a primary horror object, the site of a dangerous coherence; in the Henry James novella, for instance, the governess's notebook must wait for years and pass through other narrators before it can be transcribed into the real-world medium of print.[2] In the two best horror films released in 1981, Tobe Hooper's *The Funhouse* and Joe Dante's *The Howling,* most of these concerns are at issue, and the "book of the vampire" is no longer a book but the tradition of the horror film itself.

It should be said at the outset that *The Funhouse* is the better of these pictures, the more rigorously self-enclosed, and by far the more frightening, while *The Howling* is the more socially committed, an oddball combination of Corman-level silliness and acute political insight. The question both address is how to deal with real horrors when one has been encouraged, particularly by horror films, to expect any danger to be imaginary, to be fun, to be presented within the frame of an institution (the carnival in *The Funhouse*) or genre (the Disney cartoon and *The Wolf Man* in *The Howling*). In both cases the institution turns out to be the danger. In *The Funhouse* this boils down to "you get what you pay for" and "you pay for what you get": the audience wants to have fun being scared in the "funhouse" of the genre, and the director (whose surrogate, as the credits make explicit, is an overweight, chuckling doll) has the last laugh. In *The Howling,* on the other hand, the real-world horrors are pornography, irresponsible journalism, and the neurasthenic impact of the media in general as they make money out of presenting atrocities, encouraging their audience to take only the merchandising angle seriously, and to disregard — or not adequately confront — the suffering they report. *The Funhouse* points out the danger of modeling one's life on a horror film (especially in its opening sequence, a parody of *Halloween* and *Psycho*) because, after all, one's fantasies have a way of coming true — i.e., one often precipitates into being that which one authentically desires. *The Howling* points out the danger of complacency, of assuming that horrors are only media creations instead of noticing that the world does sometimes behave like a horror film and that many of the media's creations are horrific. For both, however, the principal warning texts are horror films, and the implication in both is that their warnings ought to be taken more seriously, like the attractive note on the side of a pack of Camels.

Joe Dante learned the business from Roger Corman and did his first memorable work as co-director of *Hollywood Boulevard,* a send-up of Corman pictures that hilariously detailed the problems of a film crew who are being systematically murdered as they make a violent movie. The emblematic scene in that film shows the heroine being raped by the projectionist at the drive-in premiere of her picture while a sex scene plays on the screen — a bitter reflexive joke reminiscent of the climax of Peter Bogdanovich's best film, the Corman-produced *Targets.* In *Piranha* — of which I wrote the first positive review, and there were not many — Dante teamed with ace screenwriter John Sayles (*The Return of the Secaucus Seven*) to examine how people who have seen *Jaws* are less prepared than they ought to be to watch out for dangerous fish. At first glance this might seem like an artificial problem, if not simply a joke (for awhile after working on *Piranha,* Dante seriously contemplated making a film to be called *Jaws 3, People 0*), but this problem gained relevance through the careful ways it was paralleled with the dangers of media control by the military-industrial complex, and it culminated in the spectacle of a salesman's trying to stop a television crew from conveying the truth to his audience: a scene as reminiscent of Peter Watkins's allegorical *Punishment Park* as it was of network coverage of the Vietnam War. In *The Howling* Dante abandoned both Gary Brandner's original novel and a screenplay by Terence H. Winkless to work with Sayles again and to explore much the same problem. But this time the problem turned out to be not the military but the general problem of desensitization, coupled with a timely parody of such commercialized sensitivity therapies as *est* and Primal Scream.

The protagonist in *The Howling* is Karen White (Dee Wallace), a media superstar who anchors a Los Angeles news program and who is committed to searching out and reporting the truth. The film opens with a video interference pattern over which one can hear snatches of dialogue from the entire film, a good image of prophecy and of the potential failure of communication, as well as a systemically self-conscious acknowledgment (since these snatches could be available only if the events and the film had somehow already been completed; another way to say this is that the film is scanning itself, and still another is that the audience's task — to tune this in as precisely as possible — is here being announced). The film closes, equally appropriately, with a clip from *The Wolf Man* (Maria Ouspenskaya's "Go now, and heaven help you!") that dismisses the audience and reminds them of the burden of what they have learned — a particularly interesting quotation since in *The Wolf Man* this scene has no reflexive implications — and a blip of scrambled video; these two closing shots are an emblem of the dialectic within which this film functions: dangerous knowledge and dangerously failed communication.

Karen is first seen on her way to meet Eddie Quist, a bestial sex murderer whose calling-cards are those insipid yellow "happy-face" decals; she is wired for sound, but because of "all that neon out there" (an obvious but still relevant symbol) the crew at the station is unable to receive her signals; thus from the start Karen is presented as someone whose trust of communication/media/openness is dangerously inappropriate, a trust that in the end will prove genuinely, ennoblingly tragic. She meets Eddie in a booth in a pornographic movie arcade, and he turns out to be not only a werewolf but also an unsettlingly quiet fellow with a couple of brilliant lines. Standing behind her, he puts a quarter in the slot and tells her to "just watch" a film in which a young woman is stripped and raped by several men. "She didn't feel a thing," he says. "They're not real, the people here, they could never be like me." So far this is reminiscent of Daffy Duck's rationalization for turning Bugs Bunny over to the Abominable Snowman — "I know it's a despicable thing to do, but I'm different from other people: pain *hurts* me" — and I bring that in not for a joke but because it is the one thing a rapist or murderer has to believe, because it is at the base of any attempt to deny the being of the victim and is the root impulse of fascist self-absorption, as Nazi camps and pornography houses equally demonstrate. But Eddie goes on: "You're different; I watch you on TV; I know how good I could make you feel . . . I want to give you something." For Eddie the television image is somehow more seductive, more tied to reality and to his own self-concept, than the pornographic film; it is *because* it is believed that television news is dangerous here, whereas by the end of the film it is when it shows the truth that it is *not* believed. Because the media (as we now have them) trade in the half-truth of commercialized communication, they fail to live up to their potential as a positive social force. (In retrospect, it turns out that what Eddie really means is that normal people do not enjoy sex as much as werewolves do, and that he senses Karen has the potential to respond in his terms.) Eddie changes into a wolf — the "gift" he has in mind is bestial sex, or freedom — and is shot by police, later to regenerate and return; Karen suffers temporary amnesia, but has dreams in which she almost remembers what happened. These dreams are significantly of the pornographic film and of the figure of Eddie backlit by the projector. When she goes on the air to report her experience, she sees the pornographic film in the lens of the television camera and is unable to continue; that is the symbolic highpoint of the film, a brilliant condensation of its message.

Eventually the story takes her and her husband to "the Colony," an Esalen-type retreat run by a werewolf doctor by the name of George Waggner (after the director of *The Wolf Man*), whose intention is to help his lycanthropic clients learn to channel their bestial impulses into relatively social expressions; one of his most lovable patients is named Erle Kenton (after the director of *The Ghost of Frankenstein*), played by John Carradine; other veteran actors in this film include Slim Pickens, Dick Miller, Kenneth Tobey (*The Thing*), and Kevin McCarthy (*Invasion of the Body Snatchers*). For a while it seems as if the film will be overwhelmed by its spectacular makeup effects — designed by Rob Bottin with help from Rick Baker, and indebted to the work of Dick Smith[3] — especially in a daring sex scene between two werewolves; but the dark, reflexive humor is never offscreen for long.

Two of Karen's colleagues, Terry and Christopher, visit an occult bookstore and begin to suspect that werewolfery is part of the story. The proprietor shows a cache of silver bullets that a client had requested but never claimed (guess why . . .); when they ask whether he believes in the legends, he answers, "What am I, an idiot? I'm making a buck here." Terry and Christopher get further hints from a late-night showing of *The Wolf Man*, and Terry goes to the Colony to help Karen. When Terry calls Christopher to let him know what is really going on up there, Christopher is watching a cartoon in which a wolf traps a lamb, and this cartoon is crosscut with Terry's being brutally murdered by a werewolf; ironically Christopher does not switch off the set, and the two sound tracks overlap (making the point that many of the characters in this film and their real-world counterparts may not be able to sort out reality from fantasy and so may fail to be aware of the reality of those dangers the media have trivialized — an echo of *Piranha* and its critique of the coverage of the Vietnam War). By the time Christopher calls the sheriff (who is of course one of Them) and buys the silver bullets, it is too late to save Terry. Eventually he does save Karen, but in their escape she is bitten and so must herself become a werewolf — and the counterculture point is hammered in that this last disaster would not have happened had they not both trusted the sheriff once too often.

All this leads to the marvelous climax of the film, where Karen decides to make her audience believe in the danger of rampant bestiality and fascist control in the culture by changing into a wolf on camera and having herself shot by one of Christopher's silver bullets. She cries while she does this and emerges as a media saint, committed to the last to the communication of truth. The horrified producer (McCarthy) cuts to a dogfood commercial, and Dante cuts to snatches of audience reaction: a man looking at the *TV Guide* to find out what category of program this is; two kids who believe what they see; the bookseller shaking his head; and a barroom where one man accepts, without getting worried about it, that her transformation and death were real, while others dismiss the whole thing as "special effects." The film of which all this is finally most reminiscent is not a horror film but *Act of the Heart,* with its painful examination of the problem and value of the sacrificial gesture in a culture that does not know how to pay attention.

Now it is certainly true that the majority of horror films in the past few years have contributed not to this level of consciousness-raising but to the brutalization of the audience. Some, like *Motel Hell,* are redeemed by an E. C. Comics brand of humor; some, like *Jaws,* score social-relevance brownie points by attacking bureaucrats and validating paranoids; and some, like *Halloween,* are redeemed by sheer relentlessness and technical skill. But most of them have no purpose beyond that of encouraging their audiences to participate in fantasies of victimization and destructive aggression. As Roger Ebert observed in a fine article on *I Spit on Your Grave,*[4] the crucial influence of *Jaws* and *Halloween* has been to validate the use of subjective camera for the visual viewpoint of the horror object; whereas in earlier decades the audience tended to share the viewpoint of the victim and to see the monster, in the 1970s it became commonplace for the audience to share the viewpoint of the killer or monster, and with this came an emphasis on the isolated female as primary victim. (In this context, it is significant that in *The Funhouse* and *The Howling* the seeker-figures whose perspectives turn out to be justified are women.) Most of these films, whose ranks include *Friday the 13th, He Knows You're Alone,* and *My Bloody Valentine,* are clearly part of the backlash against the feminist movement as well as an extension of pornography into the media mainstream, and what they take from *Psycho* is an overwhelming interest in the psychology of the sex murderer. This is altogether different from the sympathy one was encouraged to feel for Frankenstein, the Wolf Man, King Kong, or the Mummy, whose alienation was usually tied to society's rejection of their impulse to love, and which was presented in the context of their clearly inappropriate expressions of that impulse. Kong never set out to kill Ann, the Wolf Man did everything in his power to protect Gwen, the Frankenstein monster intended to play with the little girl because she reminded him of a flower, and the Mummy's project was always to reunite with his beloved Princess Ananka. Although Alfred Hitchcock's intention in *Psycho* was, typically, to implicate the voyeurism of his audience, that film was apparently endorsed as a glorification of the psychotic. The combination of *Carrie* and *Psycho,* together with the new vistas of violence opened by *Night of the Living Dead* (another good movie that proved easy to exploit) and the misogynist *Straw Dogs,* which received an "intellectual" stamp of approval in the vicious *A Clockwork Orange*—all led to the cult of the misunderstood woman-killing psychotic, the "poor me" murderer typified in *Prom Night* and *Terror Train.* In *The Exorcist* and *The Omen* there was some attempt to belie the presentation of children as monsters by implying that these particular children were unusual incarnations of the demonic, and *Halloween* continued that by having its child-then-adult murderer be in fact "the boogeyman." But *Halloween*'s use of subjective camera, courtesy of *Jaws,* undeniably made the link between audience and murderer without any of Hitchcock's irony or Steven Spielberg's *Enemy of the People* Ibsenism. When socially conscious horror films like *Alien* and *Dawn of the Dead* came into this audience context, they were embraced for their violence and terror at the expense of their other attributes and indirectly contributed to the momentum of the worst aspects of the genre. But when Werner Herzog resurrected the beautiful and visionary aspects of the horror film in his *Nosferatu* he found practically no audience, and the heritage of F. W. Murnau and Carl-Theodor Dreyer receded even further. It remains to be seen whether *The Howling* will find an audience simply on the merits of its special effects—though that does seem, unfortunately, likely—or whether it will remind the audience of the value of the genre as a means of dealing with the institutionally and psychologically repressed; for horror films are one of our important ties with the mythic, with the visionary, and their best goal has historically been — as in the analogy of the Freudian dream — to bring to consciousness that which has been repressed, so that integration and wholeness, both personal and societal, might become a real possibility. The therapist in *The Howling* is a deliberate caricature of the cult of the eruption of the bestial who pays lip service to integration, and its heroes are those who are lovers or vegetarians (Karen's husband) not because they are out of touch with any bestial nature but because they have *chosen* to love.

The Funhouse may well contribute to this return to the better energies and impulses of the genre, though again it is entirely possible that audiences will watch it for its tentshow dancing girls and two murdered women (it is hardly a redeeming issue that there are also three murdered men). It may do so because of its reflexivity — its relentless emphasis on the victims' having chosen to go to the equivalent of a horror film — and because of its ruthless caricatures of phallic aggression, which is absolutely never validated as it is in *Halloween*. To take an explicit example: the father/barker who owns the funhouse (played by Kevin Conway, last seen in *The Lathe of Heaven*) is killed by being thrust onto a sword held by a mannequin; it protrudes through the front of his belly, and he grasps it like an erection. In a slightly reversed echo of Malory's *Morte d'Arthur* (Mordred's killing his father by hauling himself along the spear that has impaled him), the barker tries to kill but only wounds the male good guy, Buzz, by forcing him belly first onto that sword, in a homoerotic patriarchal nightmare that could not possibly please the audience. To take another example: the monster in this film (played very well by the mime Wayne Doba, with special makeup executed by Craig Reardon and designed by the ubiquitous Rick Baker) is an unlovable child on the model of the Frankenstein monster, and about halfway through the film he tries to buy the sexual favors of the palm reader, Madame Zena (Sylvia Miles). He is presented as pathetic, and more than that he has a premature orgasm — which is, of course, a taboo in pornography and in similar fantasy structures: the knives in *Halloween* and *Psycho* may imply sexual dysfunction on the part of the killers, but as symbols they are always hard, and that is one reason such images may appeal to rapists, who are often impotent but who are in any case using sex only as an outlet for violent hatred. When he goes on to kill Madame Zena, he indirectly shorts out the electrical system, and the funhouse (in which the four protagonists are hiding overnight, for fun) comes momentarily to life. The point is that the funhouse/horror film is here explicitly tied to perversity and sexual frustration rather than to sexual fulfillment.

The other female killing makes a similar point in a more horrible way. It is a genre convention to pass moral judgment on the victims by killing them off in what are presented as appropriate ways. (The fellow who gets the idea of staying in the funhouse, for instance, besides being selfish, dope-oriented, and greedy, is killed just after recounting a story of how he once tried to scare his brother but was locked in a closet for his troubles; thus it seems appropriate that he should die trapped in the funhouse.) The character Liz is presented as promiscuous, and so one might expect that her punishment will be connected with her sexuality. When she is trapped by the monster, she attempts to seduce him — but it is obvious that she is terrified, that she is simply doing the cleverest thing she can think of under the circumstances (she has witnessed the scene with Madame Zena and has to distract him long enough to stab him; she does, but the wound does not kill him). Instead of the conventional spectacle of a woman's being punished for sexual activity, there is the horrifying image of her being murdered by an unimaginably ugly and impotent rapist. As in the best horror films, there is an unsettling mixture of identification with the victim and reluctant compassion for the monster. There is nothing remotely titillating about these and similar scenes, yet they cannot be called disgusting; what they have instead is a horrible beauty that has always been one of the central attractions of the genre and the core of its claim to art. Much of this is due to the dark, sharp color cinematography of Andrew Laszlo, but it is undeniable that director Tobe Hooper, who made the shocking, repulsive *The Texas Chain Saw Massacre* and the relatively tame television adaptation of *'Salem's Lot,* emerges here as a highly efficient and professional craftsman. (Auteur fetishists may enjoy noticing the tie-in with *Chain Saw* of the degenerate family, the endangered teenagers, and the lone female survivor.)

Where this all comes together is in three remarkable reflexive sequences: the opening, the conclusion, and a scene in the middle, where the father confronts his monstrous son. "As God is my witness," he says, "I don't hate the sound of your voice." Until this point the monster has been wearing a Frankenstein mask, a downright brilliant gesture, not just because the Frankenstein monster is the correct prototype (the child rejected by his creator and looking for love) but because with the mask on he appears part of the *normal* world, the world that includes horror images as elements in its playground. Now the father criticizes him so harshly that the son tears off his mask and confronts him with what he is. The horror, the audience discovers, is real; as the ads say, "There is something alive in the funhouse," and the fun in a horror film is in confronting the possibility that the horrors are not made up. In this ploy is the central difference from *The Howling,* but it must be noted that *The Funhouse* contacts reality in its analysis of the impact of horror films on the fantasy lives of their audience, and in that respect the films are not so different.[5]

The latter point is made clearly in the first five minutes. A young boy — in subjective camera — looks at a Frankenstein poster, takes a knife from his bedroom wall, puts on a clown mask, and heads for the bathroom where his sister Amy (the lead and seer-figure, played by Elizabeth Berridge) is taking a shower. The parody of *Halloween* is entirely explicit, and one cringes at the prospect of another *Boogey Man* or *Prom Night.* In shots that just as closely echo *Psycho* he pulls aside the shower curtain and jabs the butcher knife at Amy's belly — where it is revealed to be a rubber toy. The boy is a straightforward image of the child not as horror-object but as horror-audience, and if Hooper's audience finds him as harmless as their own presumed self-image, they will learn, as the boy later does, that there is more at issue than fun, that these games are connected in a meaningful way with genuine rape and murder in an unattractively perverse context. This is an image of the child that critiques the child images of *The Exorcist, The Omen,* and *Halloween* rather than reinforces them, and scorns utterly those in *Prom Night* and its ilk. Amy then goes downstairs to wait for her date, where she finds her parents watching *Bride of Frankenstein* on television, a film that by the end will be revealed as the same sort of clue provided by *The Wolf Man* in *The Howling.*

For in the end the monster tries to make Amy his bride in death. He has cornered her in the basement of the funhouse; she holds him off with a steel pole. She is distracted by a (false) skeleton that drops behind her, but has the self-possession to realize which is the real horror (as the victim in the again relevant *Targets* does not) and strikes at him. He pulls the bar away and accidentally electrocutes himself on the power plant, an echo of his killing of Madame Zena; this starts in motion the mechanism that pulls the ride's carts, which catches him in its hooks and chains. He appears to be dead, and Amy stands before him — but he revives and almost succeeds in pulling her toward him. This further echoes the recent death of his father and the business with the sword, for both of them try to destroy their destroyers on emblems of their own perverse power. But she gets away, and the monster is ground in half by the wheels of the mechanism, in one of the greatest and most vivid images in the recent history of the movies.[6] The point is that the heroine, being "normal," cannot finally destroy this monster; he can only be destroyed by his own kind, by his own metaphysical *category* (as there are only supernatural ways of killing vampires and werewolves), by his own level of imagery. What destroys him is the funhouse from which he is inseparable and which is an emblem of the horror film in general. Thus this image celebrates the self-enclosed qualities of the genre, the ways it is a law unto itself (again, like myth), which are the keys to the ways it impinges on reality.

The horror film is not a model for behavior but a categorical intrusion. If it seems to be turning more regularly reflexive in these two recent films, that may be because its makers realize the importance of its rediscovering its roots, its laws, and its genuine calling, and thus defining itself to itself in ways that may teach the sidetracked and brutalized audience what to see in it.

NOTES

1. Bruce Kawin, *Mindscreen* (Princeton, N.J.: Princeton University Press, 1978). Also see Kawin, "Right-Hemisphere Processing in Dreams and Films," *Dreamworks* 2 (Fall 1981), and Kawin, "The Mummy's Pool," ibid., 1 (Summer 1981).

2. For a discussion of the relations between reflexivity and horror fiction, see Bruce Kawin, *The Mind of the Novel* (Princeton, N.J.: Princeton University Press, 1982), 180–210.

3. See *Cinéfantastique* 10 (Winter 1980), for articles on *The Howling* and *The Funhouse,* and ibid., 11 (Summer 1981) for another article on *The Howling* and extensive information on the careers of Dick Smith and Rick Baker.

4. Roger Ebert, "Why Movie Audiences Aren't Safe Anymore," *American Film* 6 (Mar. 1981). It should be kept in mind, however, that subjective camera *had* been used for the monster's POV at least as far back as *It Came from Outer Space.*

5. Another recent film that faces this question is Vernon Zimmerman's *Fade to Black.*

6. This wheel image is taken (if I remember correctly) from *The Strange Door,* but here it has much greater complexity and beauty.

8

Through a Pumpkin's Eye:
The Reflexive Nature of Horror

J. P. Telotte

More completely than Bruce Kawin and in a manner quite distinct from Lucy Fischer and Marcia Landy, J. P. Telotte in this essay (reprinted from Literature/Film Quarterly *[1982]) examines the reflexive nature of the horror film, using* Halloween *as his prime example. Telotte's intensive study of the character's, camera's, and viewer's "modes of vision" in* Halloween *is a model of phenomenological analysis that is fully grounded in specific textual details. Horror, he asserts, is best understood not as transparent social fable or as adolescent sexual rite of passage, but as a beneficial "investigation of the nature of our conventional manner of seeing"—an investigation that can lead us to see "beneath the surfaces" of ourselves and our world and to achieve a "new level of awareness."*

A professor of English at Georgia Institute of Technology, Atlanta, and co-editor of Post Script, *Telotte has written extensively on the horror film and other popular genres for* Film Quarterly, Film Criticism, *and other journals.* Dreams of Darkness, *his book on the films of Val Lewton, was published in 1985.*

> This life's five windows of the soul
> Distorts the Heavens from pole to pole,
> And leads you to believe a lie
> When you see with, not thro' the eye.
> —William Blake

Henry David Thoreau, meditating upon Walden Pond, once described his private lake as the surrounding landscape's most "expressive feature," a sort of giant "eye, looking into which the beholder measures the depth of his own nature."[1] Today technological culture seems to have made such solitary retreats a rarity, though it does, after a fashion, still acknowledge their necessity by furnishing an alternate version of this reflective experience, one we enjoy in the movie theater. Within that dark world the viewer privately encounters familiar images of reality with which he is encouraged to identify and relate, often even in a more moving or meaningful fashion than outside the theater's confines. More important, though, the movies also bring him face to face with a kind of intelligence, alive even as Thoreau's woods were and similarly challenging him to a level of introspection. As Bruce Kawin has shown, movies all, in their own way, "imitate mindedness," that is, they confront us with images that are "the result, and the indicator, of directed attention," of another, narrating intelligence directing its perceptions to us.[2] Of course, that intelligence is essentially our own, that narration emanating from our own involvement in those projected images we so raptly follow. One consequence of this singular encounter, though, is the generation of a new manner of seeing, one in which we see not simply *with,* but 'thro' the eye," thereby glimpsing not only the world we inhabit but also our place in that context. What the best films offer us is a type of "eye contact" that, like the experience of Thoreau's pond, might prod us into seeing beneath the surfaces, even into ourselves as we are mirrored in their shimmering image patterns.

This perspective seems a particularly appropriate one to take to the horror film, for it is a genre especially concerned with conjuring up images whose existence we might previously have hardly suspected or perhaps sought to suppress from consciousness. Through its frightening scenes, R. H. W. Dillard contends, the horror film functions in a decidedly "instructive" fashion, much like a medieval morality play, teaching us to accept "the natural order of things . . . and to cope with and even prevail over the evil of life."[3] Sharing this basic understanding of the genre, Robin Wood suggests that horror films represent "our collective nightmares," and that their visual embodiment on the movie screen empowers us to cope with our subconscious fears "in more radical ways than our consciousness can countenance."[4] Most critics agree, therefore, that the terrors confronting us in these films are neither gratuitous nor designed merely to effect a catharsis; they also drive home lessons regarding our resolution of those personal and cultural problems that we are often reluctant to face outside the theater.

The specific manner in which those lessons are thrust home, however, has largely been neglected because of our more immediate concern with those nightmares that the horror film brings to light. Clearly, the horror film — perhaps more than any other genre — is designed to evoke a specific response from its audience, whether it be a shiver of fear, a vague uneasiness, or a sense of relief at the dispelling of some great threat. The manner in which the viewer is drawn into the film narrative therefore becomes a key to understanding any example of the genre. And when viewed in this light, every horror film becomes something of a reflexive text, referring back not only to its own generic workings, but also to its audience that, through its visual participation in the events unfolded, contributes to their impact and affirms our capacity to bear with such traumatic encounters.

That almost personal confrontation between the generic formula and the audience is at the heart of most horror films, but is especially evident in John Carpenter's first foray into the form, *Halloween.* Drawing heavily upon the conventions established by many classics of the genre, Carpenter has created what seems, despite its dark, threatening surface, to be one of the most limpid, pondlike of horror films, a tale whose most telling effects derive not so much from our forced encounter with its disturbing images or from our mindfulness of those half-forgotten, mythic fears associated with Halloween night, but precisely from the ways in which we are asked to see those often denied visions.

The film requires that we look through the eye of a glaring pumpkin — the symbol of both our fears and deep urge to cloak them under a mythic form; but it thereby enables us to see those human depths that Thoreau discovered in his more bucolic surroundings.

From its opening shot, a slow track-in to a hollow, gleaming jack-o'-lantern's eye, *Halloween* clearly announces that its primary concern will be with the way in which we see ourselves and others and the consequences that often attend our usual manner of perception. That pumpkin, set in relief against a field of black, looms in the darkness like a glowing mask, inside of which burns a destructive fire, as the close-up view through its triangular eye then affirms. Gaston Bachelard's description of man's visual relationship to his surroundings, that "everything that makes us see, sees,"[5] seems particularly appropriate here, for Carpenter uses that opening image to suggest an inanimate yet threatening world, which is clearly staring back at us, making us all the more conscious of the quite different way in which we normally view the world we inhabit. From this initial confrontation of points of view, there follows an investigation of the nature of our conventional manner of seeing and a stripping away of those masks behind which we so often tend to cloak the more disturbing visions that our world holds in store.

After this initial, disturbing "eye contact," *Halloween,* following the pattern of Alfred Hitchcock's *Psycho,* places its audience in a voyeuristic position to begin that task of exploring and revealing their relationship to the events here depicted.[6] While *Psycho* opens with the camera slowly tracking in through a window to intrude on two lovers in a seedy hotel room, *Halloween* goes a step further with its introductory tracking shot, lodging its audience's perspective firmly in the subjective, voyeuristic view of six-year-old Michael Myers, who watches from outside his house as his sister and her boyfriend "make out." As a result of this shift in perspective from a disembodied, narrative camera to an actual character's eye, though, we are forced into a deeper sense of participation in the ensu-ing action. The scene is Haddonfield, Illinois, on Halloween night 1963 as we walk around the outside of this two-story house, seeing entirely through Michael's eyes as he peers into the windows of his home. With the advantage of his viewpoint, we see without being seen, titillated by the adolescent sexual encounter we witness. However, as is often the case with the voyeur, we then experience frustration, being prevented from viewing the consummation of this encounter when Judy and her boyfriend leave our field of vision and go to an upstairs bedroom. A further benefit of our identification immediately presents itself, though, for Michael can enter the house and thus overcome this initial physical barrier. Donning a mask previously worn by his sister's boyfriend, he goes upstairs to her room, though too late to view the rest of their lovemaking. In any case, Michael still faces two more imposing and significant barriers—the one psychological and the other phenomenological; and it is by their agency that Carpenter then drives home the consequences of this voyeuristic iden-tification that, up to now, has seemed such a pleasant, if slightly mis-chievous activity.

On the one hand, this child with whom we have been forced to identify can hardly be expected to understand the complexities of adult sexuality, much less the fumbling uncertainties and experimentation of adolescents like his sister. Hence, whatever he does see must remain something of a harsh mystery to him, one in which one person pleasurably assaults an apparently willing victim. A corollary consequence, and perhaps a better explanation for the violence that ensues, is that through this voyeuristic perspective, Judy Myers has already been reduced to something far less than human, an object of visual interest and immature sexual titillation. These factors, seen in the context of a Halloween night when "evil" is already afoot, and through what we come to recognize as a deranged mind, result in a horrifying travesty of the sexual encounter that the child has only partially witnessed and completely misunderstood.[7] As Michael ap-proaches, his sister sits naked, staring at her reflection in a vanity mirror, this narcissistic fascination with her own image apparently preventing her from noticing her brother, who then slashes her repeatedly with a long, phallic knife. As the voyeur, the outsider who is cut off from a proper understanding of that which he has seen, finally confronts his opposite number, the insider or initiate into the mysteries of adulthood, tragedy follows.[8]

These opposite modes of seeing and the consequences that attend each are two of *Halloween*'s central concerns, just as they are implicitly major concerns in many realistic horror films. Throughout the film we see that narcissistic vision in the form of those people who refuse to see or believe anything outside of that known world, which they feel revolves totally about them; and this perspective is especially embodied in the teenagers Annie and Lynda, friends of the heroine Laurie. For them Halloween simply signals the start of a weekend of partying and provides an opportunity for them to sneak off from their parents and meet their boyfriends for a night of sex play, even though it means, in Annie's case, shunting off her responsibility for babysitting on Laurie. The voyeur's vision, which sees man as little better than an object of curiosity or pleasure, hardly able to lay claim to any human concern or sympathy, belongs preeminently to Michael, now grown into a veritable monster and escaped from the mental asylum at Smith's Grove where he has been incarcerated for the past fifteen years. It is a failure of vision on both sides, in fact, an ongoing human perceptual limitation, whose consequences *Halloween* then proceeds to lay bare for us.

Appropriately, eyes become a central focus of the film, starting with the blazing eye of the jack-o'-lantern and culminating in Laurie's attempt to put out the eye of the monster as he tries to kill her. That opening close-up of the pumpkin's flaming eye introduces the subjective murder sequence taken from Michael's point of view, thus thematically linking the two scenes and warning of the type of vision that we then see demonstrated—it is a burning, destructive view, seeing not fellow human beings but objects of curiosity, looking not into a mirror of common humanity but at a total enigma, and seeking not to participate in the mutual human drama but to parody and devastate its concerns. After Michael has killed his sister and been discovered by his parents, we are finally divorced from his perspective, yanked away to a reverse angle view of his staring, uncomprehending eyes, as the camera rapidly tracks back and up. The complete lack of comprehension in his face—which Dr. Loomis later describes as a "blind, pale, emotionless face"—suggests a mode of vision quite alien to us, as is emphasized by the sudden shift to an extreme long shot. With this shock of recognition comes almost a revulsion, accentuated by the camera's rapid acceleration away from the action, as if the viewers had just realized what they had been, if not party, at least an interested witness to. A sense of guilt, however slight, has been imparted and will linger throughout the film, even though Dr. Loomis seems to offer some measure of absolution. He makes repeated references to the boy's "evil" eyes, describing them as "the blackest eyes, the devil's eyes," and stating his belief that what lurked "behind that boy's eyes was purely and simply evil." Apparently we are to understand that vision involves a kind of morality, a right manner of seeing entailing right action, a wrong bringing chaos.

An indication of the sort of perspective that the grown Michael brings back to Haddonfield is seen in the fact that he goes about masked, as on that earlier Halloween in 1963. The almost luminous white mask that he wears through the rest of the film is neither grotesquely distorted nor natural, but more resembling the face of a dead man. It therefore functions not only to cloak his human features, but also to effectively divorce him from the world of the living, his victims. Besides the mask stolen from the local hardware store, at one point he even dons a sheet to cover his entire body, wearing over it a pair of glasses taken from his latest victim, Lynda's boyfriend Bob. When he appears before Lynda in this garb, she is hardly disturbed; in fact, she laughs rather than screams, believing that Bob is simply playing a joke on her. Little suspecting that great disparity between appearances and reality, which Carpenter has already primed his audience to expect, she describes the figure as "cute, real cute." That image — the glasses atop a full white sheet — however, provides a grotesquely ironic commentary on the way in which people see in the film. For one thing, the monster *looks* comical, but it is that very disparity between seeming and being that is so disturbing. If, after all, such a frightening reality is able to masquerade as a harmless fiction, then how safe can we ever be? On what perceptions can we really rely? At the same time, those glasses suggest a corrective for vision, a proper way of seeing reality, although on closer inspection we notice that they cover no human eyes, only a facade of whiteness, a blankness impenetrable and incapable of responding to humanity. In the course of fifteen years, that child's vacant stare has become a malevolently blank vision — akin to the "white mask" of evil that Ahab saw in Moby Dick — so Laurie's defense against this monster at the close of the film, attempting to poke out his eye, to blind him and thereby at least momentarily end his threat, seems only natural, not simply a gratuitous shock.

This emphasis on eyes and seeing is not an isolated pattern in *Halloween,* however, for Carpenter has paired it with a distinctive manner of presenting and perceiving the events that transpire here. The opening track-in to the jack-o'-lantern's eye again establishes a pattern to be followed by the ensuing introductory sequence, also a lengthy tracking shot in which the audience gradually approaches a victim and then visually participates in the unleashing of that destructive energy imaged forth in the blazing pumpkin eye. Having jolted his audience into such a disconcerting awareness about the way in which we see and the consequences that often attend a certain kind of irresponsible vision, Carpenter seldom repeats that subjective tracking shot, though every time the camera moves in a similar fashion, with that same slow, deliberate, exploratory motion, we are conditioned to expect the worst. In place of that subjective movement, he resorts to several almost equally disconcerting camera techniques designed to underscore the lesson contained in the opening murder scene. One such recurring device is a slow tracking back of the camera to suddenly discover another character whose presence we had not expected, most often to reveal Michael watching someone while remaining unseen. Such a technique forces us to acknowledge two complementary planes of action and assures that we remain aware of the limitations of any perspective that prevents us from seeing such a depth of field. Also, it functions as a visual warning, a correlative to Dr. Loomis's injunctions to the police, affirming a need to remain on guard, ready for the unexpected to suddenly intrude into this seemingly peaceful little community.

An even more unsettling variation on that opening voyeuristic tracking shot is frequently used when Michael stalks his victims. Instead of once again subjectively forcing us to identify with the murderer, Carpenter opts for an ambiguous camera placement, consistently locating it slightly behind or just to the side of his "boogeyman," so that we view part of the killer in the frame, usually in the foreground, while a potential victim, unaware of any threat, occupies the background. Consequently, when the killer follows Laurie and her friends home from school in the doctor's stolen car, we see what a passenger in the rear of the car might; instead of perceiving events as the murderer himself would, we look on as his *accomplices*, bearing our own special burden of guilt in these matters. A continuously effective ingredient of Carpenter's horror formula, then, is this subtle build-up of a guilt anxiety in the audience, which he eventually allows us to exchange only for an equally unsettling identification, that of potential victim of these horrors.

That subjective tracking shot finally recurs as Laurie crosses from the safe enclave of the Doyle household, where she is babysitting with Tommy, to the Wallace house, where Lynda and Annie are and which is, as the audience already knows, a scene where she will encounter the most violent and unexpected of horrors. We cross the street with her, in the process leaping a boundary from a circumscribed adolescent world — one not far removed from childhood — where our horrors are all safely packaged and controlled through the television screen (Dr. Dementia's six straight hours of horror movies) to a disturbing adult world where those nightmare horrors become reality itself, with ourselves as possible victims. By so implicating his viewers in these terrors, therefore, by visually forcing them through a series of unsettling identifications, first as killer, then accomplice, and finally potential victim, Carpenter emphasizes the common human responsibility for and involvement in those grisly aspects of life from which we usually like to think ourselves safely removed. Perhaps he hopes to demonstrate that, bearing our own burden of involvement in these actions, we are also the ones best placed to call a halt to the proceedings, provided, of course, that we choose to accept this very human responsibility.

This notion of responsibility, of a general complicity in the events that here unfold, is consistently linked with the modes of perception that these characters engage in. Dr. Loomis appears, at first, a decidedly ambiguous figure, for in his single-minded concern with having Michael locked away for the rest of his life, he seems almost maniacal himself. Obviously, his nurse has her doubts about his compulsiveness in this matter, despite Loomis's admonition that she "try to understand what we're dealing with here." As our surrogate, the voice of a calm and rational skepticism, the nurse has to receive "ocular proof" before she can understand the doctor's concern and his talk of "evil." So to drive home the shocking nature of this threat, Carpenter places his audience in the car with the nurse as she waits outside the asylum where their subject is being held. Along with her, we are suddenly assaulted by what we are still thinking of as a boy, now a large, grown man, who first jumps to the car's roof, staying just out of our field of view, and then suddenly smashes his hand down on one of the windows to break into the car and violate our supposedly safe perspective. More than simply an introduction to the "grown" monster, this scene reasserts the sudden, disconcerting visual threats that abound in this world and transports us from its periphery — from our secure theater seats — to within that fragile human society at which these threats are directed. Thereafter, the doctor's watchfulness, his almost manic concern with standing guard on the old Myers house, comes to seem quite understandable to us, if not to the local police; in fact, it is clearly the only responsible action he could take in the circumstances.

On the whole, however, human nature as Carpenter here depicts it seems to be plagued, in some cases perhaps mercifully so, with a limitation on its visual capacities, a limitation that at least might serve to excuse the shortcomings of some characters. The fact that almost the entire film occurs at night — on a Halloween in 1963 and another fifteen years later — naturally evokes a sense of mystery, of the unknown lurking just beyond the reach of artificial illumination, and also beyond that "light" of reason that we normally use to render the mysterious harmless. The darkness into which we are thrust, therefore, not only offers an obstacle to seeing things clearly, but it also spurs us to question whether what we do perceive is real or only a phantasm, conjured up jointly from the imagination and the collective myths surrounding Halloween.

Naturally, if we cannot be certain about our own perceptions, then we shall most probably be skeptical toward what others report seeing, hence the numerous cases of disbelief in which one character's sightings or beliefs are given no credence at all, simply because they are his views alone. If Loomis's nurse is skeptical of his views on Michael, even a bit cynical about his motives, the Haddonfield police are even more so, far less ready to accept his contention that the town's quiet family dwellings full of women and children are simply "lined up for the slaughter." Laurie offers a more pointed example, though. She believes that she is being followed, for out of the corner of her eye she repeatedly sees a mysterious stranger, trailing her in a car, hiding beside a hedge, or staring into her room from a neighbor's yard. Her friends, however, convince her that she is simply fantasizing, projecting into the real world her image of the dream boyfriend she has been too shy to pursue. Even the local sheriff, who accidentally startles her, dismisses Laurie's jumpiness as due to Halloween, a time when "everyone's entitled to one good scare." Since her impressions do not coincide with the reality perceived by the majority, she convinces herself that she has simply been working too hard at her studies and is seeing things that are not really there. Besides, she assures herself, such fears of ghosts and monsters are "kid stuff," and she "outgrew superstition" long ago. Later, Laurie applies this same approach to Tommy Doyle as she babysits with him, in this case using her age and "experience" to explain away his fears of the "boogeyman" with which his classmates have taunted him. Several times he reports seeing this creature he has been warned about, only to be assured by his sitter that there is no such thing. Of course, events finally prove the truth of his own and Laurie's original estimations, but by then we have already seen just how limited and unreliable that commonplace vision of reality ultimately is.

This sense that there exists a great disparity, particularly between what we actually see and what is potentially visible to us, pervades *Halloween*. What Carpenter seems intent on demonstrating is how consistently our perceptions and our understandings of the world around us fall short of their potential, most often because we are conditioned by our experience and culture to see less and less, to dismiss from our image contents those visions for which we might not be able to account, or those that might simply distract from our more important personal concerns. It is only natural, then, that the children in *Halloween* — Lindsey and Tommy especially — see more than do their adolescent babysitters, who in turn have a slightly more encompassing view than do their adult counterparts. If children seem to be scared more easily by the mysteries of the night, it may be because they have good reason, being more alert to the very real dangers that ever lie waiting "out there," and that they alone perceive. From the film's beginning, though, the audience has been initiated into this wider view, as we confront a discrepancy between our own understanding of that adolescent sexual encounter and six-year-old Michael's view of it. In keeping with that disconcerting opening, our perspective thereafter is frequently manipulated so as to reveal an ongoing discrepancy between our view and that of a particular character. Privileged with the information that the killer is driving a stolen stationwagon bearing the insignia of the state mental institution, we repeatedly identify that vehicle—and thus the killer's threatening, but unseen, presence—in the background or extreme foreground of numerous shots. For example, when Annie picks up Laurie to go babysitting, we recognize that the car that pulls out behind them is the one occupied by the fugitive, stopping when they stop and maintaining a discreet but threatening watch over their actions. And when Loomis makes his report to the local police, who are investigating the hardware store burglary, the discrepancy between audience and character perceptions takes on a particularly ironic note. In medium shot we see the doctor looking worried, straining for some glimpse of his stolen car and its insane occupant; he turns to the right as the car, which we immediately identify, enters the frame from the left rear, and as he turns back, it passes behind him to the opposite side of the frame, by chance eluding his persistent gaze, and at the same time, mocking the police in their search for the burglar—the occupant of that car. This broader view with which we are gifted reinforces our sense of anxiety by imparting a feeling of inevitability to all that we witness; it is as if a force that we see but that remains beyond the comprehension of these characters is bearing down on them, a force as inexorable as that "fate" that Laurie learns about in class that day.

Having established the threatening aspect of the background and periphery of his compositions, Carpenter uses that disparity between his characters' restricted viewpoints and his audience's inevitably more encompassing field of view to sustain the general atmosphere of tension and expectation. In the case of Laurie's friend, Annie, who is babysitting Lindsey Wallace, he shows the murderer threatening to attack three times, as Annie remains totally oblivious to the terror lurking nearby. While she is in the kitchen fixing popcorn for Lindsey—ironically "Jollytime" popcorn—the killer appears looking through the glass door in the rear. Carpenter then teases us into expecting an immediate confrontation between victim and killer when Annie spills butter on her clothes and exits through that same rear door in search of the washing machine to clean the stains out. Instead of a sudden climax, though, Annie reaches the laundry room and accidentally locks herself in. Again the killer hovers in the background, apparently ready to strike, as he peers in first through the glass panel of the door and then through a rear window; and in her bumbling way, Annie seems intent on making it easy for him, for she tries to use that window as an exit from the washroom. What makes the tension all the more excruciating is that Carpenter forces us to laugh at her situation, despite our anxiety and expectations, by having Annie get stuck in the window while remaining unconscious of that impending threat. That humor is apparently designed to have a slightly disarming effect, for when Annie emerges unscathed from this predicament, safely returns to the house, and closes the kitchen door, there is a sense that she may have managed to avoid what had previously seemed like certain disaster, that perhaps a providence is watching over those who completely fail to see the nature of the world in which they live. No sooner do we breathe easier, though, than that deathly white face looms out of the darkness once more, promising to finally fulfill our worst fears when Annie goes out again, this time to pick up her boyfriend, after she sends Lindsey across the street to the Doyle house. When she finally gets into her car—visually recalling for us the earlier attack on Dr. Loomis's nurse—Annie notices something wrong, frost on the inside rather than the outside of the window, but by then it is too late. Carpenter then concludes the scene with a close-up of her dead, staring eyes, open as before, but no longer able to perceive that world around her. It is a fitting image: vision taken from one who had used it so heedlessly, life violently snatched away from a person who could not see clearly enough to sustain it.

The challenge ultimately facing Laurie, then, is to overcome this visual limitation, to see beyond her immediate concerns and thereby save her life. She is introduced as being brighter, more imaginative than her friends, and probably more responsible, for her father has entrusted her with dropping off the key to the Myers house, now a rental property that his company, Strode Realty, is handling. Laurie also has her limitations, though, as she demonstrates in discounting Tommy's fears of ghosts and goblins, and later dismissing his claim to having seen the boogeyman from his living room window. When he asks her to look at this apparition, she responds like a skeptical adult, looking too late and expecting to see nothing anyway. Halloween, she assures him, is nothing more than a time "when people play tricks on each other," and when our eyes, in turn, apparently deceive us as well. As this particular Halloween night progresses, however, Laurie undergoes a visual awakening. This initiation begins with her repeated sightings of that mysterious figure, which she finds both threatening and alluring, lurking around her neighborhood. Later, along with Tommy and Lindsey, she watches two of Dr. Dementia's horror films on television, *The Thing* and *Forbidden Planet,* which sound the same basic warning, that "there are more things in heaven and earth . . . than are dreamt of" in our philosophies. And finally, moved by curiosity and a real concern for her friends who do not answer her phone call, Laurie leaves the safe confines of the Doyle house to go to the Wallace residence and try to find out just what is going on there. What she finds, of course, is an education in that constant disparity between what appears to be and what actually is, between our commonplace expectations and those complexities of reality we too often overlook.

Laurie expects to find her friends waiting in that dark house to surprise her, ready to jump out from their hiding places and have a laugh at her anxieties; in short, she thinks—or hopes—that a harmless joke lies behind the spooky appearance of the Wallace house. Thus when she enters, Laurie calls out into the darkness that "the joke's over," but her words immediately take on an ironic flavor when her friends literally begin to "pop out" from their hiding places—dead. After Bob's body falls from a closet and she discovers the corpses of Annie and Lynda, Laurie is faced with a corroboration of those "childish" fears she has previously repudiated with Tommy. These new and disconcerting discoveries force her to see more than she had ever anticipated, obviously more horrors than she thought could be harbored in her calm, midwestern community; and they soon loom all the more ominously as the killer turns his attention to her, for they become a mirror of her own potential fate. To underscore this sudden, radical transformation of her perception of reality, then, Carpenter once more returns to the subjective shot as the murderer makes his first attempt on Laurie's life. Again evoking Hitchcock, this time *Vertigo,* Carpenter has Laurie escape from her assailant by accidentally plunging headfirst down a flight of stairs. The dizzying subjective shot that results suggests both her near-fatal immersion in this horrific scene and the drastic upset of her understanding that this sudden shock has precipitated. Like Alice falling through the looking glass, Laurie's vision of reality has been radically transformed, and, given her survival, she will clearly never be able to view her world in quite the same way again.

Simply knowing that horrors do, in fact, exist "out there" is insufficient, however; the full consequences of this knowledge also have to be thrust home. Laurie barely gets back to Tommy's house ahead of the killer and locks the door behind her. She then breathes a momentary sigh of relief, as if she might have effectively drawn back into another world, one that is proof against such terrors. As in Annie's case, Carpenter employs a series of three incidents to demonstrate that, once given this special vision, having been initiated into this frightening knowledge, one can never again find such easy security. Throughout these final scenes he returns to those in-depth compositions to confront us with two planes of action simultaneously, thereby forcing us to wonder all the while when their separate actions will collide and to what effect. Within the Doyle house, Laurie cringes on the sofa in the foreground, knowing that the killer is somewhere about, but not noticing him as he rises up from the background to attack her. Despite being taken by surprise, she successfully defends herself, stabbing him with her knitting needle and apparently ending the threat. As she again turns away from the killer to see about Tommy and Lindsey whom she had hidden upstairs, he once more rises in the background to resume his stalking, making his appearance just as Laurie assures the children that the danger is over. Pursued into a second-floor bedroom, Laurie hides in a closet and when discovered jabs a makeshift lance into the monster's eye and then stabs him with his own knife. Once more she turns her back on this finally vanquished horror and sends the kids off for assistance as she sinks down on the floor, exhausted from her ordeal. As she gathers her strength and rises, though, we see in the background just beyond her shoulder the thing rising as well to renew its attack. This time Dr. Loomis, whose vigilance has finally paid off, intervenes to kill Laurie's attacker, emptying his gun into the killer and forcing him to fall from the second-story window. At this point they both turn away from the presumably dead killer, and even the audience is made to breathe a bit easier since Carpenter here abandons the dual planes of action, that visual formula he has hammered into our consciousness to represent the incessant nature of this threat, in favor of close-ups of the two principals, both shaken but alive. That feeling of security is short-lived, however, for then we cut to a high-angle shot, as Loomis looks down from the window to the yard where the murderer's body had been lying. For a final time we see the consequence of that momentary relaxation of our vigilance: it has risen and vanished into the darkness, probably to kill again. We are left then with the sound of the killer's labored breathing and a dark screen, a threat still about, even if we cannot see it.

The warning that *Halloween* so simply yet effectively posits, then, is preeminently a visual one, calling us to a new level of alertness. By the film's end, we are almost afraid *not* to see, for to avert our eyes even momentarily, it has been drummed home, might allow this terror that has several times seemed vanquished the chance it needs to reassert itself, to once again threaten what has now been revealed as a precariously stable world at best. As in *The Thing* to which *Halloween* offers homage, we have been stridently warned to "keep watching" if we value our human environment.

As Dillard has further noted, those frightening images of the horror film serve a truly vital purpose, since "evil must be known to be combated."[9] This premise holds true whether we identify that evil with a monster or catastrophe of some sort or if it springs from within ourselves. *Halloween,* I believe, successfully reaches for a disturbing combination of these possibilities, which it then seeks to make "known" to us. No satisfying explanation for Michael's actions are ever forthcoming; he is simply a monstrous "given"—"the evil," the boogeyman—placed down in the world of this film. He is simultaneously ourselves and a monster, terrifying in his total other-ness. Through his presence, though, Carpenter is able to rivet our attention on the manner in which we perceive and react to the conditions of the world we daily inhabit. He places us in a setting where dangerous lunatics are allowed to roam free in a storm and their keepers can plead, "I'm not responsible," where the sheriff is too busy to notice that his own daughter is smoking pot, and where neighbors turn off their lights and hide behind locked doors when a teenage girl comes screaming for help. It is not simply a world in which the adults are largely absent; more significantly, it is one in which that sense of human responsibility and complicity that we conventionally associate with adulthood is conspicuously missing. Here people either neglect to look about them or purposely avert their eyes for fear that they will be called upon—perhaps by some residual sense of fellow feeling—to act. *Halloween* conjures up a frightening vision of a culture largely deprived of this human concern; as a consequence its people are easily transformed into objects of voyeuristic attention, sexual pleasure, and finally homicidal mania. So how, Carpenter puts the question, should we respond to such a situation?

The challenge facing his characters is essentially the same one he poses for us: we must open our eyes more fully to our human surroundings, seeing more responsibly and staying aware of our role in the world in which we dwell. Following the example of Michael's startled parents at the opening of *Halloween,* we are called upon to rip off the masks that too often cloak our human nature and look into those complexities that lurk beneath. Only through this deeper, more encompassing perspective, through a constant human vigilance such as that thrust home to Laurie, he suggests, can we continue to exorcize the boogeyman that we often, in uneasy defense, joke about, but that, individually, in our most irresponsible moments, we can evoke to threaten our world. It is into these depths of our nature and our culture that *Halloween,* after the fashion of its best predecessors in the genre, challenges us to steadily if fearfully gaze.

NOTES

1. Henry David Thoreau, *Walden* (New York: Holt, Rinehart and Winston, 1948), 156.

2. Bruce Kawin, *Mindscreen* (Princeton, N.J.: Princeton University Press, 1978), 13. This intelligence, Kawin asserts, is the basic "principle of narrative coherence"

in the film, in its most abstract form, evidence of the tale telling or revealing itself (55). In a form that relies so heavily on audience manipulation, as the horror film does, this principle, I suggest, is all the more clearly operative.

3. R. H. W. Dillard, "The Pageantry of Death," in *Focus on the Horror Film,* ed. Roy Huss and T. J. Ross (Englewood Cliffs, N.J.: Prentice-Hall, 1972), 37.

4. Robin Wood, "Return of the Repressed," *Film Comment* 14 (July–Aug. 1978):26.

5. Gaston Bachelard, *On Poetic Imagination and Reverie,* trans. Colette Gaudin (Indianapolis: Bobbs-Merrill, 1971), 78.

6. Much of the structure of *Halloween* seems openly indebted to Hitchcock and to his *Psycho,* in particular. Like *Psycho,* for instance, *Halloween* begins with the printed titles that identify the specific place and time of the ensuing action. It consistently identifies its antagonist as a dangerous voyeur. And the male lead who saves the female from the killer is named Sam Loomis in both films.

7. A possible model for this situation, indeed, a very close parallel, can be found in Michael Winner's film about children's misinterpretation of the adult world, *The Nightcomers.*

8. As D. L. White suggests in his essay, "The Poetics of Horror: More than Meets the Eye," in *Film Genre: Theory and Criticism,* ed. Barry K. Grant (Metuchen, N.J.: Scarecrow Press, 1977), 136, what Carpenter deals with here is probably "the most pervasive" fear found in the horror genre, "that of being cut off from others."

9. Dillard, "Pageantry of Death," 40. Dillard further notes that this "knowing" is no guarantee against the recurrence of evil, but it does give us the ability to cope "with events beyond human control."

9

"The Fallen Wonder of the World": Brian De Palma's Horror Films

Allison Graham

Freudian psychoanalysis, with its insistence on interpreting the monstrous, nightmarish threat as projection and double, may indeed be, in Noel Carroll's phrase, "more or less the lingua franca *of the horror film and thus the privileged tool for discussing the genre." And several essays in this collection are at least in part Freudian-styled readings of the genre. In her essay on the horror films of Brian De Palma, Allison Graham draws her inspiration elsewhere, from the theories of Herbert Marcuse as well as the speculations of the archetypal psychoanalyst James Hillman, who equates the unconscious with the creative imagination. Films like* Sisters *and* Dressed to Kill, *Graham proposes, enact the larger cultural dilemma of the "abused imagination," as the private, interior life is appropriated by pragmatic, one-dimensional, external "reality" until only spiritual isolation and the void left by "eroded subjectivity" remain. (R. H. W. Dillard and J. P. Telotte address similar concerns.) Graham's examination of the "feminine" inner self in De Palma's films offers a different perspective from Lucy Fischer and Marcia Landy, Virginia Wexman, Robin Wood, and Vera Dika on the representation of women and the feminine in contemporary horror.*

Allison Graham, the author of Lindsay Anderson, *teaches film studies in the Department of Theatre and Communication Arts at Memphis State University, Tennessee. Her essays have appeared in* Film Criticism, Mosaic, *and the* Georgia Review. *She is currently completing a book on American film and culture since World War II.*

Because of their persistent obsession with the varieties of psychological stress, horror films seem to lend themselves most readily to psychoanalytic interpretation. While social or political critiques are inherent in the genre, they are usually assigned secondary status to what is seen as the major drama of horror: the constant confrontation of the self with its myriad fears and projections. Even when the cultural conditioning of such anxieties is most blatant (the obvious example being the fear of Communist subversion in many science fiction and horror films of the 1950s), the prevailing assumption of most critics and directors of horror films is that the seemingly endless variations on terror we can imagine for ourselves all spring from a common source: the mind that seeks metaphoric outlets for its imploding anxieties, the mind that must give symbolic form to repressed desires that would destroy its rational adjustment to society, the mind of lightness and darkness—in short, the Freudian mind.

With its logical structuring of the levels of the psyche, the Freudian model offers the most accessible way to understand the common roots of the disparate types of horror films. Thus, madness (from *The Cabinet of Dr. Caligari* to *Psycho* to *The Shining*), monsters—whether "natural" (*Nosferatu, Jaws, Gremlins*) or "synthetic" (*Frankenstein, The Car*)—and satanic possession (*Rosemary's Baby, The Exorcist*) can be interpreted as dramatizations of our fear of our own "double" nature, the projecting upon another (a dead mother, a shark, a car, the devil) the terrors and desires we cannot enact outside the realm of art or dream.

Freud's belief that the uncanny event or entity is "nothing new or foreign, but something familiar and old-established in the mind that has been estranged only by the process of repression"[1] has found general acceptance by a generation of critics and filmmakers intent on exploring the varieties of modern repression. Stanley Kubrick, for example, is reported to have studied "The Uncanny" during the making of *The Shining,* and Robin Wood, in an essay aptly entitled "Return of the Repressed," has distilled the major ideas of "The Uncanny" (as well as *Civilization and Its Discontents*) into a general critical approach to the horror genre. "In a society built on monogamy and family," he paraphrases Freud, "there will be an enormous surplus of sexual energy that will have to be repressed and . . . what is repressed must always strive to return."[2] (John Carpenter apparently agrees, claiming that his madman's horrendous behavior in *Halloween* is actually a reflection of the *heroine's* "repressed sexual energy."[3]) The double, then, becomes the repository of all we cannot consciously avow; each country, each era, each sex will create its own socially relevant forms of the double, but the essence of the horror project remains the same: to look upon, however obliquely, the "contents" of our "inner" selves.

The Freudian model clearly provides a fascinating index for decoding the "real" source of thousands of boogeymen who have haunted the screen since the turn of the century. Obviously, our imagined demons are spawned by us, and just as obviously, they can function as mirrors of us. Yet there is something oddly comforting about these projections: their very presence reassures us of our own depth, their magnitude complements our self-image. However diminished we may feel in our day-to-day relationships, these monsters testify to our "hidden" power—enough, usually, to incinerate the world (or at least to bump off anyone who has even incidentally belittled us). While laboring in the desert of modern anonymity, we can believe that we harbor within us a dense jungle of tangled motives, gnarled wishes, and fecund desires. *We* contain a world, *we* are the unconscious followers of Ishmael's advice to "live in this world without being of it."

By this point in the twentieth century, the concept of psychic levels is so ingrained in our popular culture that the unconscious itself is often assumed to be a concrete verity—an actual lower layer of the human head (or an active homunculus within the head) that is the "real me" (most people, including many psychoanalysts, forgetting, as Harold Bloom has noted, that Freud "always remained aware that the unconscious was his hypothesis or metaphor, a prime fiction of his theory"[4]). When one speculates upon the relative impoverishment in our culture of spiritual ties to family, community, and even work, one might wonder if the prospect of "another self," a self that, for better or worse, never deserts us and that furnishes us the impetus to proclaim "I gotta be me" and do things "my way" is not our final security in the face of absolute isolation. If this is plausible, then Wood's idea that the "implicit hero" of many horror films of the 1970s is the monster that destroys "the bourgeois Establishment" is particularly interesting. If we fear our society much more than we fear our own inner demons, then civilization clearly has not offered enough satisfaction to justify its escalating demands on an already overloaded psyche. *The Omen,* Wood claims, "would make no sense in a society that was not prepared to enjoy and surreptitiously condone the working out of its own destruction."[5] And it would make no sense, we might add, to an audience that did not delight in identifying with that "evil" hero—a projection, it seems, of the solitary self trapped in a deathly society.

Within this context, the modern American horror film might seem to posit a revolutionary vision: the overburdened, alienated unconscious ultimately exploding in rage against an increasingly repressive social structure. This vision, like that of the layers of the mind, is based on an image central to popular psychology: namely, the self as "container." However we choose to visualize this container—as reservoir, vessel, storehouse—we implicitly set limits on the amount of its contents. When too much is repressed, our carefully stabilized delineation between secret self and public world disintegrates—the dam breaks, the storehouse explodes, and society is engulfed in retributive catastrophe. But this interpretation ignores a major fact about such films: society may be rocked, but it is not devastated. Whatever psychic firepower we hurl at the world is finally deflected back at us, and what begins as a revolutionary intention usually becomes a reactionary fact.

Many horror films since the 1960s – films like *The Exorcist, The Shining,* and especially those of Brian De Palma – appear as somber postscripts to the 60s dreams of social revolution, ghastly reflections of our culture's decision to embrace what Herbert Marcuse called our tendency toward "one-dimensionality." Marcuse's writings throughout the 1950s and 1960s, in fact, offer an image of the American psyche that is eerily similar to that of most modern horror films: a "flattened-out" vestige of the imagination, an inner space eroded by our desire to live in the "real" world of mass communications and technology. In this space where the "Great Refusal" of the status quo should grow lies instead the specter of "the Happy Consciousness," the conviction that "the real is rational and the system delivers the goods."[6] While Marcuse believed that a "biological insurrection" could overthrow our physical and emotional identification with the values (and things) of mass culture, he realized that our alienation from our own organic disposition was probably exacerbated beyond repair. For in a society that can effectively neutralize all threats, even the erotic is stripped of its anarchic power and is exploited as another "standard feature" of the good life, and in a society that promises the fulfillment of one's deepest desires, self-actualization is an ideological act: it is assimilation into the public consciousness, the great acceptance of "the real." To one so assimilated, the inner self is an embarrassing anachronism, a slow-witted faculty that evolution has not yet disposed of. As private space gives way to mass consciousness, the demons of the personal psyche should wither away; sublimation, after all, is only possible when one harbors a wish that *cannot* be gratified directly. For the members of the "permissive society," to wish is to be gratified, for what is wished is only that which is immediately possible.

If we can understand the "unconscious" in psychologist James Hillman's sense as the "imagination," then we can see that it is the imagination itself that is most threatened by a desublimated, "permissive" society. Hillman's Jungian "re-visioning"[7] of the unconscious, in fact, bears particular relevance to a discussion of contemporary culture, for it is in part a revisioning of the relationship between the personal and collective psyches. To Hillman, our projected fears and anxieties must be understood as creative phenomena, images born from "the field of imagination." But rather than value our "inner" resources, Americans have exploited them, just as we have exploited the treasures of the "outer" world; we have, he says, strip-mined the psyche: "We burn up our psychic resources just as we burn up our natural gas, as if there were an endless supply from the so-called creative unconscious. Who said the unconscious, the depths of the psyche, is an inexhaustible creative pool? Maybe psychic burn-out results from this exploitative view—as if everything should come up and be used."[8] Hillman believes that traditional psychoanalysis, which has pervaded our culture in its pop psychology form, depletes the psyche in pursuit of rational control of the essentially uncontrollable. It is the triumph of technique over the aesthetic.

Marcuse would agree, but would see this activity as only one aspect of the large trend toward the technological and commercial manipulation of all psychological uniqueness. From either the psychoanalytic or sociological perspective, however, the contemporary state of both the individual and the collective imagination is imperiled. Even so, graphically violent examinations of this condition often provoke tremendous critical disdain, for spiritual emptiness is usually considered the exclusive thematic territory of tasteful existentialists like Ingmar Bergman or Michelangelo Antonioni, in whose films the soul may quietly agonize itself out of existence without calling unseemly attention to its death throes. But to insist that our increasing sense of loss is best expressed as a tale of horror, not angst, is to imply that there is nothing *more* tasteless than the decay of the imagination. This is a bit different from saying that the contents of our imagination are tasteless; it is to conjure the very void itself.

In *The Exorcist,* for example, a priest discovers that a child who is apparently "possessed" by countless evil presences—all of them projections of other characters' cracking psyches and hidden guilts—is really inhabited by "no one," a discovery the priest makes only by playing a tape of the "voices" backward, as if detecting an aural version of the child's mirror image (a theme continued in the more recent *The Entity,* which focuses on a woman who is terrorized by an invisible, foul rapist—a being she calls "no one"). Like Jack Torrance in *The Shining,* whose self-proclaimed responsibilities as a writer and a father become a mask for the ghoulish compulsions of a man with nothing to write and nothing to do, the possessed child in *The Exorcist* obscenely displays the nothingness at the heart of the film's horror by revealing that what is inside her is exactly what is inside her society: a spiritual and imaginative void. Every director creates different metaphors for this void, but whether they be the zombies of contemporary consumerism (*Dawn of the Dead*), the disinterred souls of suburbia haunting the living through television channels (*Poltergeist*), a reptilian slime mold infesting the empty shell of former humans (*Alien*), or a computer intent on impregnating a woman (*Demon Seed*), they all form a part of the new mythology of American hell: the collective nightmare of an objective, technological reality, the world of "real things," coiling back on itself to consume the vestiges of eroded subjectivity.

Brian De Palma shares with his colleagues in horror a conviction that in a mass-mediated society that promises (and seems to deliver) everything we can dream of, little remains of an inner life that can create an alternative reality. What *is* left inside is a twisted image of the abused imagination, whose power, because it has no place in a desublimated world, can only appear hideous. Yet while the destructive eruptions of the soul appear to be the dramatic focus of his films (and they obviously account for a large portion of his production budgets), their flamboyance masks a far more insidious activity, one that is responsible for these outbursts in the first place. For the truly horrifying aspect of De Palma's films is not the unpredictable *explosion* of repressed desire, but the all too predictable *implosion* of social information, the steady appropriation of interior life by exterior consensus. It does not seem coincidental that De Palma turned to horror (in *Sisters* [1973]) after his attempts to make socially relevant films in the 1960s (*Greetings; Hi, Mom!*) ended in disillusionment. He came to realize that, as Marcuse had been observing for two decades, American culture was capable of absorbing nearly any threat to its social and economic equilibrium. "I found myself on talk shows," he has said, "talking about the revolution, and I realized I had become just another piece of software that they could sell, like aspirin or deodorant. It didn't make any difference what I said. . . . In my experience, what happened to the revolution is that it got turned into a product, and that is the process of everything in America. Everything is meshed into a product."[9] In the wake of this great meshing, as the self becomes co-extensive with its society, it abandons any faculties that encumber its smooth assimilation into the one-dimensional fabric of reality. Disowned and devalued, the impoverished imagination hovers just beyond the flattened-out landscape of De Palma's films, longing for embodiment but remaining a permanent psychic outcast.

This image of the homeless soul is so central to De Palma's work that we need look no further than the credit sequence of *Sisters* to see how completely it dominates his concept of the horrible. In this sequence we first see a human embryo emerging from the blackness of the frame, attached by its cord to an amorphous placental mass. The subsequent images reveal the growing fetus in close-up, its face acquiring distinguishable features, its eyes appearing, in one particularly eerie shot, to open while still in the womb. Following this montage, the final image of the sequence appears: the single fetus has inexplicably—and with no visual warning—become two. Centered in the enveloping darkness, the twins float in a womb that appears to be "cracking" open, ready to deliver its contents.

Bernard Herrmann's menacing soundtrack contributes greatly to the sense of unease that pervades this sequence. But the score itself would not be nearly as effective in creating an ominous mood if it were not accompanied by an equally disquieting visual element: the brilliant, oppressive blackness that surrounds the fetus in every shot. Whatever the infants are growing within, it is not a discernible human body. In fact, the nearly impenetrable darkness of the background, against which the brightly lit womb appears as a garish neon splotch, suggests nothing so much as the cold blackness of space itself, with the few spots of light scattered throughout it looking more like cosmic matter than traces of a human womb. Even the fetuses themselves look unnatural in this context, almost extra-terrestrial (the immediate reference is, of course, Stanley Kubrick's floating fetus at the end of *2001*). In short, the sequence has a distinctly alien tone, one traditionally associated with science fiction films, and that probably owes much to the influence of Herrmann. Although De Palma wanted the revered film composer to write a score reminiscent of his work for Alfred Hitchcock, Herrmann urged De Palma to devise a new credit sequence to complement his decidedly un-Hitchcockian introductory theme. Oddly, what the theme resembles—and is almost a speeded-up version of—is the opening music of another film scored by Herrmann, Robert Wise's *The Day the Earth Stood Still* (1951), a film whose concerns in many ways mirror those of *Sisters*.

In Wise's credit sequence, during which we hear Herrmann's dramatic theme, the screen is filled with a vision of outer space, from which the earth emerges and appears to grow larger. Since there is no visible life in this sequence (and since, of course, the film was made years before a human entered space), we must infer that we are seeing this vision from the point of view of an alien being who is about to land on earth. This, as it develops, is exactly what we should infer; our identification with Klaatu's point of view is encouraged from the first moment of the film as the *only* point of view imaginable for decent, intelligent humans, for it is the humanistic alternative to a world filled with foul prejudices and petty warmongering. In this film, what is hidden and mysterious is not a raging, demonic force bent upon demolishing rational societies, but a life-affirming impulse that, by necessity, must stand in conflict with the society that represses it. In other words, what is "out there" is our "better self," which cannot be incorporated into the divisive structure of pragmatic reality. Because of its refusal to see our disowned projections as inherently evil, Wise's film cannot portray the alien's movement into earthly society as an occasion for horror. Our abandoned double (our transcendent human self) remains sublimely intact, returning home to be finally legitimized. The striking naiveté of the film (in its view of spiritual life as totally independent of political and social context) allows it to suggest that since society is capable of redemption, what returns to us after eons of repression is still pure. Acceptance of the other, under these circumstances, is fairly easy. Integration and reunion (all heralded in the credit sequence) become the necessary conditions for the film's final exhortation: to make the great move outward—toward the community of humankind, toward an acceptance of all others in the world.

Sisters, however, offers no such millennial vision. Unlike Klaatu, De Palma's fetal twins are hardly the harbingers of spiritual unity. While the refined alien is born from an empyrean of universal harmony and order, the infants seem to be born from the void that surrounds them. The mystery of their genesis is further compounded by their peculiar state: they are, we later discover, Siamese twins. If this sequence can be seen as a preface to the rest of the film (and even to the rest of De Palma's work in horror), then what we have witnessed is a tragic parable of the disconnected self. Connected to no visible human mother, the initial fetus seems to be suspended in a most suspicious isolation. Visually born from nothing and apparently nourished by nothing, it is almost a parody of the ultimate inner event: the mysterious creation that should be growing inside a human being is, in fact, taking form *outside the body.* As if in reaction to its extreme desolation, this detached self, this isolated fact, duplicates its own creation and gives birth in turn to a companion—its mirror image. Stranded in space, the alienated self and its double await delivery into the void that spawned them, the void, it turns out, of the contemporary imagination.

De Palma's variations on the theme of depleted imagination center on the motif of voyeurism, but not as a semi-pornographic technique (although he definitely alludes to pornography), nor as simply a "strategy" (as Pauline Kael has called it[10]) of cinematic self-reflexivity. As the central way of seeing in his films, voyeurism is inextricably bound to the horrific vision, the privileged glimpse into terrorized privacy. The credit sequence of *Sisters,* of course, is a foreshadowing of his particular kind of voyeurism, for what appears to be a vision of a miraculous occurrence turns out to be a vision of a growing monstrosity. Furthermore, what appears to be a remarkable glimpse into the secrets of the human body turns out to be a kind of trompe l'oeil: the inner event is entirely external, detached from the body and displayed as a repellent oddity.

The subtlety with which De Palma introduces the idea of voyeurism gives way to broad satire in the next sequence, as we watch an apparently lecherous man spying on an apparently blind woman who is undressing in a bathhouse changing room. Just as she begins to remove her under-garments, the camera zooms out from the man's freeze-framed face to form the shape of a television screen. Immediately we are in the midst of a television game show, "Peeping Toms," in which contestants—and "all you Peeping Toms at home" — try to guess "what our unsuspecting subject will do." All of the contestants guess that he will continue to watch the woman undress, but when the "hidden camera" continues its story, we see that the "chivalrous" man (as the host calls him) turns away. De Palma's supremely horrific joke is the connection he makes between this sequence and its ostensibly unrelated predecessor. For the blind girl, Danielle, is none other than one of those floating infants from the credit sequence, recently separated from her Siamese twin and employed as a decoy for "Peeping Toms"; and the void those twins were about to be expelled into in that sequence turns out to be none other than the "vast wasteland" of television itself. A game show whose premise (like that of its model, "Candid Camera") is the inherent consumer appeal of anyone's most private moments and whose assumption is that any event can be packaged into a marketable format is, of course, a show perfectly in tune with its medium. De Palma does not simplify the nature of this kind of psychic erosion by implying that our mass media are its cause; it is *our* flight from privacy that calls forth the instruments of psychic destruction. It is we who have created the illusion of a desublimated world in which nothing, from goods to acts, is denied the consumer; it is we who have turned inner reality into simply another manipulatable object in a completely externalized world.

In *Dressed to Kill* (1980) television appears again, but in such a subtle way that its correlation to the film's concerns may be missed. In a split-screen scene, both Liz (a prostitute) and Dr. Elliott (a psychiatrist) watch Phil Donahue interview a transsexual about her previous life as a man. The thematic focus of the scene seems to be the mysterious link between Liz and Elliott; we feel that Liz, because she has glimpsed Kate Miller's murderer, will also be attacked shortly, and that Elliott is protecting the killer, who is his patient. The link, of course, is stronger than this. The killer Liz has seen is Elliott's own "second self," his "woman trapped inside a man's body," whose sole mission, it appears, is to destroy anyone (including Liz) who arouses the "external" man. Elliott, we later learn, is himself preparing to undergo a transsexual operation but cannot make "the last step"; in simple terms, he will not allow his *inner* self to become his *outer* self. Liz, however, has confronted what Elliott himself cannot face. Her privileged vision of his tortured, repressed self seals her fate: she, and her knowledge, must be eradicated.

There is, however, another element in Elliott's desire to kill Liz. She is a prostitute, a woman who earns her living by externalizing men's fantasies, by calling forth and embodying hitherto private visions. Ironically, Elliott's form of therapy appears to be an abstract version of the hooker-client relationship. We discover, for example, that in his session with Kate,

Elliott's "male" self was being stimulated by her rather depressing confessions. Liz's session with Elliott, however, is a joke, an erotic act performed by a detached woman for the purpose of diverting Elliott's attention. Her fantasies, as opposed to the fantasies of the sincere Kate, are a sham, enacted before several audiences: Elliott, Kate's son Peter (outside with binoculars), a policewoman who has been following her, and us. But while the format of psychoanalysis comes to bear a great resemblance to that of a prostitute's trick — a timed, professionally regulated sequence of events — it is more subtly similar to that of the "Donahue Show," which provides the background for Liz's and Elliott's early activities. While Kate unknowingly performs for Elliott, Liz consciously parodies the search for a real self beneath layers of personae. As her performance in Elliott's office makes clear, the talk show of television only mirrors the talk show of therapy; it is simply another bogus glimpse of the psyche. The transsexual who has so proudly merged his inner self with his outer self and has transformed himself into the image of his innerness has become pure image, his inner life now a consumer product for the "Peeping Toms" at home.

When De Palma extends this theme to his own art in *Blow Out* (1981), questioning the complicity of film (and horror films in particular) in this massive assault on the integrity of the private vision, he creates the final chapter to the television sequence of *Sisters*. In *Blow Out* everyone is set up, everyone is spied upon, everyone is both usable and disposable. From the first sequence — a rip-off horror film-within-a-film (entitled *Coed Frenzy*) — De Palma repeatedly and cynically suggests that even the worst horror film is an accurate reflection of our collective perception of the world. When the director of *Coed Frenzy* tells his sound engineer, Jack, that "this is our finest film," he is, in a peculiar way, probably right. For the subplot of *Blow Out* concerns their successful quest for "the perfect scream" for a *Psycho*-styled murder, which leads them to the ultimate source of their images' power: a *real* death scream, taped and overheard by a lost and frantic Jack. Arriving on the murder scene too late to help the victim, Jack ends up using his tape in *Coed Frenzy* ("Now *that's* what I call a scream," the director exclaims when he hears Jack's handiwork). Having passed judgment on politicians and newspeople for capitalizing on others' misery, Jack ironically becomes the film's final appropriator and manipulator of psychological reality.

Returning to *Sisters,* we can see that Danielle's role is similar to Jack's. Born from the void, a creature of a totally externalized world, she functions well within it, genially cooperating in the great demystification of privacy going on around her. In contrast, however, Philip (her unsuspecting subject in "Peeping Toms") persists in distinguishing between private and public, inner self and outer persona. His refusal to consume her image before the hidden camera, his hesitation about accepting her invitation to dinner, and his unwillingness to take sexual advantage of her all mark him as clearly doomed in De Palma's one-dimensional universe. He does not attempt to have sex with Danielle until she invites him to, and in the morning, he does not enter Dominique's room even though he hears her voice arguing violently with Danielle. For Philip's chivalrous behavior, for his constant refusal to deny Danielle her autonomy—her private space—he is rewarded with murder (more specifically, a stab in the groin from Danielle's new cutlery, her "Peeping Toms" prize). As he crawls across the apartment floor to write "help"—backwards—on a window in his own blood, he is seen by another "Peeping Tom," Grace, a journalist living across the courtyard. (De Palma's split-screen here, in which we see both Philip's and Grace's points of view simultaneously, emphasizes, in contrast to the slickness of the television show, the excruciating difficulty of communicating an inner experience to an observer.) Philip's fate is clear from the beginning of the film: used as commercial fodder by television and as bait by Danielle to show Emil, her ex-husband and doctor, that she is free, Philip is doomed by his inability to manipulate his own image (and De Palma's decision to cast a black in this role was perhaps an evocation of this theme, as well as an archetypal association of darkness with interiority). His "help" is the last word of the dying private man, his invitation to anyone to look into his private anguish. That Grace does look dooms her as well, for her mission throughout the rest of the film is to publicize, or at least legally validate, her vision of private hell, to understand it as more than a passing moment, a mirage (or a television show, if you will).

If Philip represents the privacy of acts, Grace represents the privacy of intellect; both suffer appropriate ends. Stuffed into the couch on which he made love to Danielle, Philip becomes the final unsuspecting subject in the film, as a detective spies on the unclaimed couch at a rural Canadian depot. Literally taken into nothingness in his consummation with Danielle, he *becomes* nothing—consumed, invisible. Grace's fate is more complicated. Like Jimmy Stewart's character in Alfred Hitchcock's *Rear Window,* she comes to identify with the criminal whose activity she has witnessed, becoming Danielle's alter-ego. By the end of the film she has, in hallucinations induced by Emil, actually *become* Dominique, Danielle's dead Siamese twin.

To understand the logic of this exchange, we must understand the role Dominique plays in Danielle's life. Already dead by the time the film proper begins, Dominique is reduced to an off-screen voice during Philip's stay in Danielle's apartment, functioning the way Norman Bates's mother functions in *Psycho,* as a second personality of the main character. Grace learns from a documentary film that Dominique was the withdrawn twin, while Danielle appeared "so sweet, so responsive, so normal," although, as a doctor claims, "Danielle can only be so *because* of her sister." Orphaned while babies, reared in an institute, the twins were supervised by Emil, who (as he later suggests to Grace) became attracted to Danielle. Dominique became a physical and emotional obstacle to his advances and was drugged (at Danielle's urging) to be gotten out of the way. When Danielle became pregnant, Dominique attempted to kill the fetus, necessitating a separation that killed both her and the baby. Instead of psychologically integrating Dominique's spirit into a new, whole personality, Danielle became pathologically fragmented, retaining her sunny persona (Danielle) while suppressing her inner self (Dominique), a self obsessed with revenge for her banishment from the world. Her shattered personality in many ways resembles what R. D. Laing has called the "divided" or "unembodied" self. This schizoid condition, in which "the individual experiences his self as being more or less divorced or detached from his body," arises from the desire to achieve security in a terrifying world. "The body," Laing has stated, "is felt as the core of a *false* self, which a detached, disembodied, 'inner,' 'true' self looks on at [*sic*] with tenderness, amusement, or hatred, as the case may be."[11] All that matters to the divided self is the equilibrium of the hermetically sealed inner self, yet what is valued as the real self is, of course, *unreal,* an apparition born from — and maintained through — fear.

That Danielle's inner self is so barbarously destructive — responsible for the murders of both Philip and Emil — is presaged in the title sequence. Her mirror image, created in the void, can only reflect what she herself cannot admit: her terror of loneliness and her displaced anxiety about spiritual isolation. To acknowledge unity with this monster would be to acknowledge her emptiness, to understand that what grows inside her is, like her fetus, dead. Danielle's grotesque separation scar on her hip is visual proof of the disastrous proportions of her displacement, yet it is a scar created by Emil, who himself bears a large, red scar on his forehead. What intellectual monster, it seems reasonable to ask, has given birth to Emil? It is under his scientific direction that Grace completes her identification with Dominique. Through his hypnotic suggestion, her own conscience is erased; in its place is a totally programmed set of responses. Although Emil dies, his role as progenitor of an externalized world is ultimately successful, for by the end of the film Grace can only repeat to the police the words he has implanted in her unconscious: "It was all a ridiculous mistake. There was no body, because there was no murder." And, of course, the final image proves her right: there *is* no body, only an unclaimed couch. Grace is also correct when she claims there was no murder, for the crime not only was seen by someone who no longer exists (the fully conscious Grace), but was committed by someone equally insubstantial (the dead Dominique). The entire sequence was, in effect, a tragic, ghostly reenactment of "Peeping Toms": apparitions spying upon apparitions, with private life becoming the ultimate joke. Philip's invisible, rotting corpse that haunts the last image is De Palma's final comment on voyeurism: there is, quite literally, nothing to see.

"What a culture can't assimilate, it destroys," a character says in *The Fury* (1978), and there can be little doubt about what De Palma sees as unassimilable in our culture: the unpredictable power of the unconscious, the uncontrollable urges of a severely repressed innerness. In light of his consistent portrayal of this force as inherently — and grotesquely — female, however, we might reasonably ask, as many feminists have, whether it is not De Palma himself who is destroying that which *he* cannot assimilate into his aesthetic vision. We need only think of the castrating ghost of Dominique hiding in Danielle's psyche (a *female* ghost, we should remember); the repressed anima of Dr. Elliott; or, most pointedly, the horrendous telekinetic power that appears to be a by-product of Carrie's first menstrual period (in *Carrie,* 1976). Clearly, what comes from *within* has the power to destroy what is *without;* chaotic, violent, and *organic,* the feminine energy of the inner self is a constant threat to the synthetic structuring of mass-mediated society. De Palma, though, cannot allow the known, however repressive, to be defeated by the unknown. His horror, then, becomes self-perpetuating: in an atrophied inner world, only monstrosities can grow (mutant fetuses, schizoid psyches, lethal energy), but only the release of these monstrosities can destroy the forces that engendered them. Either choice — repression or liberation — promises a psychic debacle. De Palma's films, in fact, reveal a consciousness politically stranded at the crossroads of critique and ideology, terrified by the power of a deadly consensus reality, yet equally mortified by the prospect of violent change, and the horror they reflect becomes a documentary vision of our historical moment.

Hillman has said that contemporary America suffers from "psychotic concretism," in which "exterior determines interior."[12] To him, psychoanalysis must begin to focus on what is outside individuals as well as what is inside them, for "pathology is 'out there' . . . on the highway . . . in the car . . . buildings are anorexic . . . the language is schizogenic . . . 'normalcy' is manic, and medicine and business are paranoid." "The whole world," he claims, "must become a patient." De Palma's vision is similar, for what is inside his characters is, quite simply, the pathology of the real world, the sickness of a "soulless concreteness." In *Dressed to Kill,* for example, Kate Miller's son Peter invents a new circuit for his computer, and Kate jokingly suggests that he name the circuit after himself; "I'll tell your grandmother you're working on your Peter," she tells him. Her humorous identification of sexuality with technology, however, is not an innocent observation (especially considering her own description—and De Palma's depiction—of her sex life with her husband as highly mechanical). The technological vision of the world as an assemblage of dead objects and manipulatable things has become, in De Palma's films, the dominant vision of the spirit as well.

"I want what's coming to me—the world and everything in it," Tony Montana says in De Palma's *Scarface* (1983), and, ironically, the world *does* come not only to Tony but to the rest of De Palma's characters as well, its soulless matter forming the basis of their reality. In such a world the inner circuitry of the computer becomes an appropriate model for the psyche: a self-referential system whose feedback is predictable and whose functions are controllable. In the progressive leveling of ambiguity such a system entails, "The Peter" (and Peter himself) becomes a programmed circuit. The inner world, in effect, becomes a mirror of the outer world, and the promptings of the unconscious are simply (like the events on "Peeping Toms") reprogrammed into unthreatening formats. Thus, Grace's memory is replaced by a data bank supplied by Emil; Robin and Gillian's telekinetic powers are redirected by the Paragon Institute in *The Fury,* while Carrie's similar powers are channeled, under the aegis of her gym teacher, into a middle-class fantasy of popularity; and Dr. Elliott's submerged real self, Bobbie, is committed to analysis by Elliott himself and denied all access to her male host except through a telephone answering machine. It is little wonder there are so few fathers in De Palma's films, for the true fathers in his world are the abstract forces of masculine technocracy (and their representatives: the evil agent in *The Fury,* Emil, and Elliott). It is these forces that embark on the great appropriation of the psyche, stripping inner life of its mysteries, neutralizing the power of the imagination, and transforming the spiritual terrain into usable space. Philip Slater would call these forces "psychic excretions," projections of our paranoid and murderous fantasies that have been given material form. According to Slater, our desire for control, itself a reaction to a world perceived as "unloving, ungiving, and unsatisfying," has "proceeded to the point where the parts of ourselves that we have extruded into [the world] keep backing up and flooding the personality with its own rejected components."[13]

This projected fantasy of the totally externalized life in which all that is inside us is brought out, examined, classified, and incorporated into the technological landscape can only be a concretized death wish. "It's like being on Mars," Carrie says of her absurd confection of a prom, and she is right, for the dreams of De Palma's characters are oddly disconnected from any sense of psychic vitality—products, like *Coed Frenzy,* of a terrorized and withered imagination. Kate Miller's masturbatory revel in *Dressed to Kill,* for example, turns horrifying as her own imagination seems to betray her; her afternoon tryst—a paradigm of a fantasy pick-up—turns bitter and finally tragic; Liz's fabricated dream confession to Elliott backfires; and, most tellingly, her career of manipulating *others'* fantasies returns to haunt her as she dreams of her own death (at the hands of Elliott) in a dead woman's bed, itself the site of Kate's resentful sex act with her husband at the beginning of the film. When Carrie incinerates her high school and classmates, she destroys her entire notion of reality and desperately embraces her mother's sin-obsessed Christianity as a last salvation. If the world is unreal, then the spirit must be the only—and final—reality. Her mother's stab in the back proves the fallacy of this belief, for locked away in that Gothic labyrinth of a house has not been the soul's dark secret, but only its dark emptiness.

The world of these characters *is* a kind of nothingness, but only because it has sprung from their *desire* for nothingness. As *The Fury* shows clearly, our internal power can only destroy, and the closing image in each of De Palma's horror films—from the concealed murdered body in *Sisters,* to Carrie's own reaching out of the grave in Sue Snell's nightmare (and Sue's waking hysteria), to the agent's exploding head in *The Fury,* to Liz's death dream and subsequent fright in *Dressed to Kill*—shows precisely what we might fear most in our culture: that to look inside ourselves, to find our real selves, is to find an image of death. What is repressed has become nothing, for our demons have been exorcised into the world. The world has become the landscape of fear, the mirror of anxiety, the projected void of the imagination. In Don De Lillo's *The Names,* a child writes a short story whose final lines could serve as a coda to De Palma's horror films. "This was," he writes, "worse than a retched nightmare. It was the nightmare of real things, the fallen wonder of the world."[14]

NOTES

1. Sigmund Freud, "The Uncanny," in *Sigmund Freud: Collected Papers,* 4, trans. Joan Riviere (New York: Basic Books, 1959), 394.

2. Robin Wood, "Return of the Repressed," *Film Comment* 14 (July–Aug. 1978):27.

3. Todd McCarthy, "Trick and Treat," *Film Comment* 16 (Jan.–Feb. 1980):23.

4. Harold Bloom, "War within the Walls," *New York Times Book Review,* May 27, 1984, 3.

5. Wood, "Return of the Repressed."

6. Herbert Marcuse, *One-Dimensional Man* (Boston: Beacon, 1964), 84.

7. I am using this word as James Hillman does in his book, *Re-Visioning Psychology* (New York: Harper & Row, 1975).

8. James Hillman, *Inter Views* (New York: Harper & Row, 1983), 32.

9. Jean Vallely, "Brian De Palma: The New Hitchcock or Just Another Rip-Off?" *Rolling Stone,* Oct. 16, 1980, 39.

10. Pauline Kael, "Master Spy, Master Seducer," in *Taking It All In* (New York: Holt, Rinehart and Winston, 1984), 37.

11. R. D. Laing, *The Divided Self* (Chicago: Quadrangle, 1960), 71.

12. Hillman, *Inter Views,* 127. Subsequent quotations in the paragraph are from 136 and 121.

13. Philip Slater, *Earthwalk* (Garden City, N.Y.: Anchor Press/Doubleday, 1974), 14–15.

14. Don De Lillo, *The Names* (New York: Random House, 1983), 339.

10

Made-for-Television Horror Films

Gregory A. Waller

By examining a particularly devalued and yet surprisingly resilient form, the made-for-television horror film, Gregory A. Waller offers a perspective on modern horror that differs from the other essays included in this collection. Given the economic, narrative, programming, and censorship constraints of primetime commercial television, made-for-television horror has tended to be suggestive rather than explicit, stylistically conventional, focused on the personal and the intimate, and particularly given to narratives that feature an isolated victim, psychic investigator, endangered young wife, or a threatened middle-class family. The representation of both the monstrous and the normal in telefilms, Waller suggests, provides a revealing contrast to theatrical horror films of the 1970s and 1980s.

Waller teaches film and popular culture at the University of Kentucky, Lexington. In addition to his recently published The Living and the Undead: From Stoker's Dracula to Romero's Dawn of the Dead, *he is the author of* The Stage/Screen Debate: A Study in Popular Aesthetics *and articles in* Film Criticism, Journal of Popular Film and Television, *and* South Atlantic Review.

In an essay on "The Fact of Television," Stanley Cavell argues that "an immediate difference presents itself between television and film," for "what is memorable, treasurable, criticizable" in television "is not primarily the individual work, but the program, the format." Television, Cavell concludes, "works aesthetically according to a serial-episode principle," and many critics of popular television narrative would agree.[1] From this perspective, 90- to 120-minute made-for-television movies that belong to neither serial nor series are more movie than television or are at best a mongrel form.

Almost all the apologists or critics who do discuss telefilms accord a privileged position to those made-for-television movies like *Brian's Song* (1970), *That Certain Summer* (1972), *Born Innocent* (1974), and *Some-*

thing About Amelia (1984) that dramatize controversial, highly topical social problems or transform medical case histories into profiles of pathos and courage. Whether seen as great tradition or exploitational problem-of-the week programming, this telefilm canon explicitly excludes virtually all other made-for-television movies, from obvious pilots for potential series and nostalgically reflexive sequels (i.e., *Return of the Beverly Hillbillies* [1981]) to remakes of classic Hollywood productions and telefilm variations on popular film and fiction genres like the western, private eye, disaster, or horror story. In this essay I consider the most interesting of these telefilm genres, the made-for-television horror movie.

The linking of horror and television is hardly confined to the made-for-television movie. *Poltergeist* (1982) and *Videodrome* (1983), for example, picture the television set itself as a source of horror—a notion less imaginatively pursued by certain opponents of television, like Jerry Mander. Mander's *Four Arguments for the Elimination of Television* can be read as something of a horror story in which television is an evil, Caligari-like monster that insidiously isolates and manipulates viewers, transforming them into mindless, enslaved zombies.[2] Mander's arguments would have provided a compelling—if somewhat clichéd—scenario for an early 1960s episode of "Alfred Hitchcock Presents," "The Twilight Zone," or "The Outer Limits," all series that on occasion included ironic tales of horror. "Night Gallery" (1969), "Trilogy of Terror" (1975), and other made-for-television anthologies continue this tradition, as does "Tales from the Darkside" (1984-present), a syndicated series produced by the same company that produced *Dawn of the Dead* (1979) and *Creepshow* (1982). Best-selling horror novels have been adapted for the multi-episode format of mini-series like *'Salem's Lot* (1978) and *The Dark Secret of Harvest Home* (1978), and, more recently, horror films have inspired a host of popular rock music videos, including "Thriller," "Dancing with Myself," and "Somebody's Watching Me." All these works in different ways provide an important backdrop for the over 100 made-for-television horror movies that have premiered on primetime network television since 1968.

This diverse, durable genre is both a corollary and a counterpoint to the evolution of horror in novels and motion pictures of the past fifteen years, for the made-for-television horror film includes: adaptations of classic horror fiction (*Dracula* [1974] and *The Sins of Dorian Gray* [1983]) and contemporary horror fiction (*When Michael Calls* [1972] and *Cry for the Strangers* [1982]); imitations of big-screen horror (*The Spell* [1977] and *The Initiation of Sarah* [1978], two telefilms about teenagers with telekinetic power, both released in the wake of *Carrie*'s success); sequels (*Look What's Happened to Rosemary's Baby* [1976] and *Revenge of the Stepford Wives* [1980]); stories torn from the pages of tabloid journalism (*Beyond* the *Bermuda Triangle* [1975], *Satan's Triangle* [1975], and *Bermuda Depths* [1978]); updated versions of traditional monsters like the vampire (*The Night Stalker* [1972] and *I, Desire* [1982]) and the werewolf (*Moon of the Wolf* [1972] and *Scream of the Wolf* [1974]); the creation of new movie monsters (*Gargoyles* [1972] and *Snowbeast* [1977]); films of alien invaders (*Night Slaves* [1970] and *The Aliens Are Coming* [1980]), of a malevolent natural world (*The Savage Bees* [1976] and *The Beasts Are on the Streets* [1978]), of satanic evil (*Satan's School for Girls* [1973] and *The Devil's Daughter* [1973]), of haunted houses (*The House That Would Not Die* [1970] and *Something Evil* [1972]), of psychopathic killers (*Scream Pretty Peggy* [1973] and *Someone Is Watching Me!* [1978]), and of exorcists (*The Possessed* [1977] and *Good Against Evil* [1977]).[3] While there are few, if any, unacknowledged masterworks or cultural milestones to be found in the sprawling and often monotonous landscape of made-for-television horror, a closer look at these telefilms can help us to understand the shape of horror as a popular genre from the Vietnam years to the age of Ronald Reagan and to assess certain narrative and ideological assumptions that inform primetime television programming in general and the made-for-television movie in particular.

Both Douglas Gomery and Gary R. Edgerton offer convincing definitions of the generic rules, commercial requirements, and narrative strategies of the made-for-television movie. These critics note, for example, how this form operates within obvious restrictions on language and on the representation of so-called adult situations and how it must be tailored to accommodate temporal and budgetary limitations as well as commercial breaks. Gomery identifies the made-for-television movie as a version of "classic narrative cinema," which features a small number of clearly delineated individual characters—heroes and villains—who are "causal agents" in plots that logically move toward a closed resolution with no "questions or enigmas" left open.[4] The visual style of the typical telefilm is unobtrusively subordinated to "telling the story"; hence the reliance on close-ups and medium shots, high-key lighting, continuity editing, and functional sound. Such an "invisible" style is well suited, Edgerton argues, for the "video realism" of the telefilm, in which "themes are generally played out by no more than a handful of protagonists on a very personal level."[5]

Certain of the technical limitations that affect all telefilms are particularly telling for made-for-television horror. The relatively poor definition of the standard television image, for example, hampers, if not prohibits, telefilms from disclosing to the viewer a complex mosaic of vivid, mysteriously charged details—as Robert Altman does in *Images* (1972), Nicolas Roeg in *Don't Look Now* (1973), and Peter Weir in *The Last Wave* (1977).

Similarly, on most television sets, shadows and darkness become murky, textureless areas that lack the ominous blackness so often favored by horror film directors.

More significant is the influence of network censorship codes. Since the Motion Picture Association of America instituted its "Industry Code of Self-Regulation" in 1968, the horror film has been a predominantly R-rated genre that has, in fact, expanded the boundaries of what can be shown under the rubric of an R-rating. From *Night of the Living Dead* (1968) and *The Exorcist* (1973) to *Friday the 13th* (1980) and the spate of gore movies in the 1980s, this genre has explicitly visualized graphic violence and taboo subject matter to a degree unprecedented in the commercial American cinema. Made-for-television horror, in contrast, rarely offers what would qualify for a PG-13, much less an R-rating.[6] However, the same powerful network censorship restrictions that separate telefilms from the mainstream of contemporary theatrical horror films put made-for-television horror in the position of carrying on what Ivan Butler, S. S. Prawer, and other commentators praise as the "restrained" tradition of horror that is based on suggestion and indirection. Such an aesthetic of restraint and suggestion foregoes "excessive exposure to crudity and violence" in favor of "leaving the ultimate terror to the imagination."[7] In principle, if not in practice, the made-for-television horror movie is the heir to Victorian ghost stories, Val Lewton's RKO productions in the 1940s, and classics of "indirect" horror like *Dead of Night* (1946) and *The Haunting* (1963).[8]

From this perspective, the commercial interruptions demanded of all telefilms could be said to have a legitimate narrative function as a means of enforcing restraint and censorship. (As John Hartley and John Fiske note, commercials and programs together form "part of the *same kind* of naturally continuous field" and should be "decoded" as such.[9]) Commercial breaks do in fact often occur in made-for-television horror movies immediately after a suggestive yet incomplete glimpse of the horrific; however, the commercials themselves leave little to the imagination, for they dissipate horror by transporting us to a clean, safe, brightly lit, quotidian normal world in which solving problems is simply a matter of buying the right product.

The budgetary limitations and abbreviated shooting schedules under which virtually all telefilms are made also pose unique problems for made-for-television horror. For example, these limitations in part account for the caliber of special effects in television movies, which lag far behind state-of-the-art effects in both verisimilitude and ingenuity. As befits a narrative form that evokes horror by indirection and suggestion, made-for-television movies less often rely on the creation of elaborately detailed monsters and the simulation of bloody death scenes than on the distortion of the television image through the use of slow motion, over-saturated colors, negative exposure, and superimpositions. Ironically, most of the techniques used in telefilms to signify the intrusion of the dangerous, supernatural, and horrific are familiar elements of the basic video vocabulary of newscasts, commercials, sportscasts, and other forms of non-narrative, nonfictional television. Certain rock music videos—themselves influenced by horror film—suggest the possibilities for distortion and disorientation that are untapped, yet at least theoretically available to made-for-television horror movies.

Whatever their merits, the special effects in made-for-television horror seem at odds with what Edgerton and Gomery identify as the functional, invisible style of "video realism" that characterizes the telefilm. In the contemporary cinema, horror has proven to be a genre that accommodates and encourages a heightened sense of stylization in editing, camera movement, and mise-en-scène. The films of Brian De Palma, John Carpenter, and, most impressively, Joe Dante, David Cronenberg, and Larry Cohen all bear witness to this fact, as do the almost obligatory hand-held subjective camera movements in slasher films. The made-for-television horror movie seems to be one of the few types of television drama (as opposed to television comedy) that allows for some degree of stylization and some measure of intentional disruption.[10] For instance, Steven Spielberg's flashy manipulation of cross-cutting and shifting point of view in *Duel* (1971) shares little with the anonymous video realism of most issue-oriented telefilms.[11] Unfortunately, overt stylization in made-for-television horror movies all too often becomes simply a matter of predictable mood music and sound effects in concert with the sort of special effects I mentioned earlier and the repetitive use of zoom-ins to single out an ominous or meaningful detail. Carried to its extreme in a telefilm like *The Strange Possession of Mrs. Oliver* (1977), this exclamatory style comes to signify the presence of an omniscient director who continually reminds us of his knowledge of the hidden truth—which hardly seems to merit all the fanfare with which it is revealed.

In addition to overstepping certain restrictions of "video realism," made-for-television horror movies often provide open endings in lieu of the closed resolutions that are, according to Gomery, characteristic of the telefilm format. In the concluding sequence of *Vampire* (1979), for example, the monster escapes into the darkness, leaving unresolved the struggle between the living and the undead, and in the final shot of *I, Desire* the camera moves away from the human survivors to show us a previously unseen vampire lurking in the shadows.

Whether their endings are open or closed, made-for-television horror movies overwhelmingly adopt a narrative form based on the personal adventures of an individual protagonist or a small group. An obvious example of this preoccupation with the intimate is *Duel,* which focuses on the confrontation between one man (appropriately named Daniel Mann) and one malevolent truck on an isolated stretch of desert highway. This life-or-death duel has no effect on and is of no interest to society at large. However frightening, the horror is localized, identified as a singular incident. We can, of course, take Daniel Mann to be an allegorical stand-in for everyman, but Mann's encounter with horror remains a personal episode that alienates this ostensibly normal protagonist from normality's seamless routines and thus reinforces his individuality and our close-up perspective on his dilemma.

Comparably intimate situations recur throughout the genre: in, for example, *The Norliss Tapes* (1973) and other stories of the solitary investigator who stalks an equally solitary monster, and in *Death Moon* (1978) and other stories of the cursed or haunted man or woman. Quite unlike the apocalyptic tradition in the contemporary horror film, which draws upon Revelation or enacts what Robin Wood calls the "disintegration" of America's "dominant ideology,"[12] in these intimate made-for-television movies the monstrous threat does not arise from, manipulate, or assault social conventions, institutions, and beliefs. Instead it duels or preys upon one human being whose situation falls outside the province and the power of socially sanctioned authorities. Telling horror stories on what Edgerton refers to as the "personal level" of the made-for-television movie not only reduces the stature of the monster (in their telefilm incarnations, Satan, killer bees, and the Bermuda triangle all pose surprisingly small-scale threats to humankind), but also demonstrates that Daniel Mann's most severe test will be a private one that means nothing to American society.

Duel has obvious affinities with later made-for-television movies like *Killdozer* (1974) and *Death Car on the Freeway* (1979), as well as with theatrical horror films like *The Car* (1977) (not to mention *Jaws* [1975]). For my purposes, however, more significant than Spielberg's presentation of the monster is the extent to which *Duel* is perhaps the quintessential example of the intimacy and narrow scope that characterize most telefilms — and most network programming in general according to Horace Newcomb and a host of other critics.[13] *Trapped* (1973), for example, retells *Duel* by pitting bloodthirsty guard dogs against a lone man who is accidentally wounded and locked inside a closed department store. A similarly personal focus on the fate of one reasonably intelligent, middle-class, white, adult male is found in *Death Moon* and *The Norliss Tapes,* which do not document a solitary struggle for survival. The businessman become werewolf in *Death Moon,* cursed by the crimes of his ancestors and plagued with nightmares, is a primetime version of the monster-as-victim. In living out his private fate, he leaves society behind, traveling from a contemporary urban setting to die on a desolate Hawaiian beach. In *Death Moon,* as in *Duel,* horror is a personal affair that augurs no cataclysmic social breakdown.

The narrowly personal focus of much made-for-television horror is equally evident in telefilms that feature some type of psychic investigator, a figure who rarely assumes a prominent role in motion pictures of the 1970s and 1980s (pace *Ghostbusters* [1984]).[14] Carl Kolchak, old-style newspaperman on the trail of a monster in *The Night Stalker* and *The Night Strangler* (1973), is the most well-known of these investigators, though the role can also be filled by a private detective (*Curse of the Black Widow* [1977]), a criminologist (*Spectre* [1977]), a defrocked priest (*The Possessed*), or an author dedicated to debunking the supernatural (*The Norliss Tapes*). All of these telefilms include glimpses of the monstrous — in the form of, say, a latter-day vampire, a giant spider, or an ancient demon brought to life — yet the limited scope of these works renders the monster, however deadly, comparable to the standard television series image of the criminal whose actions affect only a handful of unlucky, innocent victims. Since *The Norliss Tapes* and similar made-for-television movies insist that the investigator is destined to undertake other, equally bizarre adventures, what is announced as a tale of horror slips almost imperceptibly into the well-worn trappings of a television cop show case. Perhaps in this way made-for-television horror acknowledges commercial television's affinity for the series format, which always presupposes a stockpile of eight million potential stories. Significantly, *Fear No Evil* (1969) — arguably the first made-for-television horror movie — features as its protagonist a psychiatrist/expert in the occult who successfully rescues a beautiful young woman from the supernatural forces called forth by a satanic cult. This self-styled "doctor to the bedeviled" reappears in *Ritual of Evil* (1970), in which he challenges another manifestation of evil. As much as in "Marcus Welby, M.D." or "Baretta," in *Fear No Evil* and *The Night Stalker* the individual male hero and the narrowly defined case is the frame of reference — evil in these telefilms is a ubiquitous, multifaceted problem, but it it nonetheless simply a problem, on the order of illness for Marcus Welby or crime for Baretta.

In addition to the psychic investigator, who, regardless of his personal quirks and the strange creatures he encounters, is readily recognizable as a version of the authoritative, skilled, experienced male hero of prime-time action series, and the lone, entrapped man, who becomes cut off from any occupational, social, or familial context, the made-for-television movie offers another version of personal horror centering on the fate of a child-less, married woman, twenty to twenty-five years old, who is before all else identified as a wife. *Rosemary's Baby* (1968) is one obvious model for this particular telefilm subgenre. (As would be expected, the influence of Roman Polanski's film can be seen in several made-for-television horror movies, from stories of satanism and possession like *The Devil and Miss Sarah* [1971] and *The Devil's Daughter* [1973] to *The Stranger Within* [1974] and *Night Cries* [1978], which draw upon the fears associated with pregnancy and childbirth.) However, with the notable exception of Richard Loncraine's *The Haunting of Julia* (1976), there are few recent theatrical horror films that take as their central protagonist a young wife. Instead, big-screen horror offers victimized divorced women (*The Hearse* [1980] and *The Entity* [1983]), successful, independent, and vulnerable career women (*Eyes of Laura Mars* [1978] and *Visiting Hours* [1982]), and, above all, middle-class teenagers or college coeds (*Halloween* [1978] and *He Knows You're Alone* [1981]). While the young wife seldom appears as the principal figure in contemporary horror films, she is immediately recognizable as a common female stereotype of the 1950s who continues to thrive in somewhat updated style in television commercials and telefilms like *She Waits* (1972), *Don't Be Afraid of the Dark* (1973), *The Strange Possession of Mrs. Oliver* (1977), and *The Haunting Passion* (1984).

In this group of made-for-television horror movies, the young wife becomes a prized possession, battled for by opposing forces, and her fate implicitly comments on the value of marriage and personal independence, as well as on the nature of female desire and male heroism. Without a great deal of rhetorical fanfare, these telefilms become as ideologically pointed as any issue-oriented television melodrama about rape or divorce.

For example, *Don't Be Afraid of the Dark,* a version of the haunted house story, and *The Strange Possession of Mrs. Oliver,* a story of split personality, both depict an affluent, upper-middle-class environment (complete with maid) in which the wife purchases her empty freedom and lack of material concerns at the expense of loneliness, since the husband devotes his time and energy to his work as a lawyer. Sally, the heroine of *Don't Be Afraid,* fashions her own destiny—against the wishes of her husband and for no reason this telefilm deems bona fide—by choosing to live in the Victorian house she has inherited from her grandmother, by ignoring an elderly handyman's repeated warnings about the danger of willfulness and curiosity, and by being dissatisfied with her role as wife and hostess. Once she has chosen to open up the sealed fireplace in a long-locked room and thereby allowed the gnomelike creatures trapped inside to escape, her own fate is sealed. The diminutive creatures claim Sally as one of their own, and not even her husband, much less her well-meaning female friend, can rescue her. As punishment for not heeding the advice of the men in her life and not settling comfortably into the natural course of domesticity, shopping, and motherhood, Sally becomes isolated forever from the natural world, crying out for freedom while she is imprisoned in the darkness with a brood of monstrous children. (For a striking sense of just how tame made-for-television horror generally is — in its manipulation of audio-visual techniques as well as in its psychological and cultural assumptions — contrast *Don't Be Afraid* with David Cronenberg's *The Brood* [1979].)

Strange Possession is a different sort of cautionary tale, more overtly contemporary in its concerns with female identity and self-determination than is *Don't Be Afraid*. Troubled by nightmares that picture her own funeral and stifled by her wealthy, staid husband's insistence that she remain at home and begin raising a family, the repressed, spinsterish Mrs. Oliver finds herself inexplicably donning a blonde wig and a tight-fitting, low-cut blouse and adopting the persona of a swinging single. Dialogue, disorienting subjective inserts, and innumerable zoom-ins to her face (particularly when it is reflected in a mirror) all raise the possibility that she may be going mad or unconsciously responding to her feeling of "dying inside," or that she may be the target of malevolent supernatural forces. What could potentially be a modernization of Charlotte Perkins Gilman's classic feminist horror story, "The Yellow Wallpaper," becomes instead a tidy, reactionary fable that explains away all traces of ambiguity and horror. The denouement of *Strange Possession* unequivocally informs us that Mrs. Oliver's problems are caused by neither her husband nor the deadly sterility of her environment, nor by the institutions and ingrained sexism of American society, but instead by her own sense of guilt for the tragic death of her best friend several years before. After being suitably frightened, she is rescued by her husband, without whose protection she would die. Once again safe, Mrs. Oliver declares: "Now I know who I am," as she seeks the solace of her husband's embrace. She has learned who she is — a wife, a no-longer strange possession.[15]

As well as its narrative focus on one person's isolated and idiosyncratic descent into horror and its ideological sidestepping of quasi-, or perhaps better put, pseudo-feminist concerns, the commitment in *Strange Possession* to clarifying the ambiguous and logically explaining apparently supernatural phenomena also makes it typical of one strain of made-for-television horror. (Perhaps the purest example of this type is *Daughter of the Mind* [1969], in which an American scientist's visions of his dead daughter are proven to be illusions produced by wily Soviet agents.) The reassuring revelation that horror is ultimately the result of sleight-of-hand or entirely explicable natural occurrences has been a staple of Gothic fiction since

Ann Radcliffe's novels. However, there are few such texts in recent motion-picture horror, in which we are far more likely to witness the eye-opening punishment of the skeptical rationalist (as in *Don't Look Now* and *Amityville: The Demon* [1983]). In *Strange Possession,* the working out of the heroine's identity crisis, the reunion with her husband, and the logical explanation of a situation that seems extraordinary or supernatural all contribute to a strong sense of closure. (Recall Gomery's comments on "classic narrative cinema" that I cited earlier.) Mrs. Oliver's newfound clarity is our clarity as well, and we are encouraged to embrace this telefilm's restoration of normality as unthinkingly and wholeheartedly as Mrs. Oliver embraces her husband.

Both *Strange Possession* and the 1982 telefilm, *The Haunting Passion,* begin as tales of what Tzvetan Todorov calls the "fantastic," for these telefilms force the viewer and the protagonist to "hesitate" in the face of ambiguous events that could be interpreted either as "reality or dream, truth or illusion." *Strange Possession* dispels ambiguity by explaining this case of possession as an example of the "uncanny . . . which may be readily accounted for by the laws of reason."[16] *Haunting Passion* creates a comparable effect by demonstrating that the haunting it depicts is a "marvelous" event that actually involves the supernatural. *Haunting Passion* is thus more directly linked than *Strange Possession* to Gothic tales of otherworldly lovers and passionate hauntings, and at the same time it is more self-consciously au courant in its presentation of marriage and sexual roles.

Julie, the heroine of *Haunting Passion,* is beautiful, self-assured, and artistic, while her troubled husband, Danny, is undergoing a mid-life crisis during the year after his professional football career ends. Explicit references to his impotence and her sexual fantasizing give this made-for-television movie an air of topicality that often passes for relevancy on network television. However, it is not Danny's psychological problem, but Julie's weakness in the face of a domineering, masculine ghostly presence that almost wrecks their marriage and destroys their enviable life-style. She is at once not responsible for her actions (the woman as helpless, weak, easily tempted) and guilty of being attracted to the grand passions associated with an exciting, long-past era (the woman as naive romantic, victim of her own emotions). Julie is, in effect, punished for the sexual pleasure she experiences from the ghost's adulterous embrace—pleasure that often looks masturbatory. On the brink of committing suicide to join her ghostly lover, Julie is awakened from her self-absorbed trance by Danny's avowal of love after he has violently forced his way into their locked house. A healthy dose of jealousy and a burst of heroic action restore his virility, enabling Julie—like Mrs. Oliver—to come back to herself after her husband's last-minute appearance. The spell cast by illicit passion is broken, and thus the marriage and the couple's "dream house" are preserved.

What this brief look at *Don't Be Afraid, Strange Possession,* and *Haunting Passion* begins to suggest is the way traditional horror story situations — the haunted house, the split personality, and the ghostly presence — are adapted for a telefilm format that defines American life as a collection of discrete, unrelated, personal histories.[17] While it obviously puts a premium on intimacy and the individual moment, this format does not promote a uniform, stable, easily paraphrased system of values.[18] Even those telefilms that focus on the fate of the young wife vary in their depiction of normality and marriage and their identification of what constitutes the truly horrific. It is not reductive uniformity we should seek in made-for-television horror or any other genre of popular art, but rather the interplay between similarity and difference that reinforces and expands the generic context.

From the solitary victim, the masculine investigator, and the vulnerable wife, let us move to the besieged suburban nuclear family, another embodiment of the personal life in made-for-television horror. In telefilms like *Stranger in Our House* (1978) and *Invitation to Hell* (1984), the family's adventures both complement and in certain ways correct the thematic preoccupations and ideological underpinnings of texts like *Duel* and *Haunting Passion.*

It is entirely predictable that made-for-television horror would take the suburban family as a primary subject, since, as John Ellis convincingly argues in *Visible Fictions,* "TV programmes are addressed to a generalised audience which is conceived in a very specific way: as isolated nuclear families in their domestic settings."[19] A small but significant number of recent theatrical horror films — *The Amityville Horror* (1979), *Amityville II: The Possession* (1982), and *Poltergeist* (1982), for instance — explore a comparable subject, though these films (and to a lesser extent, *The Shining* [1980]) insist that the domestic setting is haunted by evil supernatural forces whose presence predates the arrival of the modern family. Defined principally as victims who are called upon to pay for the sins of the past or to suffer because of their own rather minor flaws, the normal families in *Amityville Horror* and *Poltergeist* find their grotesque doubles in the predatory, perversely imaginative, monstrous families in films like *The Texas Chain Saw Massacre* (1974) and *The Hills Have Eyes* (1977).[20]

Though the closest network television has come to the monstrous family has probably been "The Munsters" and certain oily, ambitious clans on nighttime soap operas, made-for-television horror has its share of nuclear families that move to an old, isolated, evil-ridden house (*Crowhaven Farm* [1970] and *The House That Would Not Die*). What makes *Stranger in Our*

House, Invitation to Hell, and *Devil Dog: The Hound of Hell* (1978) especially noteworthy is that in these telefilms, the house itself—and with it the suburban domestic setting and affluent California life-style for which this household is a metonymy—is inherently safe. Horror comes from outside the house and the family, infiltrating normality just as effortlessly and invisibly as the television programs that appear in our living rooms. (In a telling instance of reflexive self-criticism, *Devil Dog* and *Invitation to Hell* both contain examples of demonically possessed children who are captivated by televised images.) Without the intrusion of external, unambiguously evil, supernatural forces, the family would continue its uneventful, unruffled course—with no antagonism between affectionate children and their well-educated, well-meaning parents, and no rupture between the hard-working, caring husband and his supportive, talented, and independent-but-not-too-independent wife. However, once evil, clothed in some innocent and familiar guise, has been invited in, the average family (which is "average," needless to say, only according to primetime television) proves susceptible to temptation and corruption. What these telefilms enact is the fall and the redemption of the ostensibly stable, isolated nuclear family—a group of people who have less in common with the atypical households featured on situation comedies in the wake of "All in the Family" and "Three's Company" than with the families in, for example, other made-for-television movies and in commercials for insurance and toothpaste.

The stranger in *Stranger in Our House,* directed by Wes Craven (also director of *Invitation to Hell* and theatrical horror films like *Last House on the Left* [1972] and *Deadly Blessing* [1981]), is Sarah, a teenage girl from the Ozarks who is actually a witch with the power to cast spells and survive fiery car crashes. Posing as an orphaned relative, she is taken into the unwary household and enchants all of the family except for Rachel, the teenage daughter. Most disturbing, given commercial television's emphasis on clear-thinking, trustworthy, mature men (as newscasters, talk show hosts, sports announcers, and so on) is that Rachel's father, like her boyfriend, is sexually captivated by Sarah's wiles and begins to live out what this telefilm implies are not simply adulterous, but incestuous desires. Accused by her parents and brothers of being jealous and juvenile (which she is), Rachel turns for advice to an elderly professor—a male figure of authority who is better informed and less corruptible than her father. At the risk of her own life, she breaks Sarah's spell over the family. (That Rachel is played by Linda Blair, the much put-upon victim in *The Exorcist* and in the highly publicized made-for-television movie, *Born Innocent,* underlines by way of contrast her assertive, heroic role in *Stranger in Our House.*) For her efforts Rachel is rewarded with the return

of her boyfriend and her trouble-free adolescence. Her family gathers
around her; their home is intact; the sun shines: life will proceed as it was
before Sarah's arrival. Dad offers his apology, though he admits that he
remembers almost nothing of the bizarre episode — suggesting that none
of the family has learned anything. Aside from the fact that these people
belong to a family and look so unassumingly normal (in television terms)
and enviably comfortable in their upper-middle-class style of life, there
is no reason why they deserve to be saved from Sarah and from a full
realization of their own weaknesses.

The domestic world in Curtis Harrington's *Devil Dog* is also preyed upon
by outside forces, in this case a satanic cult that ritualistically calls forth
a demon to impregnate a German shepherd. The cult manipulates events
so that the unsuspecting, harmless Berry family takes in one of the possessed pups. Harrington plays this potentially ridiculous idea perfectly
straight and thereby insists that even so common a creature as a pet dog
can bring the stable, loving suburban family to the brink of destruction.

The dog quickly becomes the master of the two previously innocuous
Berry children, transforming them into spiteful, duplicitous conspirators
ready to stop at nothing to achieve their ends. What could be understood
as adolescent rebelliousness is thus explained as the work of the devil. The
wife, too, easily falls under the influence of the hell hound, though a strate-
gically placed commercial break prohibits us from seeing exactly what
happens after she is trapped with and by the dog behind a closed bedroom door. The wife's transition — or better put, her fall — is immediate:
she becomes as voluptuous, sexually aggressive, immoral, and self-serving
as any soap opera villainess. Unlike in *Stranger in Our House,* in *Devil
Dog* the burden of saving the family falls to the father, Mike, who suffers
the patriarch's most-feared nightmare when his wife and children disregard
his threats and ridicule his moral imperatives — worst of all, they simply
ignore him. "My family's changed," he confesses to a doctor, become
"strange, cold, somebody else. I can't even recognize them anymore."

Like one of the vampire hunters in Bram Stoker's *Dracula* or Stephen
King's *'Salem's Lot,* Mike must leave his everyday concerns behind, gain
the requisite knowledge of the monster (his solitary quest first takes him
to an occult bookstore, then to Ecuador on a pilgrimage to an aged
shaman — far indeed from the spacious suburbs of Los Angeles), and risk
his life to destroy the beast. Significantly, the final confrontation takes
place at the aerodynamics plant where Mike works; his income maintains
the domestic setting, yet by spending so much time at his white-collar job
he has left his household vulnerable to evil influences. The defense of his
family becomes his true work. Once Mike has used a magic talisman to
kill the hell hound, he returns to the arms of his shaken, now-normal wife,

who declares: "Thank God, you're home." Though *Devil Dog,* like *Stranger in Our House,* concludes with a brief coda, revealing that some form of the monstrous evil still exists, ready to infiltrate other equally innocent and naive families, Harrington insists that the Berrys have emerged unscathed and apparently unaltered, with their familial roles and their home intact. The family can weather all storms — God and right are on its side.

Stranger in Our House and *Devil Dog* issue no overt ethical warnings, principally because Craven and Harrington present the eminently corruptible family members as innocent victims of vicious supernatural forces. At the conclusion of these telefilms, a tableau of the restored family reminds us that evil is to be located outside the normal self, family, and home. In contrast, the wages of sin and moral weakness are exacted with a vengeance in *Invitation to Hell,* which becomes something of a sermon against the dangers of greed, ostentatious affluence, status seeking, corporate machinations, and misdirected (i.e., egotistical) ambition. Despite its topical trimmings — the family lives in a thriving area modeled on Silicon Valley, where the father works for a high-tech firm designing a computerized space suit — *Invitation to Hell* is oddly nostalgic in its recycling of themes and broadly liberal values more popular in the 1960s than the 1980s. After all, evil in this telefilm makes its home not in a graveyard, swamp, or haunted house, but in a posh, exclusive, Yuppie-filled country club, which serves quite literally as a gateway to hell. (Ironically, not only is the narrative of *Invitation to Hell* interrupted by commercial breaks, but its moral is undercut as well by advertisements that associate material possessions and personal fulfillment with the luxurious pleasures of the good life — pleasures accessible to anyone with a MasterCard.)

The act of invitation and, by extension, the free choice to accept or refuse, is essential in *Invitation to Hell.* Here, the casual, seemingly content nuclear family is threatened by the wife and mother, Pat, for she is the most enticed by the allure of luxury and elite social status, which she sees as her just deserts. Against the wishes of her husband, Matt, who is satisfied with simple pleasures and homey comforts, Pat takes their two children through the demonic country club's mysterious initiation rites. In effect, she carries out a divorce for no reason other than her own selfish desires. Matt immediately notices the transformation of his family into "strangers" seemingly in league against him. Very much like the possessed wife in *Devil Dog,* the fallen Pat becomes a perverse, dangerous version of the "total woman," heavily made-up and sexually aggressive. She replaces the family's well-worn, comfortable furniture with an impersonal, coldly elegant, dark blue decor that seems absurdly out of place in a split-level suburban home.

Matt much prefers his formerly harmless kids and "the gentle Pat I used to know" to the stylish vixen and nasty brats they have become. To regain his true family he must become the solitary man of action. Protected by his computerized space suit, he confronts Satan (in the guise of Susan Lucci, who plays a beautiful vixen on "All My Children," and so is an apt opponent for Mike, played by Robert Urich, erstwhile hero of "Vegas" —the casting of *Invitation to Hell* helps guide and simplify our interpreting of this telefilm and exemplifies the "allusiveness" that David Thornburn finds in television drama).[21] "I want my family!" Matt yells as he ventures into the burning caverns of hell, and his will power, faith in himself, and love for his wife and children ensure his triumph. He frees his loved ones from their torment and recaptures the past. With their unpretentious furniture back in its rightful place and sunlight streaming into the living room, the family members all embrace. "Dear God, it's okay," Matt reassures them, "We're home. We're together." From the front yard of their home—which looks as if it belongs in the same suburban subdivision as the haunted house in *Poltergeist*—they see the smoke rising from the ashes of the country club that is now "all gone." Unlike the survivors in *Poltergeist,* however, the family at the end of *Invitation to Hell* can go back inside to recommence daily life, for their home is once again perfectly safe.

Having been to hell and back, the viewer can also proceed with life as usual, staying tuned for the 11:00 news and the never-ending stream of programs that have been advertised during the telefilm's commercial breaks. Watching in the well-lit, familiar confines of our homes, we know that television—life—goes on. Even more than the happy, reconciliatory, restorative endings of virtually all the telefilms I have mentioned, the commercial breaks in made-for-television movies serve to dissipate—to deny— horror by predicting the future and by insisting that problems are solvable, and happiness, safety, health, security, and pleasure are attainable. Daniel Mann can elude a malevolent semi, Mrs. Oliver's strange possession can be exorcised, and Matt can free his family from hell, but made-for-television horror cannot escape the peculiar limitations of the telefilm format and the overarching structure of primetime commercial television. In fact, made-for-television horror would seem to be by definition impossible. Yet the genre exists, throwing motion-picture horror into high relief, occasionally questioning primetime's version of normality, and illuminating certain shadowy corners in television's intimate, personalized America.

NOTES

1. Stanley Cavell, "The Fact of Television," in *Themes Out of School: Effects and Causes* (San Francisco: North Point Press, 1984), 239, 242. See also Fred E. H.

Schroeder, "Video Aesthetics and Serial Art," in *Television: The Critical View,* ed. Horace Newcomb, 2d ed. (New York: Oxford University Press, 1979).

2. Television, Mander writes, "is a machine that invades, controls and deadens the people who view it" (*Four Arguments for the Elimination of Television* [New York: William Morrow, 1979], 158)—one of the many images in this book that evoke the conventions of the horror story.

3. Alvin H. Marill's *Movies Made for Television* (New York: Da Capo Press, 1980) is an indispensable reference work that provides credits and brief plot summaries of telefilms released from 1964 to 1979. Additional information specifically about made-for-television horror movies is found in two annotated filmographies: Donald C. Willis's *Horror and Science Fiction Films II* (Metuchen, N.J.: Scarecrow Press, 1982), and John Stanley's *The Creature Feature Movie Guide* (New York: Warner Books, 1984).

4. Douglas Gomery, "*Brian's Song:* Television, Hollywood, and the Evolution of the Movie Made for Television," in *American History American Television: Interpreting the Video Past,* ed. John E. O'Connor (New York: Frederick Ungar, 1983), 218–21. As Gomery notes, much of his definition of "classic narrative cinema" derives from David Bordwell and Kristin Thompson's textbook, *Film Art: An Introduction* (Reading, Mass.: Addison-Wesley, 1979). Gomery also discusses the business history of the made-for-television movie in "Television, Hollywood, and the Development of Movies Made-for-Television," in *Regarding Television,* ed. E. Ann Kaplan (Frederick, Md.: University Publishing of America, 1983), 120–29.

5. Gary Edgerton, "The American Made-for-TV Movie," in *TV Genres,* ed. Brian G. Rose (Westport, Conn.: Greenwood Press, 1985), 165.

6. Bill Kelley, " '*Salem's Lot:* Filming Horror for Television," *Cinéfantastique* 9 (1979):9–21, suggests a good deal about the censorship of made-for-television horror by the networks' own departments of Standards and Practices. For example, Kelley quotes Richard Kobritz, producer of *'Salem's Lot* (and of films like *Christine* [1983]), who declares: "A television movie does not have blood or violence. It has atmosphere" (16).

7. S. S. Prawer, *Caligari's Children: The Film as Tale of Terror* (New York: Oxford University Press, 1980), 48; and Ivan Butler, *Horror in the Cinema* (New York: Warner Paperback Library, 1970), 15.

8. One particularly straightforward made-for-television ghost story is *The Ghost of Flight 401* (1978), which includes several sequences filmed from the ghost's point of view. By endorsing an unqualified faith in benevolent "cosmic energy" and life after death, this telefilm not only underplays, but ultimately dispels all terror.

9. John Fiske and John Hartley, *Reading Television* (New York: Methuen, 1978), 167.

10. Even the BBC-PBS production of *Count Dracula* (1979), which includes video special effects seldom seen in the "Masterpiece Theater" tradition, suggests the extent to which horror allows for stylization.

11. *Duel* is one of the few made-for-television horror movies to receive any critical acclaim; it is most often singled out as a technical tour-de-force that proves what a budding auteur can accomplish within the strict limits of the telefilm format.

See, for example, Douglas Brode, "The Made-for-TV Movie: Emergence of an Art Form," *Television Quarterly* 18 (Fall 1981):59–60. For information on Spielberg's career as a television director, during which he directed a segment of "Night Gallery" (1969) and the made-for-television horror movie, *Something Evil* (1972), see Alvin H. Marill, "Films on TV," *Films in Review* 26 (Mar. 1975):173–75. The screenplay for *Duel* was adapted by Richard Matheson from his story of the same title, and a comparison of the two texts reveals how little the telefilm version relies on the interior monologues and the allegorical reminders found throughout the story.

12. Robin Wood, "An Introduction to the American Horror Film," in *American Nightmare: Essays on the Horror Film,* ed. Robin Wood and Richard Lippe (Toronto: Festival of Festivals, 1979), 23. See also Charles Derry, *Dark Dreams: A Psychological History of the Modern Horror Film* (New York: A. S. Barnes, 1977), 49–82.

13. Horace Newcomb, *TV: The Most Popular Art* (Garden City, N.Y.: Anchor Press, 1974). See also Brode, "The Made-for-TV Movie."

14. The psychic investigator in made-for-television horror movies has his literary antecedents in figures like William Hope Hodgson's Carnacki, "the Ghost-Finder," and Algernon Blackwood's John Silence. These heroic investigators have a much grander stature than the workaday parapsychologists in films like *The Amityville Horror* and *The Entity.*

15. *Strange Possession,* in turn, begs comparison with *The Stranger Within,* another telefilm written by Richard Matheson that focuses on a young wife and the disruption of a well-to-do domestic environment. When the "perfect" woman in *The Stranger Within* becomes pregnant, she is transformed into an eccentric, indeed schizophrenic, harpy who ignores housework and her husband's emotional needs in favor of taking solitary walks and speedreading college textbooks. Her desire for independence and knowledge—which might in a different context be deemed a sign of liberation—is not freely chosen, for she is simply a victim of the extraterrestrials who have impregnated her from afar.

16. Tzvetan Todorov, *The Fantastic: A Structural Approach to a Literary Genre,* trans. Richard Howard (Ithaca, N.Y.: Cornell University Press, 1975), 25, 46.

17. Cf. Herbert Zettl's conclusion that "television encourages us to become introspective, to look at our private actions, conflicts, tensions, rather than those of society at large" ("Television Aesthetics," in *Understanding Television: Essays on Television as a Social and Cultural Force,* ed. Richard P. Adler [New York: Praeger, 1981], 130).

18. See Fiske and Hartley on the "dynamism" of the "myths" television presents and the "ambivalence" of the "cultural text" (*Reading Television,* 43, 157).

19. John Ellis, *Visible Fictions: Cinema: Television: Video* (London: Routledge and Kegan Paul, 1982), 115.

20. See Tony Williams, "American Cinema in the 1970s: Family Horror," *Movie* 27/28 (1981):117–26.

21. David Thornburn, "Television Melodrama," in *Understanding Television,* ed. Adler, 82.

11

More Dark Dreams: Some Notes on the Recent Horror Film

Charles Derry

Charles Derry's essay is a postscript to his 1977 book, Dark Dreams: A Psychological History of the Modern Horror Film, *which traced the emergence of three subgenres of modern horror: the horror of personality, of the demonic, and of Armageddon. Here Derry provides an overview of these subgenres during the past decade, singling out particularly significant films (including* Dressed to Kill *and* Scanners*) and suggesting the diversity of modern horror as it undergoes historical transformation. Like a great many commentators, Derry begins with the assumption that horror films can be usefully analyzed as public nightmares that speak "to a culture's anxieties." In contrast to the "cultural" reading of the genre by Allison Graham and Vivian Sobchack, for Derry the relationship among shifting social mores, historical events, "shared" fears, and horror films is relatively unproblematic.*

Derry, who received his Ph.D. from Northwestern University, teaches film at Wright State University, Dayton, Ohio. In addition to Dark Dreams, *he is the co-author of* The Film Book Bibliography: 1940–1975 *and the author of the forthcoming study,* The Suspense Thriller. *Derry has also directed two films,* Cerebral Accident *and* Joan Crawford Died for Your Sins.

Why are horror films so popular? Certainly horror films connect with our profound and subconscious need to deal with the things that frighten us. In the way they work upon us, films are much like dreams, and horror films are like nightmares. Some horror films deal with our fears more directly than others, but in general, horror films speak to our subconscious and — as do our dreams — deal with issues that are often painful for us to deal with consciously and directly. In a sense, the B-film accouterments so long associated with the horror film — low budgets, few stars, primitive production values, less than literate dialogue, and exploitative advertising — serve to displace and disguise what might be termed the genre's rather profoundly affecting psychoanalytic discourse. Many reason-oriented adults, so sensitive to the lack of sophisticated surface, often take a defensive and negative attitude toward this culturally devalued genre, finding the films merely distastefully unpleasant or unimportant and silly. Other adults, more sensitive and less oblivious, may be rather hostile to the psychoanalytic discourse itself, which is regarded, so to speak, as an uninvited intruder upon the viewer's own carefully guarded psyche. Children, on the other hand, less connected to the value judgments of a culture, often take an attitude of joyful anticipation and enthusiasm toward horror film, even though the films sometimes traumatize them. As well, children have not yet learned to civilize and repress their fears: they know that there are monsters in the closet who will kill them if the nightlight goes out. Children's response to the psychoanalytic discourse in the Friday night "Creature Features" programmed by local television stations across the country is as direct as to the underlying discourse in the nightmares they will tell over the Saturday morning breakfast table. Among the most common of all dreams, particularly among children, is the dream in which one is chased by a large dog or monster and, as if drugged or in slow-motion, one can't seem to lift one's feet to run – an archetypal scene replicated in recent films such as *Night of the Living Dead* (1968) and *The Omen* (1976). And for teenagers, perhaps the major audience for horror films, these films represent not only a rebellious rejection of the adult values, but also a titillating glimpse into the forbidden contents of the id, especially the sexual and violent impulses that so dominate the contemporary genre. If dreams are personal, then films – offering a shared rather than solitary experience – are social, produced for a large, public audience and screened in a public place where one can be aware of the responses of others. Horror films speak, therefore, to shared fears, to a culture's anxieties. The atomic bomb, the Holocaust, the social cataclysms brought about by World War II, and the accelerated pace in the last three decades of scientific developments and social change have irrevocably altered the horror film. By the 1960s, the old horror film – as represented by *Frankenstein* (1931) and *Dracula* (1931) – had been by and large supplanted by the new horror film. In *Dark Dreams,* published in 1977, I documented three primary subgenres of contemporary horror, which I call the horror of personality, the horror of the demonic, and the horror of Armageddon.[1] Since 1975, there have been interesting developments in each of these subgenres.

In the traditional pre-1960 horror film, the monster never really looks like a human being; there is always something that sets the monster apart: an odd manner of dress, facial disfigurement, or an animal appearance. In the first subgenre of the new horror film – the horror of personality –

the monster is invariably a man or woman who looks as normal as the average person on the street. The seminal film, of course, is Alfred Hitchcock's ultimately exhaustively analyzed *Psycho* (1960). *Psycho*'s monster is Norman Bates, the apparently dutiful son, shy and unassuming, protecting his mother's reputation. *Psycho* is modern, too, in that it extended and redefined the iconography of horror. Traditionally, acts of horror took place in old dark houses with lots of shadows; although *Psycho* presents a dark house, the most horrible act takes place in the whiteness of a shower stall; *Psycho*'s world is the contemporary one of motel rooms, real estate offices, hardware stores, and interstate highways. Other films that ascribe to this more modern sensibility include *What Ever Happened to Baby Jane?* (1962), *Strait-Jacket* (1964), *Hush Hush Sweet Charlotte* (1964), and *Pretty Poison* (1968). Invariably these films emphasize the anxiety of living rather than the fear of death; violence is the norm, and fear of bodily mutilation is very strong. Conventional, sexually fulfilled role models are strikingly absent in most of these films; and everyone is potentially insane ("We all go a little mad sometimes. Haven't you?" asks Norman Bates), thus making any assumption of psychological stability problematic and dangerous. Other generic elements include the monstrous crime or secret uncovered from the past; the obsessive and twisted relationship between two individuals, often women; the use of split personalities and alter-egos; an authoritarian, often crippling parental figure; a scene in which an investigator is killed, often on a stairway; and the ultimate reversal in which a disguised monster is shockingly revealed. Weapons in these films are generally technological extensions of claws—that is, knives, hatchets, axes. Why had Anthony Perkins replaced Boris Karloff as horror icon? These films emerged from a society traumatized by race riots, assassinations, and violence in the streets. Charles Whitman had killed passersby from a Texas tower; Richard Speck had killed nurses in Chicago. These human monsters were more scary than the Frankenstein monster, because they were not readily recognizable as dangerous; it was as if at any moment, anyone could go berserk. *Psycho* was seminal because it anticipated the social catastrophes and upheavals that subsequent horror films so thoroughly reflected.

What is surprising about these films is not that they dominated the 1960s, but that they continued so forcefully through the 1970s and 1980s within a society in which random violence and mass murder were now so common and expected as to go routinely unreported by the media (unless, of course, a specific violent act were to take more victims than any previous violent act or to incorporate some mind-boggling and grisly variation theretofore unheard of, in which case the news media would exploit it in an almost Guinness-Book-of-World-Records style). If films such as *Friday the 13th*

(*I, II, III,* and *IV;* 1980, 1981, 1982, and 1984) and *Halloween* (*I, II,* and *III;* 1978, 1981, and 1982) seem somehow to be less artful and more exploitative than their predecessors, they seem also, as many commentators have pointed out, to be generally much more sex-obsessed. Indeed, these films' presentation of punishment for teenage promiscuity seems especially relevant to a society that has gone beyond the early exhilaration of the sexual revolution to the anxiety associated with the disturbing record outbreaks of a variety of venereal diseases. The recent horror-of-personality films seem to reflect as well a disturbing hostility toward women, which seems a direct response to the feminist movement; consequently it is hard to respond to or praise very many of these films enthusiastically, without also feeling or expressing reservations.

Oddly enough, no recent horror film has been attacked as sexist more than Brian De Palma's *Dressed to Kill* (1980), one of the more stylish of recent horror-of-personality films, and, on one level, a film actually less misogynist than many others. Robin Wood has suggested that the violence in many of the horror films of the 1960s and 1970s can be seen as a reflection of America's increased dissatisfaction with its traditional sexual roles and the nuclear family.[2] In this context, the violence in certain films can be revealed not as reactionary, but as a release of social tensions, perhaps even a necessary first step toward a more liberated society with more responsive social and familial structures. De Palma's Kate, the protagonist in *Dressed to Kill* (played by Angie Dickinson), is a tragic figure because she is unable to understand the source of her problems. She retains a naive and stupid faith in the American family, despite the fact that her marriage seems not particularly happy and her husband not especially equipped to fulfill her sexually. Kate is reduced to fantasizing and prowling museums in search of some man to provide her fulfillment. Kate's error, of course, is in looking outward, toward a man for her happiness; and indeed, her encounter with the museum pick-up proves ultimately no more satisfactory than her dealings with her husband. Her discovery that she has probably contracted a venereal disease works as a concrete example of the new morality with which innocent, naive Kate is quite incompetent to deal. To view her murder (and it is not a rape-murder, as many have falsely claimed)[3] as a sign of violence against women is to misunderstand the structure of the film: Kate is a representation not of Everywoman, but of woman as victim, woman as helpless creature without a strong man to protect her. It is interesting to note that it is only at the moment of her own murder that Kate reaches out for help toward another *woman,* who successfully (if too late) removes the murder weapon from the clutches of the killer.

What many have failed to note about *Dressed to Kill* is that De Palma quite clearly provides an alternative to Kate in the character of Liz (played by Nancy Allen). Like Kate, Liz is a woman stalked by the killer; unlike Kate, however, Liz is able to survive. If Kate's reactionary identity is symbolized by her status as bored housewife, Liz's liberated identity is symbolized by her status as enterprising and highly paid call-girl. And although one can argue that the hooker option for women — long a Hollywood staple — is itself sexist and limiting, Liz's hooker is nevertheless by no means a passive victim. Indeed, the cursing, tough Liz, in so many ways the antithesis of Kate, is the independent, active protagonist of *Dressed to Kill*. The explicit transference of the narrative from Kate to Liz is marked by the extraordinary close-up of Liz in the elevator sequence: her horrified eyes responding to the unbearable suffering of Kate. It is courageous and direct Liz, the least vulnerable of would-be victims, who provides the film with its hard-edged moral force and dominates the second half of the narrative. And indeed, it must be pointed out that although Kate and Liz, while in showers, are both associated with imagined acts of violence, only Kate's shower scene represents a personal fantasy. For Liz, violence is a nightmare that is not yearned for in the slightest. Liz — in contrast to Kate — rejects the male idea that women wish to be victims; in fact, Liz even attempts to take a razor and return the violence in kind upon her male attacker. Too, it must be pointed out that although Liz does not elude the killer completely on her own, it is, at the final moment, another *woman* who saves her and brings an end to the tyranny of man's violence. And yet to call "man's violence" the subject of *Dressed to Kill* may itself be somewhat misleading. Although the killer is a man, the killer's transvestitism implies a split sexual identity, which indicates that gender-role confusion — and the subsequent anxiety associated with changes in sexual mores and sex roles — may be closer to the film's subject.

The horror film and the suspense thriller have a long, if unfortunate, tradition of using women as victims: in 1944's *Gaslight,* for instance, Ingrid Bergman is the hysterical victim of her husband's plot to drive her crazy; in 1960's *Midnight Lace,* Doris Day is similarly traumatized. In the traditional thriller, woman is seen as victim because of at least two factors: her physical inferiority to man in terms of simple strength, and, more insidiously, her "archetypal innocence." Because it was necessary in the past for the good woman to be seen as virgin, woman's lack of sexual sophistication often resulted in a view of women as helpless, naive creatures. (And it is not coincidental that De Palma's Kate, cut from this cloth, should be dressed completely in white, whereas Liz, at least in her first appearance, should be dressed in grays and black.) Ingrid Bergman, Doris Day, and Angie Dickinson are, in these films, significantly dumb, slow to realize what is actually going on, requiring the help of a strong, smart man to rescue them. The error of the heroines in *Gaslight* and *Midnight Lace* is not that they put their faith in a man, but that they put their faith in the wrong man. The three adult men in Kate's life — husband, pick-up, psychiatrist — all offer silence and betrayal in varying degrees. It is unfortunate that Kate should insist on putting her faith in any man, let alone the one whose appearance of strength and support should ultimately be revealed as only cosmetic; when this man turns against Kate so violently, it becomes clear that in our contemporary society, traditionally chauvinist sexual roles can no longer be counted on — for in *Dressed to Kill,* to expect masculine protection is to damn oneself to cosmic vulnerability. The only truly positive male role model in *Dressed to Kill* is Kate's teenage son, a would-be protector who is neither controlling nor patronizing to women, but one who accepts female strength and thereby becomes an embodiment of a new, potentially more acceptable masculinity. Indeed, what might be found most objectionable is not that Kate comes to a violent end, as that the expressive style of the museum sequence, which promotes such empathy with Kate, itself contradicts the deep structure of the film by reflecting an almost nostalgic attitude toward female vulnerability.

Oddly, *Dressed to Kill* is, if more violent, less sexist than Hitchcock's 1960 *Psycho* — upon whose narrative De Palma rather ingeniously rings variations. It is also less sexist than Hitchcock's own more recent horror-of-personality film, *Frenzy* (1972), which casually presents the female body as analogous to discarded food and depicts a horrifying rape-murder with a disturbingly clinical detachment. Ultimately, De Palma's film is most notable for its style. The museum sequence with Kate, virtually without dialogue, is expressively beautiful; and the exuberance with which its 110 separate shots are edited together to form a unified whole (which later finds its parallel/opposition in the subway sequence with Liz) is incredibly fetching. Noteworthy, too, is the formal perfection of the film, with its constant parallelism and mathematical doubling of scenes, and the way De Palma uses color and camera movement. With everyone spying on everyone else and characters constantly framed through windows or doorways, *Dressed to Kill* reveals its organizing concept of voyeurism, which De Palma relates not only to his bravura use of the point-of-view shot, but also to the rather reflexive use of the film within the film, which inherently comments on the voyeurism of the movie audience as well as of the characters.

Another film in this subgenre is *The Hills Have Eyes,* directed by Wes Craven in 1977. *The Hills Have Eyes* presents a representative American family traveling across the desert in their recreational vehicle. The American family — father, mother, grown children, infant grandchild, and dog — comes in conflict with a nether-family of monstrous and misshapen cretins who lust after violence and cannibalism. Once when I showed the film in a seminar on horror film, one woman retreated after the screening to the corner of the room, where she began sobbing quietly. "I don't understand these things," she said to me later, "I'm only a housewife." By the end of the quarter, however, she had written that *The Hills Have Eyes* was indeed her favorite film of the quarter, because once she had examined her incredibly emotional response, she was put — perhaps for the first time, so directly — in touch with her deepest-rooted feelings and fears. Upon reflection, she realized that the values of the American family in the film (and, by extension, potentially her own family) were inordinately disturbing: the father is a racist, clear and simple; the mother, a simpering housewife with virtually no personality whose death is mourned by the family much less emotionally and extensively than the death of the family dog. In fact, so little is the mother respected that her dead body is set afire and used by her son as a weapon against an attacker. And finally, the most horrifying, violent acts are not committed by the monsters, but by the members of the American family, who give in to the violence with an enthusiasm that is genuinely frightening. A film like *The Hills Have Eyes* shows how contemporary horror films can almost effortlessly reflect the tensions within the American family. And for this older student, the film represented a full-scale attack on the values that, as reflected by her decision to begin pursuing a college degree, she had heretofore been only slowly coming to reject.[4]

A second subgenre of the new horror film — the horror of the demonic — includes such popular films as *The Exorcist* (1973) and *The Omen* (1976). If the horror-of-personality films suggest that life is horrible because human beings are crazy, these demonic films suggest life is horrible because evil exists as a tangible entity. The films in this genre run the gamut from the most stylized and fantastic (*The Mephisto Waltz* [1971]) to the most apparently naturalistic (*Rosemary's Baby* [1968]). In this demonic universe, nothing innocent can survive: the little girl Regan in *The Exorcist* turns into a cursing, fetid horror who masturbates with a crucifix; the child Damien in *The Omen* is presented as evil, corrupt, indeed, the Anti-Christ; the vulnerable and sensitive Rosemary is raped by the devil and her world turned topsy-turvy. Other recurring elements in these films include the idea of vengeance (often the archetypal vengeance of the devil against God); the concept of mystic possession; and the use of an all-pervasive Christian symbology, which serves both to reinforce and to pervert Christian belief. This subgenre grew, it seemed, in response to certain religious events or issues of the 1960s: the election of a new pope in 1964; the well-publicized notion of "God Is Dead"; the crisis in the Catholic church as so many priests and nuns left the church; the explosion of interest in astrology, horoscopes, and Eastern religion; and the sense in the United States of a special need for a spiritual connection at a time when church attendance had decreased and the country was undergoing social cataclysm. Is it any wonder that children in these films are presented as no longer innocent when the young were out on the street protesting the Vietnam War? *The Exorcist,* which deals with the balance between good and evil, perfectly reflected the concerns of its audience: if we could not find God reflected in the modern world, perhaps we could at least find the devil. In a strange way, *The Exorcist* became a social phenomenon (indeed, almost a rite of passage) as well as a genuinely religious film.

In the 1970s and 1980s these demonic films no longer seem to have either the relevant cultural energy or the sincerity of their forebears. The existence of *Look What's Happened to Rosemary's Baby* (1976) or *The Final Conflict* (1981) or *Amityville 3-D* (1983) seems less to reflect a social need as much as to reveal Hollywood's characteristic insistence on exploiting such needs financially until a film cycle is indisputably dead. In fact, the majority of recent demonic films — *Ghost Story* (1981), *Cat People* (1982), and *Something Wicked This Way Comes* (1983) — have not been financially successful. Even those films based on the novels of Stephen King — *Cujo* (1983), *Christine* (1983), *The Dead Zone* (1983), *Children of the Corn* (1984), and *Firestarter* (1984) — have not been widely successful. One would not, I think, be wrong to ascribe the commercial failure of these films — despite some sophisticated special effects and often interesting narratives — to the return in America of a certain groundswell of popular religious belief. In an era in which Ronald Reagan and the Moral Majority have emerged as prominent, in which school prayer is being advocated in the legislature, in which abortion seems potentially soon to be outlawed, and in which the Catholic church is now being headed by a popular, anti-Communist Polish pope who upholds conservative sexual values, it is difficult to contend that "evil" (if unfairly confused with or disguised as liberal humanism) is as metaphorically ascendant as in the 1960s. In fact, one can argue that if the predominantly liberal-moving America of the 1960s and early 1970s was dominated by the pessimistic, mystic mode of horror, then the predominantly conservative-moving America of the late 1970s and 1980s is being dominated by the optimistic, mystic mode of fantasy, as reflected by the spate of films such as *Star Wars* (1977) and *E.T.—The Extra-Terrestrial* (1982).

Indeed, it is noteworthy that the most popular recent demonic horror film has been the remarkably benign *Poltergeist* (1982), a considerably reactionary film that views suburban life and American values as predominantly good and demonic spirits as anomalous and ultimately vanquishable. In *Poltergeist* parents are loving and nurturing; conventional consumerism is valorized rather than criticized; and the source of the film's violence is unambiguously derived from outside the family and its political structures. The upbeat ending of *Poltergeist* contrasts strongly, for instance, with the downbeat endings of *Rosemary's Baby, The Omen,* and *The Other* (1972), which invariably suggest that "good" is irrevocably imperiled and that evil will have an even greater victory down the line. A recent example of the demonic genre is Joe Dante's *Gremlins* (1984; produced, as was *Poltergeist,* by Steven Spielberg), which views its title spirits as often as lovable and comic as horrible. The violence in *Gremlins,* in direct opposition to the graphic violence of, say, *The Omen,* seems to reflect a comic-book sensibility; none of the protagonists we empathize with is killed or seriously injured, and the most flamboyant death is reserved for the female villain (a cross between the villainous capitalist in Frank Capra's *It's a Wonderful Life* and the Wicked Witch in *The Wizard of Oz*) for whom we have little empathy. Films like *Poltergeist* and *Gremlins* certainly seem to indicate that the cultural tensions that initially spawned these demonic films have been considerably dissipated and displaced.

It is not surprising, therefore, that when a truly demonic film emerges now, such as the Dutch film, *The Fourth Man* (1984), it seems more to reflect the personal obsessions of its makers than any majority social sentiment. Directed by Paul Verhoeven with a genuinely contemporary sensibility that takes its protagonist's sexual preference as a premise rather than a problem, and based on a novel by Gerard Reve, *The Fourth Man* has been described by one rather astute critic as "the first gay, Catholic, horror film"[5] — which is, indeed, precisely what it is. Verhoeven's witch is a contemporary seductress, a siren who leads men to their doom, including, perhaps, the protagonist, who is a bisexual man clearly more interested in the witch's boyfriend than the witch herself, whose identity as a demonic force is only gradually revealed. What makes *The Fourth Man* especially interesting — despite its misogyny (typical for a horror film) that turns women into symbols, updating the typical archetypes of the whore and the virgin into the super-archetypes of the she-devil and the Virgin Mary — is that the gay orientation of the protagonist is presented as a positive moral alternative to the heterosexuality offered by the woman. Indeed, one almost delirious fantasy scene (in a dense film packed with provocative and surreal images) shows the protagonist kissing and embracing the near-naked boyfriend who is hanging Christ-like from a crucifix in the church. That this scene works not only to provide an erotic thrill but also to foreshadow the surprising ending in which the identity of the fourth man is revealed testifies to this film's formal and skillfully organized structure.

Perhaps, however, the most interesting of the three subgenres that dominated the horror film in the 1960s is the horror-of-Armageddon film. These films have a mixed parentage: on the one hand, descended from the low-budget science-fiction films of the 1950s and inspired by atomic bomb anxieties; on the other hand, descended from the theater of the absurd and inspired by avant-garde sensibilities. These horror films invariably present an apocalyptic image of Armageddon, as the world is destroyed by proliferating, nonindividualized, nonhuman creatures. The seminal work of this subgenre is, of course, Alfred Hitchcock's *The Birds* (1962), which was quickly imitated by a host of films in which the world was destroyed by bees, bats, cats, plants, rats, rabbits, frogs, snakes, ants, apes, and cockroaches. Some of these films suggest a world ecosystem gone awry; others an apocalypse somehow related to the atomic bomb; still others develop a passionately bleak and existential worldview. Virtually all of these films emphasize the themes of proliferation, beseigement, and death. In the 1970s and 1980s these apocalyptic films have proliferated, though in a much greater variety and without such specific adherence to the narrative structures codified by *The Birds*. George Romero's 1968 cult horror film, *Night of the Living Dead,* for instance, was followed by his 1979 *Dawn of the Dead,* in which the violence became almost comically excessive and the black-and-white horror of the original was replaced by a gaudy color social satire in which apocalypse was played out against the excess of a suburban shopping mall.

One of the most notable directors to work within this genre in the last decade is the Australian Peter Weir, virtually all of whose films seem to express a rather apocalyptic sensibility. *The Last Wave* (1977) is an especially evocative horror film, taking as its subject the dreamworld of the Australian Aborigines and their conflict with Western civilization—a conflict that augurs, ultimately, to the "Last Wave," that is, an actual final tidal wave that would end all civilization. What proliferates in *The Last Wave* are not creatures, but different manifestations of the natural element of water: from the opening scene, in which hailstones fall from an absolutely clear sky, to a scene in which overflowing water from a bathtub comes pouring down the stairs to find the protagonist (played by Richard Chamberlain); from a fantasy-vision, in which the protagonist drives his submerged car as people and cars float by, to the final, terrifying image of an approaching tidal wave. In *The Last Wave* the conventions and basic pyrotechnics of the horror film, with its expected visual effects, are wedded to an essentially Jungian worldview to create a riveting fable about a society punished for having lost touch with its collective unconscious, with its soul. Like *The Last Wave, Picnic at Hanging Rock* (1975) has an apocalyptic vision as well: portending, as it does, the end of the Victorian era. Sexual liberation, lesbianism, psychic violence, and authoritarian repression come to a confluence so shrouded in mystery and ambiguity that apocalypse becomes all but inevitable. People die or disappear mysteriously; the girls' school must close; above it all, like the sword of Damocles or Hitchcock's birds, rests Hanging Rock—a symbol for the unknowable mysteries of nothingness and existence. Not surprisingly, Weir's non-horror films share the same kind of apocalyptic vision: *Gallipoli* (1981), which, in its horrifying climax shows large numbers of men senselessly massacred during World War I because of the misplaced imperialist pride of the rather villainous British; and *The Year of Living Dangerously* (1983), which shows the apocalyptic end of the Sukarno regime in Indonesia, overseen by the metaphorical little person, Billy Kwan, as well as by the characters of Indonesian myth and puppet theater. Weir's sensibility is somewhat shared by his Australian countryman, George Miller, whose *The Road Warrior* (1981) and *Mad Max* (1980), its predecessor, were hugely successful and presented a semipunk vision of an apocalyptic, post-atomic future in which all values have disintegrated, gasoline is routinely killed for, and leather-garbed musclemen roam the land to loot and plunder.

With the Reagan era, too, has come the apparently definitive end of détente and the renewal of a variety of specific atomic bomb anxieties, which have been expressed in a variety of films on a fairly literal level: *The Atomic Cafe* (1982), a satirical documentary about the early atomic education of the American public by its government; *Testament* (1983), which harrowingly shows a family dying in the aftermath of a nuclear war; *WarGames* (1983), a compelling and juvenile thriller about the potential for computer-activated apocalypse; *Special Bulletin* (1983), a made-for-television fictional film that not only explores the possibility of terrorists detonating the atomic bomb but also examines the potential media coverage of such an event; *The Day After* (1983), a highly hyped television movie that attempts to show the reality (through fairly conventional horror tricks of makeup and special effects) of a nuclear bomb dropped on Kansas City; and *Countdown to Looking Glass* (1984), a fictional HBO film-for-television that shows newscasters broadcasting late-breaking news on a Persian Gulf crisis that eventually leads the world to the brink of global thermonuclear destruction. Some of these films, like *Testament,* recall science fiction-inspired horror films of the 1950s, like *Five* (1951) and *On the Beach* (1959); all inevitably play upon the audience's anxiety in relation to daily life—the exploitation of everyday anxiety, in all its guises, being perhaps the hallmark of the contemporary horror film.

And, finally, it seems that no discussion of contemporary horror film can conclude without reference to the films of David Cronenberg, which are consistently derived from Armageddon and apocalyptic sensibilities. These films seem to resonate — in a genuine and sincere way — with contemporary life as it is presently being lived and is evolving. Cronenberg's films, which seem to exploit some of the issues raised in Susan Sontag's *Illness as Metaphor,* show human beings whose bodies are transformed by disease or mutation into a more advanced, if psychologically traumatizing, state. The illness or mutated body becomes a metaphor for secret desires or social impulses as well as an other to be feared. Ultimately, the body takes a kind of revenge upon the individual, who often becomes alienated from and painfully imprisoned in his or her own body. Cronenberg's films also deal with the future apocalypse, brought about by technology that is now being hailed as evolutionary, but that nevertheless may destroy civilization.

Scanners (1981) is an especially important masterwork — the *Psycho* of the present generation of horror films. *Scanners* inherently reflects the paranoid sensibility of the American post-Watergate era and skillfully exploits the contemporary fear of the carcinogenic substance. It differs from the atomic anxiety-inspired horror films in that it is not the earth that explodes, but one's head; indeed, one of the strongest images of any contemporary horror film can be found in *Scanners,* when an auditorium filled with business and government executives watch patiently, expectantly, and then with horror, as one scanner makes another scanner's head explode like a bursting balloon. Another powerful image evokes the Cronenbergian conception that we are all prisoners of our identities and obsessions: the image of a deranged sculptor who actually lives in a larger-than-life sculpture of his own head, placed on its side, divorced from its body. Underpinning this fable of science-gone-mad are archetypal story patterns — the search for a father and the Cain-and-Abel struggle between a good and an evil brother. True to form for the horror-of-Armageddon subgenre, *Scanners* ends bleakly and ambiguously, implying that the horror and destruction will continue until we have succeeded in advancing to an even greater destructive capability.

The Brood, directed by Cronenberg in 1979, suggests a different kind of apocalypse. Dealing with feminist-inspired hostility, and especially that of women toward the physical reality of childbirth and the demands of childrearing, *The Brood* argues implicitly for the nonpropagation of the species. A group of violent children, born from a sac outside the mother's body, come eventually to embody all the tensions and hostilities that are oftentimes reposited in the nuclear family. Perhaps Cronenberg's most fascinating horror film, if not his most wholly successful, is *Videodrome* (1982), which predicts for humankind a sadomasochistic sexual future and contemplates our virtual destruction as we lose our humanity and, almost literally, turn into videocassette recorders. Indeed, the image of a man growing a kind of deformed vaginal slit for a videocassette is one of the most frightening in all horror film, balancing Cronenberg's earlier image, in *Rabid* (1977), of a woman growing a kind of deformed pineal set of jaws under her arm. Ultimately, it seems that it is this last subgenre of horror, that of Armageddon, especially as practiced by Cronenberg and Weir, that is at the very center of the contemporary horror film. One looks forward to future developments to see how, in relationship to new fears, this genre will evolve.

NOTES

1. Charles Derry, *Dark Dreams: A Psychological History of the Modern Horror Film* (Cranbury, N.J.: A. S. Barnes, 1977).

2. Robin Wood, "Return of the Repressed," *Film Comment* 14 (July–Aug. 1978), and his "Gods and Monsters," ibid., 14 (Sept.–Oct. 1978).

3. When I viewed *Dressed to Kill* late in 1980 at the Little Art Theatre in Yellow Springs, Ohio, a group of fifteen or so demonstrators were protesting the film. They carried placards announcing their opposition to rape and their conviction that the pornographic/erotic aspects of the film would lead to an increase in violence against women in Yellow Springs itself. None of these protestors had seen the film, although they had been alerted to the film by local feminist leaders, who had been monitoring other organized protests around the country. Violence in this liberal and small community did not evidently increase following the screening, although a spirited dialogue centering on women's issues and freedom of expression was promoted in the local newspaper as well as among villagers.

4. A film teacher can — because of the knowledge of the filmmaking process — easily become inured to the emotional/visceral response a film can provoke. I have since refrained from using *The Hills Have Eyes* in the classroom, preferring to use horror films that tend not to break down the aesthetic distance between film and spectator quite so completely or traumatically.

5. Film director Paul Bartel, quoted in an advertisement for *The Fourth Man* in the *New York Native,* July 2–15, 1984, 28.

12

Bringing It All Back Home: Family Economy and Generic Exchange

Vivian Sobchack

An abridged version of an article that is scheduled to appear in Camera Obscura, *Vivian Sobchack's study is, like the essays by R. H. W. Dillard and Gregory A. Waller, concerned with modern horror's representation of "the familiar and the familial." Sobchack, however, is particularly interested in the way the figure of the child and the relations between patriarchy and paternity are inscribed in popular film genres that share a common "cultural context"—the "crisis experienced by American bourgeois patriarchy since the late 1960s." Her sophisticated ideological analysis—that has much in common with the work of Fredric Jameson—of the ambivalent response to and re-solution of this crisis in a wide range of films differs from the essays by Lucy Fischer and Marcia Landy, Robin Wood, and Charles Derry in that Sobchack insists that we read modern horror not only in a cultural context, but also in the context of other popular genres, specifically family melodrama and science fiction films. Her speculations about the historical transformation of each of these genres and about the convergence of and exchange among horror, family melodrama, and science fiction raise essential points about individual films and genres and about the complex intergenre workings of American popular culture.*

Sobchack teaches at the University of California, Santa Cruz, and is currently president of the Society for Cinema Studies. She is co-author of An Introduction to Film, *and her articles have appeared in* Quarterly Review of Film Studies, American Quarterly, Semiotica, *and other journals. Among her forthcoming publications is* Screening Space, *an enlarged edition of her 1980 study,* The Limits of Infinity: The American Science Fiction Film, 1950–75.

Two very special babies were born to the American cinema in 1968: Rosemary's and Stanley Kubrick's. One was born in a horror film, the other in a science fiction film. One stared up from a cradle toward its earthly mother, the other down from space toward Mother Earth. Nonetheless, both the "devil's spawn" and the "starchild" condensed the *visible sight* of cultural difference, social change, and historical movement into the single and powerful figure of a child — one marked as an enigma by virtue of its strange eyes, and estranged, alien vision.

Both infants also signaled the replacement of previous generic displacements. In their bodies and through their eyes, those far-off and imaginary spaces that once characterized and differentiated traditional horror and science fiction films were replaced to the homesite from whence they were first envisioned. The *visual site* of horrific attraction and repulsion, of utopian wonder and dystopian anxiety, was redirected back toward that domestic structure of social relations — the nuclear family. Thus, despite their reversed visual perspectives and differing generic locations, the two newborns figured in *Rosemary's Baby* and *2001: A Space Odyssey* had a good deal in common. Born at — and as — the end or final cause of the narratives in which they were conceived and (re)produced, both babies not only infused a new flow of representational energy into their respective genres, but also marked the beginning of an extremely interesting and historically situated generic convergence.

In this essay I explore the cultural meanings that the figure of the child narrativizes as it is exchanged and transformed between the contemporary horror and science fiction films, and as it creates an adherence between these two genres and a third — the newly revitalized family melodrama. In all three genres, by virtue of its implication of domestic space, generational time, and familial structure, the privileged figure of the child condenses and initiates a contemporary and pressing cultural drama. That drama emerges from the crisis experienced by American bourgeois patriarchy since the late 1960s and is marked by the related disintegration and transfiguration of the traditional American bourgeois family — an ideological as well as interpersonal structure characterized, as Robin Wood so frequently points out, by its cellular construction and institutionalization of capitalist and patriarchal relations and values (among them, monogamy, heterosexuality, and consumerism), and by its present state of disequilibrium and crisis.[1]

Although historically asymmetrical in their major periods of production and popularity, the traditional horror and science fiction films have tended toward a structurally symmetrical relationship marked by *opposition*. The two genres have been connected but differentiated by what seems a systemic and binary reversal of themes, iconographies, and conventions of narrative, dramatic, and visual representation. As I have elaborated elsewhere, both genres deal with a grand-scale chaos that threatens "the order of things," but the nature of that order is differentiated: "the horror film deals with moral chaos, the disruption of natural order (assumed to be God's order), and the threat to the harmony of hearth and home; the SF film, on the other hand, is concerned with social chaos, with the disruption of social order (man-made), and the threat to the harmony of civilized society going about its business."[2] As well, the two genres can be differentiated by the primary modality of their "dreamwork" — those processes of condensation, displacement, and secondary elaboration that metaphorically and metonymically constitute narrative momentum and iconographic imagery. Repression seems the dominant strategy of the traditional horror film. And, as we all know by now, what is repressed returns in condensed and displaced form to threaten and challenge and disrupt that which would deny it presence. On the other hand, sublimation seems the dominant strategy of the traditional science fiction film. Libidinal energy is transferred into the creation of wondrous special effects and is displaced and condensed into dramas of technological (re)production and/or grand-scale destruction. Contemporary examples of both genres, however, tend to deny the generally neat symmetrical opposition of their traditional cinematic ancestors. In the context of the ambivalent horror and wonder provoked by the social upheavals of the last two decades and by complementary upheavals in the entertainment industry, a convergence and conflation of generic difference has occurred.

Indeed, many recent horror and science fiction films have been marked as contemporary not only on the basis of their release dates, but also on the basis of their mutual spatial relocation to the American landscape and temporal relocation to the present, their mutual figuration of the Other as both the "same" as well as "different" from ourselves and somehow implicated in family life, and by their common and preconscious thematic recognition that the social world can no longer be conceptualized and dramatized as an opposition between private and public concerns and spheres of action.[3] Figures from the past and the future get into the house, make their homes in the closet, become part of the family, and open the kitchen and family room up to the horrific and wondrous world outside this private and safe domain. A man's home in bourgeois patriarchal culture is no longer his castle. In the age of television the drawbridge is always down; the world intrudes. It is no longer possible to avoid the invasive presence of Others — whether poltergeists, extraterrestrials, one's own alien kids, or starving Ethiopian children.

Since the 1960s, then, the events of family life and social life have been commonly and increasingly experienced as convergent. Thus, it is not surprising that contemporary generic articulations of horror and science fiction have tended to complement, rather than oppose, each other. Their previously binary relation has been transformed into an analogue that includes the family melodrama—a genre whose representations are governed not by the conventions of the fantastic, but by those of realism. In the currency of today's generic economy, the once markedly different representational registers of the fantastic and the realistic are more easily able to circulate and commensurably represent similar thematic and dramatic material. Thus, even as their distinction is seemingly still held sacred, the fantastic and the real pervade each other and insist on a closer and closer equivalence.

This triadic adherence of horror, science fiction, and family melodrama also entails a temporal and spatial exchange. The past, that temporal field usually grounding the horror film, is commensurable with the future, usually associated with the science fiction film—and both are commensurable with the present, usually the temporal field of the family melodrama. Correlatively, previously distinct narrative sites become contiguous or congruent. The exotic, decadent European world of the traditional horror film, the wondrous, alien outer space of the science fiction film, and the familiar, domestic, and traditionally American space of the family melodrama become closely associated. Exotic, decadent, and alien space geographically conflates with familiar and familial space. The displaced "There" has been replaced "Here," and "Then" and "When" have been condensed as "Now." Thus, the time and place of horror and anxiety, wonder and hope, have been brought back into the American home. It is within the home and family that the institutionalization and perpetuation of the bourgeois social world begins—and ends. This is the common place, the present world, shared by horror films such as *The Exorcist, Carrie, The Fury, The Amityville Horror,* and *Poltergeist,* and science fiction films like *Close Encounters of the Third Kind, E.T.,* and *Starman,* and family melodramas like *Ordinary People* and *Shoot the Moon.*

At a time when the mythology of our dominant culture can no longer resolve the social contradictions exposed by experience, the nuclear family has found itself in nuclear crisis. Rather than serving bourgeois patriarchy as a place of refuge from the social upheavals of the last two decades (many of which have been initiated by the young and by women), the family has become the site of them—and now serves as a sign of their representation. Not only has the bourgeois distinction between family members and alien Others, between private home and public space, between personal microcosm and sociopolitical macrocosm been exposed as a myth, but also the family itself has been exposed as a cultural construction, as a set of signifying, as well as significant, practices. The family and its members are seen, therefore, as subject to the frightening, but potentially liberating, semiotic processes of selection and combination—and their order, meaning, and power are perceived as open to transformation, dissolution, and redefinition.

The contemporary genres of horror, science fiction, and family melodrama converge in their dramatization of these processes that test and represent the coherence, meaning, and limits of the family as it has been constructed in patriarchal culture. Historically asymmetrical in regard to their peak periods of production, each genre to some degree maintaining a discrete archetypal core of generic structures and motifs, the three have nonetheless come together in common response to their shared cultural context and the similar social malaise that surrounds and supports their current popularity.[4] Engaging in an urgent and dynamic exchange, whose goal is ultimately conservative, the three genres attempt to narratively contain, work out, and in some fashion re-solve the contemporary weakening of patriarchal authority and the glaring contradictions that exist between the mythology of family relations and their actual social practice. In all three genres those contradictions are most powerfully condensed and represented in the problematic figure of the child.

I began this essay by invoking two newborns: Rosemary's baby and Kubrick's starchild. My interest is in their cinematic offspring: the babies, children, and childlike figures who have been born to the cinema in their generation and eventually transformed the cinematic shape of both patriarchy and the nuclear family. First, however, I must clarify the way in which I am using the concepts of *figure* and *figuration*.[5] Not simply "motifs," "symbols," or rhetorical "additions" to narrative discourse, figures visibly represent the origin and process of narrative. "Discussion of figures," Dudley Andrew tells us, "wants to flow back to the moment in which a particular meaning was shaped."[6] Figures coalesce, condense, embody, enact, and transform the trouble in the text, the narrative problematic. Their emergence and presence in the text serve not only to give visible form to the narrative problem, but also to alter it, to describe it differently from its previous visible articulations, to change its structure, its dynamic, and its meanings.

Figures, therefore, are metaphoric in function and event — if, as Andrew suggests, "metaphor is conceived of not as a . . . substitution but as a process resulting in the redescription of a semantic field."[7] The term figuration reminds us of this process. Figuration entails the figure actively engaged in transforming the text and being itself transformed through its work: adjusting the system of representation and the demands of the psyche and culture each to the other. The figure, then, is by nature and function unstable, problematic, and productive of new meanings and new interpretations. Following Paul Ricoeur, Andrew tells us that in its most vital work, the figure forces us to put into play all the possibilities of the sign and then leap to a new possibility, the one that will change the context itself and make us see it through the "improper and impertinent" sign. This is what produces a seismic shift in the contextual field. In politics we call such condensation "revolution," in psychoanalysis "transference," and in artistic and religious experience "insight." Figures are thus more than shortcuts by way of association and substitution; they have the power to disrupt the relation of context to sign and reorient not only the discursive event but the system itself which will never be the same afterwards.[8]

It is within this context that the production and emergence of the visible figure of the infant at – and as – the end of both *Rosemary's Baby* and *2001* can be said to have disrupted and reoriented not only the cultural meanings attached to representations of infants and children, but also the articulations, structure, and meanings of the two genres in which they appeared.

The secular baby and child have held a privileged place in bourgeois and patriarchal mythology since the nineteenth century. Infancy and childhood have been represented as the cultural site of such "positive" virtues as innocence, transparency, and a "pure" and wonderful curiosity not yet informed by sexuality. Representing these virtues, the baby has been culturally produced as a figure of poignant sweetness – helpless, vulnerable, and dependent not only because of its physical immaturity, but also because of its lack of the "corrupting" knowledge necessary for survival in the social world. This "lack," however, is represented as "hope" and "promise." Not yet having been *subjected to* the lessons of experience and history, the infant and child signify the *subject of* an experience and history still to be enacted and inscribed. In this way the child becomes the *signifier* of the future. But the child is also the *signified* of the past. Its familiar identity and family resemblance are produced as visible traces of the past's presence in the present and ensure the past's presence in a future safely contained and constrained by tradition and history. At best, it will carry the father's name forward, at least, his seed. Thus, in its representation of the infant and child, bourgeois mythology has constructed a sign of the future that is sweetly traditional and safely adventurous, open yet closed. The infant and child as sign evoke nostalgia. What seems a looking forward toward the possibilities of the future is a longing backward toward the promise once possessed by the past – a longing for inexperience, for potential rather than realized action, for an openness to the world based on a lack of worldliness.

Both *Rosemary's Baby* and *2001* ended up delivering infants to the screen who interrogated this mythology by their very presence, their bodies figuring a visible site of ambiguity, ambivalence, and contradiction.[9] The two newborns were as alien as they were human; calling up familiar and familial feelings by their "baby-ness," they were, nonetheless, not wholly the culture's own. Rosemary's emerged from the outer limits of bourgeois notions of time—from an historic coupling of primal, diabolic "negativity" with human being. Kubrick's emerged from the outer limits of bourgeois notions of space—from the "infinite and beyond," from a posthistoric coition of extraterrestrial openness with human being. Given their alien parentage (Satan in one instance, a transcendental and superior unknown in the other), the innocence and lack of knowledge of both babies were certainly questionable. Given the opacity of their eyes, their transparence and sweetness were also suspect. In addition, both newborns, while appearing vulnerable and dependent in their "baby-ness," clearly possessed special power and were not as helpless as their bodies suggested. An irrational, unthinkable past and an unimaginable future collapsed into their visible infantile presence; they evoked no nostalgia. Indeed, the children in these films threatened the mythology they represented and figured "childhood's end." In sum, the future these two children promised in their representation was not the safe future as traditionally envisioned and expected, but rather a radically transformed future, an apocalyptic and/or revolutionary future, an unimaginable future—perhaps no future at all. What they have delivered, however, is quite something other than radical.

Rosemary's baby has gone on to grow up in the horror film, inscribing dramas in which those negative aspects of childhood and parenthood repressed by bourgeois mythology are played out in ambivalent representations. Diachronically, this ambivalence can be bracketed between two generic declarations. "There's only one thing wrong with the Davis baby. It's alive!" pronounces the ad for *It's Alive* in 1974 (the same year that gave us the diabolic rage of the possessed but powerful Regan in *The Exorcist*). "Part of being a parent is trying to kill your kids," says the teenager in 1983's *Christine* (the same year that saw adults plotting to kill millions of American children in *Halloween III*). Over a ten-year period, the horror film has obliquely moved from the representation of children as terrors to children as terrorized. Unnatural natural infants or demonically possessed children become sympathetic victims whose special powers are justifiably provoked or venally abused. And, where once teenagers threatened an entire populace and its social regulation with their burgeoning sexuality and presumption to adulthood, in recent years they have been solipsistically annihilating each other in a quarantined and culturally negligible space. (Indeed, a subgenre solely devoted to teenagers watching and awaiting their own senseless annihilation emerged with *Halloween* in 1978 and *Friday the 13th* in 1980. These slasher movies seem to appeal to adolescent feelings of rage and helplessness—feelings always present, but specifically articulated in apocalyptic terms in an age marked by generalized nuclear fear and the particularly brutal events of the 1960s youth and anti-war movements. These films abstract and ritualize adolescent isolation, rage, and helplessness, and it is particularly interesting to note how they rigorously repress the presence of parents and families, the latter's impotence and failure an absence that necessitates and structures the violence of the narratives.)

From the early to mid-1970s and coincident with bourgeois society's negative response to the youth movements and drug culture of the late 1960s and early 1970s, generic emphasis was on the child not as terrorized victim, but as cannibalistic, monstrous, murderous, selfish, sexual. The child was figured as an alien force that threatened both its immediate family and all adult authority that would keep it in its place — oppressed and at home. While runaway children provided the narrative impetus, but not the focus, for such precursors of the new family melodrama as *Joe* (1970) and *Taking Off* (1971), the horror film focused on children not run away, but run amok. Their resentment, anger, destructiveness, aberrance, and evil were seen as unwarranted and irrational eruptions — extrafamilial and precivilized in origin. The bodies and souls of such children as appear in *The Other* (1972), *The Exorcist, The Omen* (1976), and *Audrey Rose* (1977) are "possessed" by demonic, supernatural, and ahistoric forces that play out apocalypse in the middle-class home — most often graphically represented by "special effects" that rage in huge and destructive temper tantrums across the screen. Thus, while these children are verbally articulated as "possessed" and "victims," they are visually articulated as in possession of and victimizing their households. Family resemblance notwithstanding, these kids are not their fathers' natural children. They are figured as uncivilized, hostile, and powerful Others who — like their extracinematic counterparts — refuse parental love and authority and mock the established values of dominant institutions. They are "changelings" — the horrifically familiar embodiment of difference.[10] Fascinating the culture that also found them abhorrent, these children collapsed the boundaries that marked off identity from difference and exercised a powerful deconstructive force dangerous to patriarchal bourgeois culture. Their figural presence and work on the screen and in the home restructured and redefined the semantic field of the generation gap — articulating it in vertiginous imagery, as *mise en abime*.[11]

In the mid-1970s, however, *Carrie* (1976) transfigures and softens the demonic and murderous child into a familiar Other whose difference is marked not only by her telekinetic power, but also by her relative innocence. Adolescent Carrie is a pitiable victim of her culture who evokes sympathy. She is a nerd whose outrage, however horrific and excessive its expression, is a response to a comprehensible betrayal.[12] Like Robin and Gillian who follow her (*The Fury* [1978]), Carrie's fury is as justified as it is frightening—irrational in its power and force, perhaps, but rationally motivated. While Damien and Regan grow up in possession of relatively predetermined sequels that continue to ascribe the cause of children's abuse of their parents and adult authority to extrafamilial, diabolic, and prehistoric forces, the apocalyptic destruction wrought by the likes of Carrie, Robin, and Gillian seem as much generated by familial incoherence and paternal weakness as the cause of it. They come from broken homes. They appear oppressed and vulnerable—exposed to harm and exploitation because of the apparent weakness and instability of the bourgeois family structure deemed responsible for their protection and nurturance. Their special powers are abused, and the apocalypse that follows from their provoked and childishly unselective fury is seen as somehow deserved.

Here, it is pertinent to note that sandwiched between *Carrie* and *The Fury*, a 1979 family docu/melodrama made for television—*The Death of Richie*—plays out an opposed but also complementary narrative within the representational register of the realistic. As Leonard Maltin summarizes: "A family is torn apart by teenaged son's drug addiction. . . . straight-arrow father . . . brings himself to kill the boy."[13] Who is responsible for apocalypse here? Who destroys the family—child or parent? Although guilt is perceived as shared, *Richie* sympathetically stresses the anger and despair of the monstrous father rather than the monstrous child. Both structurally complementing and radically opposing *Carrie* or *The Fury*, in this realistic melodrama, it is a monstrous but sympathetic father who responds to betrayal by using his special power to annihilate his child.

Correlatively, we can see the horror film's earlier representation of parents as bewildered, foolish, and blindly trusting victims of their ungrateful and aberrant children undergoing a transformation as the figures of those children change. From the terrifying Davis baby or Damien to the terrifying but terrorized Carrie, Robin, and Gillian, to the terrorized Danny (*The Shining* [1980]) or Carol Ann (*Poltergeist* [1982]), we can trace a visible shift in the ascription of responsibility for the breakdown of traditional family relations. That responsibility has been transferred from child to parent. As horror film children grow smaller, younger, and less adolescent, their special powers slowly diminish from apocalyptic fury to a relatively helpless insight (the "shining" of Danny's prescience or Carol Ann's "vital" innocence). What deserves note, however, is that this transference of apocalyptic familial fury is generically specific. Contradictory to the most popular contemporary family melodramas and contrary to certain trends in the science fiction film, the horror film moves either to quarantine helpless teenagers in the carnivalesque summer camps, holidays, and prom nights of slasher movies, or to single out Dad as the primary negative force in the middle-class family.

It is in the late 1970s that the genre begins to overtly interrogate paternal commitment and its relation to patriarchal power. In 1978, strong-jawed and iconic Kirk Douglas (playing Robin's natural father in *The Fury*) proves weak and ineffectual; he is unable to save his son from the unnatural father who would exploit him in the name of the law — except by killing the child and himself (albeit accidentally). The following year shows us a weak and possessed straight-arrow father taking to the axe and after his children. *The Amityville Horror* is figured not only as the haunted middle-class family home, but also as the haunted middle-class family Dad — who, weak, economically beleaguered, and under pressure from his corrupt and demanding dream house in a period of economic recession, terrorizes his children. (This corruption of paternal responsibility and perversion of paternal love follows a trajectory forward not only to the *Amityville* sequels in 1982 and 1983, but also to the ethically lax, real-estate salesman Dad whose willful ignorance of the ground of his business practice jeopardizes his children in 1982's *Poltergeist*.)[14]

The repressed in the genre is no longer the double threat found in the traditional horror film: an excessive will to power and knowledge, and unbridled sexual desire. Rather, the repressed is patriarchal hatred, fear, and self-loathing. As the culture changes, as patriarchy is challenged, as more and more families no longer conform in structure, membership, and behavior to the standards set by bourgeois mythology, the horror film plays out the rage of paternal responsibility denied the economic and political benefits of patriarchal power. The figure of the child in the genre is problematic and horrific because it demands and generates the articulation of another figure. Father is the synchronic repressed who, first powerfully absenting himself, returns to terrify the family in the contemporary horror film. He is the one who, in 1968, willingly yields his paternity and patriarchal rite to Satan. He is the one whose absence powerfully marks the households of Regan and Carrie, who engenders these daughters' rage in their lack, but is not there to culturally constrain it within the Law of the Father.[15] Dad is also the one who — in the canny casting of John Cassevetes — carries his patriarchal pact with the devil (at Rosemary and her baby's expense) forward into his surrogate and exploitative fatherhood of Robin and Gillian. By 1980 the return and figuration of the repressed Father become fully explicit — iconically realized in the leering, jeering, mad, child-abusive hatred of Jack Torrance in *The Shining*. Looking backward with the dull but still malevolent gaze of dead Jack, frozen in a labyrinth from which he could not escape, we can see in *Rosemary's Baby* the radical beginning of patriarchal failure: of paternity refused, denied, abandoned, hated; of patriarchy simultaneously terrified and terrorizing in the face of its increasing impotence; of patriarchy maddened by a paradoxical desire for its own annihilation. In the contemporary horror film the sins of the fathers are truly visited upon the sons – and daughters.

If the contemporary horror film dramatizes the terror of a patriarchy without power and refuses or perverts paternal responsibility when it is not rewarded with the benefits of patriarchal authority, the contemporary family melodrama plays out an uneasy acceptance of patriarchy's decline. The mode of the most popular films in the genre tends to be elegiac or comic. On the one hand, 1979 gave us *The Great Santini,* which found the exaggerated authoritarian power of its family patriarch excessively and pitiably inappropriate and impotent, but also celebrated its loss with a conservative nostalgia. On the other hand, the much more popular *Kramer vs. Kramer* gave us a father without practical authority, a father lovably and lovingly bumbling to an acceptance of paternity without traditional patriarchal benefit (which includes the surplus value of a wife/mother). Dustin Hoffman's Ted Kramer is – if I may pun – a "little" big man, hardly taller than his son: a sign of fatherhood just barely intelligible to patriarchal law and hardly able to represent it. Any real rage Kramer may feel toward runaway mom, toward his dependent son, toward his loss of familial power and its benefits is as repressed in the text as his wife's past labor and those moments in which the adorable kid throws up or makes the bedroom look as if Regan has been there. If the horror film shows us the terror and rage of *patriarchy in decline* (savaged by its children or murderously resentful of them), then the popular family melodrama shows us a sweetly problematic *paternity in ascendance.*[16] The two genres exist in schizophrenic relation. Indeed, Greg Keeler's *"The Shining:* Ted Kramer Has a Nightmare" brilliantly elaborates this relation by viewing the mad, murderous, bad father, Jack Torrance, as carrying out all of the negative patriarchal fury and paternal desire repressed by the nurturant "good father" in the previous year's *Kramer vs. Kramer.*[17]

It is also worth noting that *Ordinary People* wins the Academy Award in 1980, the year *The Shining* is considered a "disappointment." The good father in the uncomic melodrama of *Ordinary People* makes more explicit the patriarchal problematic of power, which demands a hierarchy of strength and weakness. If the good father in the family melodrama is now inscribed as not only caring about his child, but also as caring for it, in assuming what has been previously defined as a maternal function, he is ambivalently figured as soft and weak, if not servile.[18] Consistent with the systemic rules of patriarchal relation and its economy, the mother in the family melodrama becomes hard, strong, and selfish. From the tall, aristocratic, neurotic intelligence of Meryl Streep to the brittle yet steely coldness of Mary Tyler Moore (whose subsequent warmth as a single mother in 1982's *Six Weeks* is interestingly suspect in light of this previous role), the inability of patriarchy to cope with its loss of authority, to admit an equal distribution of familial power and responsibility, is inscribed in the opposition of bad mother and good father. Inverting the horror film, these two most popular family melodramas attribute the destruction of the nuclear family to Mom. It is she who goes on in later films to deprive Dad of his paternal right by taking off with his kids (*Hide in Plain Sight* [1980]) or to selfishly absent herself, abandoning her kids to the care of a father who comically tries to assume the role of what *Ms. Magazine* used to call "Superwoman" (*Author! Author!* [1982]). *On Golden Pond* (1981), the only other extremely popular family melodrama of the period, resolves family tensions through a surrogate child and leaves Mom and Dad, doddering on the brink of death, elegiacally reassuring themselves that "the kids are all right."

The new family melodrama emerges right around the time when the horror film Father begins his active and hostile return from the repressed, and the special powers of his furious and alienated children begin to weaken in the face of his paternal hostility. In direct contradiction to the horror film Father, the most popular Dads in the family melodrama-cum-comedy are little more than children themselves. When Mother is the "absent one,"[19] these Dads are given license to indulge themselves in feeling and ineptitude. They are innocents abroad in the home. But their bumbling ignorance, while endearing, is disempowering. Ted Kramer does not know how to make French toast. *Mr. Mom* (1983) is terrorized by a vacuum cleaner. In addition, their children conduct a running and critical, if finally indulgent, commentary on Dad's ineffective assumption of maternal labor.

The special power possessed by horror film children and deconstructively directed against their parents and adult authority is transformed and softened in the family melodrama. In the pathetic films, that special power becomes insight, making the child prescient and sensitive, but also vulnerable and fragile (as in *Ordinary People* and *Shoot the Moon*). In the comedic films, it becomes a cute, invincible precocity (as in *Kramer vs. Kramer, Author! Author!,* and innumerable contemporaneous television sit-coms). In both cases, however, it is the child who has the power to authorize the family, who evaluates Dad's abilities and performance, who denies or legitimates the particular family's existence as a viable structure. As Marina Heung points out: "What is striking in recent films . . . is the way . . . the child not only acts as humanizer, but also as the overseer of familial roles and responsibilities. Thus, the child is a contradictory blend of precocity and vulnerability, often helpless in controlling his own situation, but instrumental in influencing the actions of adults. In fact, his control over familial relationships is so great that it is practically parental."[20] All those "little adults" and insightful teenagers let Dad off the hook by themselves representing patriarchal law in the genre's families. And Dad, in giving up patriarchal power and authority to his children, in becoming merely paternal, is himself reduced – and liberated – to the status of a child.

As true of Calvin in *Ordinary People* as of more comically articulated fathers, Dad's figuration in the genre works to represent him as positively innocent, transparent, lacking in practical knowledge, and essentially unerotic. He thus becomes a figure of poignant sweetness – helpless, vulnerable, and dependent on his children not only because of his physical ineptitude in the home, but also because of his lack of corrupting knowledge necessary for his membership and survival in the exterior patriarchal bourgeois social world. If all this seems familiar, it is so because I have previously used these terms to characterize the privileged figure and positive lack of the infant and child in bourgeois mythology. Thus, an unresolvable paradox is figured in the genre. If Dad must become as an innocent child to represent the hope and promise of an imaginable future for patriarchy (which, in these versions of a single-parent family, accepts paternity), he must also give up his patriarchal power, his authority, to his children, retaining only its illusion, its image (and that at their indulgence).

Both the horror film and the family melodrama play out scenarios that do not resolve the dilemmas faced by a contemporary patriarchy under assault. The former genre dramatizes patriarchal impotence and rage, the latter patriarchal weakness and confusion – both generated by the central and problematic figure of the child. If the child is figured as powerful at the expense of the father, then patriarchy is threatened; if father is figured as powerful at the expense of his child, then paternity is threatened. In both cases, the traditional and conceivable future is threatened – for if patriarchy is willfully destroyed by its children, no tradition will mark the future with the past and present, and if paternity is willfully denied by a patriarchy that destroys its children, then the future will not be conceived. This dilemma is more than Oedipal; in fact, it demonstrates a crisis of belief in the Oedipal model. Once conceived of as identical in bourgeois capitalist culture, patriarchy and paternity have been recently articulated as different – one powerful effect of white, middle-class feminist discourse. This difference, however, clearly poses a problem when patriarchy as a political and economic power structure and paternity as a personal and subjective relation both locate themselves in the same place (the home) and seek to constitute the same object (the child). Both genres cannot end happily—even when they are comedies; their dramatic victories are always Pyrrhic.

It is in one dominant strain of the contemporary science fiction film that patriarchy and paternity seek to happily re-solve their relationship. The resolution is as ingenious as it is predictable and, finally, ingenuous. Rather than struggle for occupation of the same place (the home), they (temporarily) leave it; and rather than struggle to constitute the same object (the child), they (temporarily) become it. Before "phoning home," patriarchy and paternity conflate in a single figure that is both powerful and lovable: the innocent extraterrestrial who is at once childlike, paternal, and patriarchially empowered. It is in much recent science fiction that the good/weak father of the family melodrama attempts to regain his political power and patriarchal strength by moving *outside* or *beyond* the space of his natural family and being born again as an adorable child with the special power to again effect both familial and global events. Rather than the synchronic repressed who, first powerfully absenting himself, returns to the horror film to terrorize his family, Dad is the synchronic transformed of the science fiction film. And while he, too, seems at first to abandon and deny paternity and family, he—unlike his horror film counterpart— returns not to savage it, but to salvage it.

The figural development of the science fiction starchild took longer than its counterpart in the horror film. Nonetheless, in both genres, the figure of the child was first introduced as embodying a suspect miscegenation of alien and human characteristics. It bears remembrance that parallel to the birth of Rosemary's baby as the cinematic production of an ahistoric and demonic hallucination, the birth of the starchild was the cinematic production of a posthistoric and "spaced-out" (drug) trip through the Star Gate. Although their delivery is delayed, the first science fiction babies are negative figures of the same generation as their horror film counterparts; born in the late 1970s, they are, nonetheless, hostile, threatening, and alien children of the late 1960s. The narrative cause for the child's negative (re)production is, of course, characteristic of science fiction: a powerful, dangerous, and cooperative science and technology are responsible for the child's alien-ation. Thus, the petri-dish paternity of *Embryo* (1976), the computer conception of *Demon Seed* (1977), and even the retrograde cloning of *The Boys from Brazil* (1978).

Almost immediately, however, this negative imagery is overtaken by a more positive dramatization, which emerges from what I have suggested is bourgeois culture's attempts in the 1970s to reinterpret its ineffectiveness and failed aggressivity as childlike innocence and vulnerability. Initially, that movement toward the conflation of the American male adult with the child and alien is marked by the 1977 release of *Close Encoun-*

ters of the Third Kind. The film clearly valorizes the bourgeois myth of the little, innocent, vulnerable child and transcends and empowers it as a mythology of the little, innocent, benevolent alien, who is also awesomely powerful and invulnerable. By emphasizing its own vision as childlike and reveling in its own technology as do the aliens, *Close Encounters* also disavows alliance with traditional patriarchal institutions and traditional paternal behavior. The government and the military are viewed as deceitful and stupid, lacking in imagination and vision, and contemptuous of those they profess to protect. The traditional bourgeois family is seen in terms of failed paternity (this failure made even more painful in the special edition of the film).

In the Guiler family, Dad (like God) is dead. Jillian is a widow raising her son as a single parent. She is the first of a number of unattached mothers or mothers-to-be in the genre's contemporary films, including *E.T., Starman,* and *The Terminator.*[21] (The single-parent family in current science fiction thus tends to reverse the structure of parental presence and absence found in the seriocomic family melodrama.) In the Neary family Dad literally abandons his paternal responsibility in an eventually successful attempt to regenerate his childhood. Misunderstood by his humorless wife and unappreciated by his conventional kids, Roy Neary's playfulness and curiosity are viewed as threatening and contemptible by his family; they are embarrassed by his childish behavior almost as much before his close encounter as after. Literally alien-ated from traditional family structure, Jillian and Roy join together in their complementary desire to relocate the innocent and playful child they have differently lost — and, in the process, they form a surrogate family unit, one "elevated as the counterpart and alternative to the biological family."[22] Nonetheless, the differences they represent, their opposing motives, signal the necessarily temporary nature of their union — for Jillian's journey to Devil's Tower is an assertion of maternity, while Roy's is a negation of paternity. Jillian wants to regain her child; Roy wants to regain his childhood.

These are irreconcilable differences insofar as they concern the hierarchical structure and function of the bourgeois family and its traditional relations of power. Nonetheless, the film reconciles them in the figure and mythology of the child, in the relocation of personal innocence and cultural simplicity. It is telling that both Jillian and Roy inhabit a world of material abundance encoded as overwhelming clutter, and in a world of communicative complexity encoded as jargon and noise. In their search, however, clutter yields to the wide-open, underdetermined, and undeveloped spaces of sky and western landscape. Jargon and noise are drowned out by a universal music of the spheres. (Indeed, Devil's Tower resembles the Tower of Babel painted by Breugel the Elder. Upthrusting from the barren Wyoming landscape, its flattened top an aborted reach to the sky, it is an iconic figure that both represents and reverses the biblical narrative of failed communication.) Irreconcilable difference sublimated in their journey, Jillian and Roy's quest converges not only in their search for the innocence and wonder of childhood, but also in their flight from an incomprehensible, obstructive, overdeveloped, grown-up world.

Thus, children unadulterated by sophistication and language, childlike purity and simplicity, innocence, wonder, transparency, and verbal inarticulateness are valorized by both the film and its central characters. And it is through the transcoding of the latter that the former is able to constitute equivalencies between the adult male father and the vulnerable and curious child, between the child and the powerful and curious alien, and between the vulnerable adult father and the childlike and patriarchally benevolent alien. By means of this transcoding, a further transformation is suggested — one whose teleology will find its major visible articulations in *Altered States* (1980), *E.T.* (1982), and *Starman* (1984). Incorporated as a child, an alien-ated and unadulterated patriarchy reappropriates its power to reproduce the future as a nostalgic image of its bourgeois past.

The transformation of children into aliens, fathers and aliens into children, and adult males into alien fathers plays out a single patriarchal narrative, cinematically dramatized with greatest energy and force in the contemporary generic articulations of horror, family melodrama, and science fiction. In their figural and transformative work of spatially and temporally redescribing the structure and semantic field of the traditional patriarchal family, the three genres have exchanged and expended their representational energy dynamically and urgently — with the "politically unconscious" aim of seeking re-solution, or at least ab-solution, for a threatened patriarchy and its besieged structure of perpetuation: the bourgeois family.[23] In sum, their mutual project has been (and is) aggressively regressive and conservative. Thus, however synchronic their intergeneric relations, the various transformations explored here seem to culminate diachronically in the current dominant popularity of the science fiction film — the genre that most visibly figures the grandest illusions of a capitalist and patriarchal cinema, and that spatially liberates powerful male children from social, political, and economic responsibility for the past and to the present.

And yet that illusion cannot quite be maintained; it keeps dissolving in the context of present structural and cultural pressure. Despite all the representational energy and urgency that have linked and revitalized the three genres in a dramatic attempt to resolve patriarchal and familial crisis in relevant but conservative narratives, there seems no viable way for patriarchy to symbolically envision a satisfying future for itself. All it can do is deny the future. There is no narrative resolution for patriarchy in the horror film—except the denial or death of the father, finally impotent and subject to the present power of his own horrific past. The family melodrama also resolves nothing; in both its serious and comic modes, its final hopeful articulations are a celebration of algorithmic paralysis, of a patriarchal present that is on hiatus. And in the science fiction film (the most hopeful of the lot), there is no resolution of patriarchal crisis that is not patently fantastic—and no fantastic resolution that does not also annihilate any real imagination of the future in its nostalgic retreat to the outer space and other time of an impossible past. All these films symbolically enact the death of the future.

Focusing on the problematic figure of the child and its transformations leads us to a historicizing and dialectical criticism that reads across generic boundaries and through cultural and narrative time. What emerges from this reading is an understanding of intertextual relations that constitute "the very locus and model of ideological closure."[24] That is, the contemporary horror film, family melodrama, and science fiction film together map "the limits of a specific ideological consciousness" and mark "the conceptual points beyond which that consciousness cannot go, and between which it is condemned to oscillate."[25] Terrorized by its own past, not able to imagine and image its own presence in the future, American bourgeois patriarchy keeps getting trapped by its desire to escape the present. Nonetheless, this failure of symbolic imagination and the boredom its repetitions will eventually generate leads one to hope. Not only do we have an active and perversely popular marginal cinema that locates future outer space in the present inner city, but we also can look forward to the debilitating effects of a symbolic exhaustion so great that imaginative failure cannot be ignored. Theater previews at the time of this writing promise we shall shortly see a science fiction film blatantly called *Back to the Future*. Surely this is ideological hysteria, the "political unconscious" of American bourgeois patriarchy teetering on the brink of babbling itself to consciousness and, perhaps, a cure.

NOTES

1. See the following articles by Robin Wood: "Return of the Repressed," *Film Comment* 14 (July-Aug. 1978):25-32; "Gods and Monsters," ibid., 14 (Sept.-Oct. 1978):19-25; "The American Family Comedy: from *Meet Me in St. Louis* to *The Texas Chain Saw Massacre*," *Wide Angle* 3 (1979):5-11; "Neglected Nightmares," *Film Comment* 16 (Mar.-Apr. 1980):24-31; and his various pieces in *American Nightmare: Essays on the Horror Film,* ed. Richard Lippe and Robin Wood (Toronto: Festival of Festivals, 1979).

2. Vivian Carol Sobchack, *The Limits of Infinity: The American Science Fiction Film* (New York: A. S. Barnes, 1980), 30. A new and enlarged edition is forthcoming in 1987 from Ungar under the title *Screening Space: The American Science Fiction Film.*

3. I would draw particular attention to my use here of the term "preconscious" rather than "unconscious." Indeed, the point is that in their traditional periods, both the horror and science fiction genres condensed and displaced their primary concerns and repressions so that dramas centering around sexuality and kinship in the horror film and ontological identity and reproduction in the science fiction film were elaborately disguised and hidden. In contemporary examples of both genres, however, such dramas are more overtly played out, are more available to consciousness — even as such consciousness is directed to look elsewhere. Displacement becomes an act of *replacement* to primary sites of trauma and condensation occurs in figures who *replicate* original sources of power: father, mother, child.

4. The horror film has probably been the most consistently popular of genres, but its contemporary period (dating from the 1960s) is particularly marked by a regular output with no particular peak years. The contemporary science fiction film, however, has a more dramatic history. Gaining particular force in 1977 (the year of both *Close Encounters* and *Star Wars*), the genre has gained in popularity and increased in number with the last two years (1983–84) marking a new peak; at the moment of this writing, the popularity and quantity of science fiction have an edge over that of the horror film — given box office reports, among other things. The contemporary family melodrama presents another history. The revitalization of the genre seems to be a result of the brief spate of liberal movies appearing in the mid-1970s, which attempted to respond to issues raised by the women's movement. From the initial focus on women protagonists, the films moved to a concern with the effects of women's liberation on the family. Certainly the success of *Kramer vs. Kramer* in 1979 marks this shift of emphasis, and thus it is from about 1980 (and *Ordinary People*) on that the family melodrama engages public interest. Still, in popularity and quantity, it lags far behind the fantastic genres of horror and science fiction.

5. For an extremely clear and useful summary of these concepts and their importance to a "symptomatic reading of American culture" through an analysis of figures and figuration, see Dudley Andrew's *Concepts in Film Theory* (New York: Oxford University Press, 1984), 157–71.

6. Ibid., 159.

7. Ibid., 167.

8. Ibid., 170.

9. It is striking that the infant does not figure at all in classic articulations of horror and science fiction before the 1960s (at least not in my memory). *The Bad Seed* seems singular in not only bringing horror into the domestic sphere through a child, but also in suggesting that infants might be evil. While young children have certainly figured in the science fiction film of the 1950s, they have generally served as unproblematic witness to — or dreamer of — alien threats (as in *The Day*

the Earth Stood Still, Invasion of the Body Snatchers, and *Invaders from Mars*), or they have been unproblematically victimized by the threat (as in *Them!* or *The Monolith Monsters*). It is worth noting that the most figurally compelling and alien-ated children appear not in American, but rather British science fiction of the period: *Village of the Damned* and its sequel, *Children of the Damned.*

10. It is worthy of note that by 1979 the "changeling" child is no longer the effect of extrafamilial and supernatural power. In *The Changeling,* a natural father murders his chronically ill son to preserve the family inheritance and himself substitutes an/Other child for his son. The child in this film no longer victimizes his parent(s), but is victimized by them — his ghostly spirit left to seek retribution and justice from perfect strangers in a lonely rented family house.

11. Although there has been an enormous and varied body of material on 1960s culture, I recommend Sohnya Sayres et al., *The Sixties without Apology* (Minneapolis: University of Minnesota Press, 1984).

12. It is interesting to note that the 1976 *Carrie* has its comedic counterpart in the 1984 *Revenge of the Nerds;* another paper remains to be written about the nature and function of the generic economy and exchange between the contemporary horror film featuring teenagers as victims/victimizers and the contemporary teen revenge comedy.

13. Leonard Maltin, *TV Movies, 1985-86* (New York: Signet, 1984), 205.

14. A brilliant analysis of the contemporary horror film's dramatization of popular fear in the face of economic crisis with particular emphasis on *Poltergeist* can be found in Douglas Kellner's "Fear and Trembling in the Age of Reagan: Notes on 'Poltergeist,'" *Socialist Review* 69 (May–June 1983):121-31.

15. Here, of course, I refer to Jacques Lacan's reading of Freud. Both *The Exorcist* and *Carrie* seem to me provocatively read in Lacanian terms; the female teenagers in these films — lacking both a phallus and the Phallus, or patriarchal Law — have no access to the patriarchal Symbolic. Unable to acquire the linguistic form of patriarchal discourse, their pubescent bodies seek expression through Other means, through menses. Indeed, the flow uncontained by the constraints of the Father, their physical and bloody rage is an apocalyptic feminine explosion of the frustrated desire to speak.

16. For a related discussion, see Dave Kehr, "The New Male Melodrama," *American Film* 8 (Apr. 1983):42-47.

17. Greg Keeler, "*The Shining:* Ted Kramer Has a Nightmare," *Journal of Popular Film and Television* 8 (Winter 1981):2-8.

18. It is interesting to contrast Calvin's weakness in the 1980s family of *Ordinary People* with that of the father in 1955's *Rebel Without a Cause.* Both are figured as more "caring" and sensitive to their son's feelings than the films' mothers, but whereas the father in the latter film is clearly and negatively coded as henpecked (wearing an apron, for instance) by an unremittingly strident and strong wife, the father in the former is ambivalently coded. Not hen-pecked, he is figured as naive and ignorant of negative feelings; he is an innocent in the face of his wife's coldness and his son's anguish.

19. We might note that here the family melodrama does not symmetrically *oppose*

the horror film. While Dad's absence is repressed in the latter genre until he returns as potential axe murderer, Mom's absence is explicitly and consciously addressed in the diegesis of the former.

20. Marina Heung, "Why E.T. Must Go Home: The New Family in American Cinema," *Journal of Popular Film and Television* 11 (Summer 1983):81. This exceptionally astute article describes contemporary family melodrama/comedy as an attempt to redefine the structure of the American family and, toward the end, relates the concerns of these films to the figure of E.T. Unlike the present essay, however, it does not discuss the family in the horror film, nor does it make generic connections between the family melodrama and science fiction.

21. Her only predecessor is Mrs. Benson in 1951's prescient and anomalous *The Day the Earth Stood Still*.

22. Heung, "Why E.T. Must Go Home," 82. The surrogate family is a central concern of Heung's article, but her discussion is primarily focused on the contemporary serio-comic family melodrama. Thus the surrogate family constituted in *E.T.* is offered as a singular culmination of a trend more generically developed elsewhere, rather than as a parallel generic figuration of the science fiction film. Nonetheless, Heung is particularly illuminating in her remarks about the distinction between the biological family and the family constituted "through circumstances or choice."

23. The reference here to the "political unconscious" is derived from Fredric Jameson's *The Political Unconscious: Narrative as a Socially Symbolic Act* (Ithaca, N.Y.: Cornell University Press, 1981). The assertion of such a concept is based on the recognition that "nothing . . . is not social and historical—indeed, that everything is 'in the last analysis' political." Jameson's articulation of the "political unconscious" calls for this political analysis, this "unmasking of cultural artifacts as socially symbolic acts" (20).

24. Ibid., 47.

25. Ibid.

Filmography

This filmography includes only those horror films released since 1968 that are cited in the essays in this collection. Each entry includes the following information: title, release date, production and/or distribution company, director (D), author of screenplay or teleplay (S), original source if adaptation, and cast (C).

Alien (1979). Twentieth Century-Fox. D: Ridley Scott. S: Dan O'Bannon. C: Tom Skerritt, Sigourney Weaver, Veronica Cartwright, Harry Dean Stanton, John Hurt, Yaphet Kotto.

Aliens (1986). Twentieth Century-Fox. D: James Cameron. S: James Cameron. C: Sigourney Weaver, Michael Biehn.

Aliens Are Coming, The (1980). NBC-TV. D: Harvey Hart. S: Robert W. Lenski. C: Tom Mason, Eric Braeden, Caroline McWilliams.

Alligator (1980). Group One. D: Lewis Teague. S: John Sayles. C: Robert Forster, Robin Riker, Michael V. Gazzo, Perry Lang.

Alone in the Dark (1982). New Line. D: Jack Sholder. S: Jack Sholder. C: Jack Palance, Donald Pleasence, Martin Landau, Dwight Schultz.

Altered States (1980). Warner Brothers. D: Ken Russell. S: Paddy Chayefsky. From the novel by Paddy Chayefsky. C: William Hurt, Blair Brown, Bob Balaban.

American Werewolf in London, An (1981). Universal. D: John Landis. S: John Landis. C: David Naughton, Jenny Agutter, Griffin Dunne, John Woodvine, Frank Oz.

Amityville Horror, The (1979). American International. D: Stuart Rosenberg. S: Sandor Stern. From the book by Jay Anson. C: James Brolin, Margot Kidder, Rod Steiger, Don Stroud, Michael Sacks.

Amityville 3-D (Amityville: The Demon) (1983). Orion. D: Richard Fleischer. S: William Wales. C: Tony Roberts, Tess Harper, Robert Joy, Candy Clark.

Amityville II: The Possession (1982). Orion. D: Damiano Damiani. S: Tommy Lee Wallace. From the book, *Murder in Amityville,* by Hans Holzer. C: Burt Young, Rutanya Alda, James Olson, Jack Magner.

Audrey Rose (1977). United Artists. D: Robert Wise. S: Frank De Felitta. From the novel by Frank De Felitta. C: Marsha Mason, Anthony Hopkins, John Beck, Susan Swift.

Awakening, The (1980). Warner Brothers/Orion. D: Mike Newell. S: Allan Scott, Chris Bryant, Clive Exton. From the novel, *The Jewel of the Seven Stars,* by Bram Stoker. C: Charlton Heston, Susannah York, Jill Townsend, Stephanie Zimbalist.

Beasts Are on the Streets, The (1978). Hanna-Barbera Productions (TV). D: Peter Hunt. S: Laurence Heath. C: Carol Lynley, Dale Robinette, Billy Green Bush.

Bermuda Depths, The (1978). ABC-TV. D: Tom Kotani. S: William Overgard. C: Burl Ives, Leigh McCloskey, Connie Sellecca, Carl Weathers.

Beyond the Bermuda Triangle (1975). NBC-TV. D: William A. Graham. S: Charles A. McDaniel. C: Fred MacMurray, Sam Groom, Donna Mills.

Blood Beach (1980). Gross. D: Jeffrey Bloom. S: Jeffrey Bloom. C: David Huffman, Mariana Hill, John Saxon, Burt Young.

Blow Out (1981). Filmways. D: Brian De Palma. S: Brian De Palma. C: John Travolta, Nancy Allen, John Lithgow, Dennis Franz.

Boogey Man, The (1980). Gross. D: Ulli Lommel. S: Ulli Lommel, Suzana Love, David Herschel. C: Suzana Love, Nicholas Love, John Carradine, Ron James.

Brood, The (1979). New World. D: David Cronenberg. S: David Cronenberg. C: Oliver Reed, Samantha Eggar, Art Hindle, Cindy Hinds.

Burning, The (1981). Filmways. D: Tony Maylam. S: Peter Lawrence, Bob Weinstein. C: Brian Matthews, Leah Ayres, Brian Backer, Larry Joshua.

Car, The (1977). Universal. D: Elliot Silverstein. S: Dennis Shryack, Michael Butler, Lane Slate. C: James Brolin, John Marley, R. G. Armstrong.

Carrie (1976). United Artists. D: Brian De Palma. S: Lawrence D. Cohen. From the novel by Stephen King. C: Sissy Spacek, Piper Laurie, Amy Irving, William Katt, Nancy Allen, P. J. Soles, John Travolta.

Cat People (1982). Universal. D: Paul Schrader. S: Alan Ormsby. From a story by DeWitt Bodeen. C: Nastassia Kinski, Malcolm McDowell, John Heard, Annette O'Toole, Ruby Dee.

Cat's Eye (1985). MGM/United Artists. D: Lewis Teague. S: Stephen King. C: Drew Barrymore, Candy Clark, Joe Cortese, Robert Hays.

Changeling, The (1980). Associated Film. D: Peter Medak. S: William Gray, Diana Maddox. C: George C. Scott, Trish Van Devere, Barry Morse, Melvyn Douglas.

Children of the Corn (1984). New World. D: Fritz Kiersch. S: George Goldsmith. From the story by Stephen King. C: Peter Horton, Linda Hamilton, R. G. Armstrong.

Christine (1983). Columbia. D: John Carpenter. S: Bill Phillips. From the novel by Stephen King. C: Keith Gordon, John Stockwell, Alexandra Paul, Robert Prosky, Harry Dean Stanton.

Company of Wolves, The (1985). ITC Entertainment. D: Neil Jordan. S: Neil Jordan, Angela Carter. From a story by Angela Carter. C: Angela Lansbury, Graham Crowden, Sarah Patterson, Micha Bergese.

Count Dracula (1977). BBC-PBS TV. D: Philip Saville. S: Gerald Savory. From the novel by Bram Stoker. C: Louis Jourdan, Frank Findlay, Judi Bowker, Susan Penhaligon, Jack Shepard.

Creepshow (1982). Laurel/Warner Brothers. D: George A. Romero. S: Stephen King. C: Hal Holbrook, Adrienne Barbeau, Fritz Weaver, Leslie Nielsen, Carrie Nye, E. G. Marshall, Ed Harris, Stephen King, Ted Danson, Viveca Lindfors.

Crowhaven Farm (1970). ABC-TV. D: Walter Grauman. S: John McGreevey. C: Hope Lange, Paul Burke, Lloyd Bochner, John Carradine.

Cry for the Strangers (1982). MGM/CBS TV. D: Peter Medak. From the novel by John Saul. C: Patrick Duffy, Brian Keith, Cindy Pickett, Lawrence Pressman.

Cujo (1983). Warner Brothers. D: Lewis Teague. S: Don Carlos Dunaway, Lauren Currier. From the novel by Stephen King. C: Dee Wallace, Danny Pinatauro, Daniel Hugh-Kelly, Christopher Stone, Ed Lauter.

Curse of the Black Widow (1977). ABC-TV. D: Dan Curtis. S: Robert Blees, Earl W. Wallace. C: Tony Franciosa, Donna Mills, Patty Duke Astin.

Damien—Omen II (1978). Twentieth Century-Fox. D: Don Taylor. S: Stanley Mann, Michael Hodges. C: William Holden, Lee Grant, Robert Foxworth, Jonathan Scott-Taylor.

Dark Secret of Harvest Home, The (1978). NBC-TV. D: Leo Penn. S: Jack Guss, Charles E. Israel. From the novel, *Harvest Home,* by Thomas Tryon. C: Bette Davis, David Ackroyd, Joanna Miles, John Calvin.

Daughter of the Mind (1969). ABC-TV/Twentieth Century-Fox. D: Walter Grauman. S: Luther Davis. From the novel, *The Hand of Mary Constable,* by Paul Gallico. C: Ray Milland, Gene Tierney, Don Murray, George Macready.

Dawn of the Dead (1979). Laurel/United Film. D: George A. Romero. S: George A. Romero. C: David Emge, Ken Foree, Scott Reiniger, Gaylen Ross.

Day of the Animals (1977). Film Ventures International. D: William Girdler. S: William Norton, Eleanor E. Norton. C: Christopher George, Leslie Nielsen, Lynda Day George.

Dead Zone, The (1983). Paramount. D: David Cronenberg. S: Jeffrey Boam. From the novel by Stephen King. C: Christopher Walken, Brooke Adams, Tom Skerritt, Herbert Lom, Anthony Zerbe, Colleen Dewhurst, Martin Sheen.

Deadly Blessing (1981). United Artists. D: Wes Craven. S: Wes Craven, Glenn M. Benest, Matthew Barr. C: Maren Jensen, Susan Buckner, Sharon Stone, Jeff East, Lisa Hartman.

Deadly Dream (1971). ABC-TV/Universal. D: Alf Kjellin. S: Barry Oringer. C: Lloyd Bridges, Janet Leigh, Leif Erickson, Richard Jaeckel, Carl Betz, Don Stroud.

Death Car on the Freeway (1979). CBS-TV. D: Hal Needham. S: William Wood. C: Shelley Hack, George Hamilton, Frank Gorshin, Peter Graves, Barbara Rush, Dinah Shore.

Death Moon (1978). CBS-TV. D: Bruce Kessler. S: George Schenk. C: Robert Foxworth, Barbara Trentham, France Nuyen.

Demon (God Told Me To) (1977). New World. D: Larry Cohen. S: Larry Cohen. C: Tony Lo Bianco, Deborah Raffin, Sandy Dennis.

Demon Seed (1977). United Artists/MGM. D: Donald Cammell. S: Robert Jaffe, Roger O. Hirson. From the novel by Dean R. Koontz. C: Julie Christie, Fritz Weaver.

Devil and Miss Sarah, The (1971). ABC-TV/Universal. D: Michael Caffey. S: Calvin Clements. C: Gene Barry, James Drury, Janice Rule, Donald Moffat.

Devil Dog: The Hound from Hell (1978). Landers-Roberts-Zeitman (TV). D: Curtis Harrington. S: Stephen Karpf, Elinor Karpf. C: Richard Crenna, Yvette Mimieux, Kim Richards, Ike Eisenmann, Victor Jory, Martine Beswick.

Devil's Daughter, The (1973). Paramount (TV). D: Jeannot Szwarc. S: Colin

Higgins. C: Belinda Montgomery, Shelley Winters, Robert Foxworth, Joseph Cotten, Jonathan Frid.

Don't Be Afraid of the Dark (1973). ABC-TV. D: John Newland. S: Nigel McKeand. C: Kim Darby, Jim Hutton, Barbara Anderson, William Demarest.

Don't Go in the House (1980). Film Ventures International. D: Joseph Ellison. S: Ellen Hammill, J. Masefield. C: Dan Grimaldi, Robert Osth.

Don't Look Now (1973). Paramount. D: Nicolas Roeg. S: Allan Scott, Chris Bryant. From the story by Daphne du Maurier. C: Donald Sutherland, Julie Christie, Hilary Mason.

Dracula (1973). CBS-TV. D: Dan Curtis. S: Richard Matheson. From the novel by Bram Stoker. C: Jack Palance, Simon Ward, Nigel Davenport, Fiona Lewis.

Dracula (1979). Universal. D: John Badham. S: W. D. Richter. From the novel by Bram Stoker and *Dracula: The Vampire Play,* by Hamilton Deane and John L. Balderston. C: Frank Langella, Laurence Olivier, Donald Pleasence, Kate Nelligan.

Dressed to Kill (1980). Filmways. D: Brian De Palma. S: Brian De Palma. C: Michael Caine, Angie Dickinson, Nancy Allen, Keith Gordon.

Duel (1971). ABC-TV. D: Steven Spielberg. S: Richard Matheson. C: Dennis Weaver.

Embryo (1976). Cine Artists. D: Ralph Nelson. S: Anita Doohan, Jack W. Thomas. C: Rock Hudson, Diane Ladd, Barbara Carrera, Roddy McDowell.

Entity, The (1983). Twentieth Century-Fox. D: Sidney J. Furie. S: Frank De Felitta. From the novel by Frank De Felitta. C: Barbara Hershey, Ron Silver, Jacqueline Brooks, David Lablosa, George Coe.

Exorcist, The (1973). Warner Brothers. D: William Friedkin. S: William Peter Blatty. From the novel by William Peter Blatty. C: Linda Blair, Max Von Sydow, Ellen Burstyn, Jason Miller, Lee J. Cobb.

Exorcist II: The Heretic (1977). Warner Brothers. D: John Boorman. S: William Goodhart. C: Linda Blair, Richard Burton, Louise Fletcher, Max Von Sydow, Paul Henreid, James Earl Jones.

Eyes of a Stranger (1981). Warner Brothers. D: Ken Wiederhorn. S: Mark Jackson, E. L. Bloom. C: Lauren Tewes, John Di Santi, Jennifer Jason Leigh.

Eyes of Laura Mars (1978). Columbia. D: Irvin Kershner. S: John Carpenter, David Z. Goodman. C: Faye Dunaway, Tommy Lee Jones, Brad Dourif, Rene Auberjonois, Raul Julia.

Fade to Black (1980). American Cinema. D: Vernon Zimmerman. S: Vernon Zimmerman. C: Dennis Christopher, Linda Kerridge, Tim Thomerson.

Fear No Evil (1969). NBC-TV/Universal. D: Paul Wendkos. S: Richard Alan Simmons. C: Louis Jourdan, Bradford Dillman, Lynda Day, Carroll O'Connor.

Final Conflict, The (1981). Twentieth Century-Fox. D: Graham Baker. S: Andrew Birkin. C: Sam Neill, Rossano Brazzi, Don Gordon, Lisa Harrow.

Firestarter (1984). Universal. D: Mark L. Lester. S: Stanley Mann. From the novel by Stephen King. C: Drew Barrymore, David Keith, George C. Scott, Martin Sheen, Art Carney, Louise Fletcher.

Fog, The (1980). Avco-Embassy. D: John Carpenter. S: John Carpenter and Debra Hill. C: Adrienne Barbeau, Hal Holbrook, Jamie Lee Curtis, Janet Leigh.

Fourth Man, The (1984). Verenigde Nederlandsche. D: Paul Verhoeven. S: Gerard Soeteman. From the novel by Gerard Reve. C: Jeroen Krabbę, Renée Soutendijk.

Frenzy (1972). Universal. D: Alfred Hitchcock. S: Anthony Shaffer. From the novel, *Goodbye Piccadilly, Farewell Leicester Square,* by Arthur La Bern. C: Jon Finch, Barry Foster, Barbara Leigh-Hunt, Anna Massey.

Friday the 13th (1980). Paramount. D: Sean S. Cunningham. S: Victor Miller. C: Adrienne King, Harry Crosby, Betsy Palmer, Mark Nelson.

Friday the 13th Part 2 (1981). Paramount. D: Steve Miner. S: Ron Kurz. C: Amy Steel, John Furey, Adrienne King, Warrington Gillette.

Friday the 13th Part 3 (1982). Paramount. D: Steve Miner. S: Martin Kitrosser, Carol Watson. C: Dana Kimmell, Paul Kratka, Tracie Savage, Jeffrey Rogers.

Friday the 13th—The Final Chapter (1984). Paramount. D: Joseph Zito. S: Barney Cohen. C: Crispin Glover, Kimberly Beck, Barbara Howard.

Frogs (1972). American International. D: George McCowan. S: Robert Hutchinson, Robert Blees. C: Ray Milland, Sam Elliott, Joan Van Ark, Adam Roarke, William Smith.

Funhouse, The (1981). Universal. D: Tobe Hooper. S: Larry Block. C: Elizabeth Berridge, Cooper Huckabee, Miles Chapin, Sylvia Miles, William Finley, Wayne Doba, Kevin Conway.

Fury, The (1978). Twentieth Century-Fox. D: Brian De Palma. S: John Farris. From the novel by John Farris. C: Kirk Douglas, John Cassavetes, Carrie Snodgrass, Charles Durning, Amy Irving, William Finley.

Gargoyles (1972). CBS-TV. D: B. W. L. Norton. S: Stephen Karpf, Elinor Karpf. C: Cornell Wilde, Jennifer Salt, Grayson Hall, Bernie Casey.

Ghost of Flight 401, The (1978). NBC-TV. D: Steven H. Stern. S: Robert M. Young. From the book by John G. Fuller. C: Ernest Borgnine, Kim Basinger, Robert F. Lyons, Gary Lockwood.

Ghost Story (1981). Universal. D: John Irvin. S: Lawrence D. Cohen. From the novel by Peter Straub. C: Fred Astaire, Melvyn Douglas, Douglas Fairbanks, Jr., John Houseman, Craig Wasson, Alice Krige.

Ghostbusters (1984). Columbia. D: Ivan Reitman. S: Dan Ackroyd, Harold Ramis. C: Dan Ackroyd, Bill Murray, Harold Ramis, Sigourney Weaver, Rick Moranis.

Ghoulies (1985). Empire. D: Luca Bercovici. S: Luca Bercovici, Jefery Levy. C: Peter Liapis, Lisa Pelikan.

Good Against Evil (1977). ABC-TV. D: Paul Wendkos. S: Jimmy Sangster. C: Dack Rambo, Elyssa Davalos, Richard Lynch, Dan O'Herlihy.

Graduation Day (1981). IFI/Scope III. D: Herb Freed. S: Herb Freed, Anne Marisse. C: Christopher George, E. J. Peaker, E. D. Murphy.

Gremlins (1984). Warner Brothers. D: Joe Dante. S: Chris Columbus. C: Zach Galligan, Phoebe Cates, Hoyt Axton.

Halloween (1978). Compass International. D: John Carpenter. S: John Carpenter. C: Jamie Lee Curtis, Donald Pleasence, Nancy Loomis, P. J. Soles, Charles Cyphers, Nick Castle.

Halloween II (1981). Universal. D: Rick Rosenthal. S: John Carpenter, Debra Hill. C: Jamie Lee Curtis, Donald Pleasence, Charles Cyphers.

Halloween III: Season of the Witch (1983). Universal. D: Tommy Lee Wallace. S: Tommy Lee Wallace. C: Tom Atkins, Stacy Nelkin, Dan O'Herlihy, Ralph Strait.

Happy Birthday to Me (1981). Columbia. D: J. Lee Thompson. S: John Saxton, Peter Jobin, Timothy Bond. C: Melissa Sue Anderson, Glenn Ford, Tracy Bregman.

Haunting of Julia, The (1976). Discovery. D: Richard Loncraine. S: H. B. Davenport, Dave Humphries. From the novel, *Julia,* by Peter Straub. C: Mia Farrow, Keir Dullea, Tom Conti.

Haunting Passion, The (1984). NBC-TV. D: John Korty. S: Michael Berk, Douglas Schwartz. C: Jane Seymour, Gerard McRaney, Millie Perkins, Ruth Nelson.

He Knows You're Alone (1980). United Artists/MGM. D: Armand Mastroianni. S: Scott Parker. C: Don Scardino, Caitlin O'Heaney, Tom Rolfing.

Hearse, The (1980). Crown International. D: George Bowers. S: Bill Bleich. C: Trish Van Devere, Joseph Cotten, David Gautreaux, Donald Hotton.

Hell Night (1981). Compass International. D: Tom De Simone. S: Randolph Feldman. C: Linda Blair, Vincent Van Patten, Peter Barton, Kevin Brophy.

Helter Skelter (1976). Lorimar (TV). D: Tom Gries. S: J. P. Miller. From the book by Vincent Bugliosi. C: George DiCenzo, Steve Railsback, Nancy Wolfe, Marilyn Burns, Christina Hart.

Hills Have Eyes, The (1977). Vanguard. D: Wes Craven. S: Wes Craven. C: John Steadman, Janus Blythe, Arthur King, Russ Grieve.

House of Dark Shadows (1970). MGM. D: Dan Curtis. S: Sam Hill, Gordon Russell. Based on the television series "Dark Shadows." C: Joan Bennett, Jonathan Frid, Grayson Hall, Kathryn Leigh Scott.

House That Would Not Die, The (1970). ABC-TV. D: John Llewellyn Moxey. S: Henry Farrell. From the novel, *Ammie, Come Home,* by Barbara Michaels. C: Barbara Stanwyck, Michael Anderson, Jr., Doreen Land, Richard Egan.

Howling, The (1981). Avco Embassy. D: Joe Dante. S: John Sayles, T. H. Winkless. From the novel by Gary Brandner. C: Dee Wallace, Patrick Macnee, Denis Dugan, John Carradine, Slim Pickens.

Humanoids from the Deep (1980). New World. D: Barbara Peeters. S: Frederick James. C: Doug McClure, Ann Turkel, Vic Morrow, Cindy Weintraub.

Humongous (1981). Embassy Pictures. D: Paul Lynch. S: William Gray. C: Janet Julian, David Wallace, Janit Baldwin, John Wildman.

Hunger, The (1983). MGM/United Artists. D: Tony Scott. S: Ivan Davis, Michael Thomas. From the novel by Whitley Streiber. C: Catherine Deneuve, David Bowie, Susan Sarandon, Cliff DeYoung.

I Spit on Your Grave (1978). Cinemagic. D: Meir Zarchi. S: Meir Zarchi. C: Camille Keaton, Eron Tabor, Richard Pace, Anthony Nichols.

I, Desire (1982). Columbia/ABC-TV. D: John Llewellyn Moxey. S: Bob Foster. C: David Naughton, Dorian Harewood, Brad Dourif, Marilyn Jones.

Images (1972). Columbia. D: Robert Altman. S: Robert Altman. C: Susannah York, Marcel Bozzuffi, Rene Auberjonois.

Initiation of Sarah, The (1978). ABC-TV. D: Robert Day. S: Don Ingalls, Kenette

Gfeller, Carol Saraceno. C: Kay Lenz, Tony Bill, Kathryn Crosby, Shelley Winters.

Invasion of the Body Snatchers (1978). United Artists. D: Phil Kaufman. S: W. D. Richter. From the novel by Jack Finney. C: Donald Sutherland, Leonard Nimoy, Brooke Adams, Jeff Goldblum, Veronica Cartwright.

Invitation to Hell (1984). ABC-TV. D: Wes Craven. S: Richard Rothstein. C: Robert Urich, Joanna Cassidy, Susan Lucci, Kevin McCarthy.

It Lives Again (1978). Warner Brothers. D: Larry Cohen. S: Larry Cohen. C: Frederic Forrest, Kathleen Lloyd, John P. Ryan, John Marley.

It's Alive (1973). Warner Brothers. D: Larry Cohen. S: Larry Cohen. C: John Ryan, Sharon Farrell, Andrew Duggan, Guy Stockwell.

Jaws (1975). Universal. D: Steven Spielberg. S: Peter Benchley, Carl Gottlieb. From the novel by Peter Benchley. C: Roy Scheider, Robert Shaw, Richard Dreyfuss.

Jaws 2 (1978). Universal. D: Jeannot Szwarc. S: Carl Gottlieb, Howard Sackler, Dorothy Tristan. C: Roy Scheider, Lorraine Gray, Murray Hamilton, Barry Coe.

Keep, The (1983). Paramount. D: Michael Mann. S: Michael Mann. From the novel by F. Paul Wilson. C: Scott Glenn, Ian McKellen, Alberta Watson, Jurgen Prochnow.

Killdozer (1974). Universal (TV). D: Jerry London. S: Theodore Sturgeon, Ed MacKillap. Based on the novella by Theodore Sturgeon. C: Clint Walker, James Wainwright, Carl Betz, Neville Brand, Robert Urich.

Last House on the Left (1972). Hallmark/American International. D: Wes Craven. S: Wes Craven. C: David Alex Hess, Lucy Grantham, Sandra Cassell, Marc Sheffler.

Last Wave, The (1977). World Northal. D: Peter Weir. S: Peter Weir, Tony Morphett, Petru Popescu. C: Richard Chamberlain, Olivia Hamnett, David Gulpilil.

Lathe of Heaven, The (1980). PBS-TV. D: David Loxton, Fred Barzyk. S: Roger E. Swaybill, Diane English. From the novel by Ursula LeGuin. C: Bruce Davison, Kevin Conway, Margaret Avery.

Lifeforce (1985). Tri-Star/Cannon. D: Tobe Hooper. S: Dan O'Bannon, Don Jakoby. From the novel, *The Space Vampires,* by Colin Wilson. C: Steve Railsback, Peter Firth.

Look What's Happened to Rosemary's Baby (1976). ABC-TV. D: Sam O'Steen. S: Anthony Wilson. C: Ruth Gordon, George Maharis, Ray Milland, Patty Duke Astin, Stephen McHattie.

Maniac (1981). Analysis/Magnum. D: William Lustig. S: C. A. Rosenberg, Joe Spinnell. C: Joe Spinnell, Caroline Munro, Gail Lawrence, Tom Savini.

Martin (1976). Laurel. D: George A. Romero. S: George A. Romero. C: John Amplas, Lincoln Maazel, Christine Forrest, Sarah Venable.

Maximum Overdrive (1986). DeLaurentiis Entertainment. D: Stephen King. S: Stephen King. From his story. C: Emilio Estevez, Pat Hingle, Laura Harrington.

Mephisto Waltz, The (1971). Twentieth Century-Fox. D: Paul Wendkos. S: Ben Maddow. From the novel by Fred Mustard Stewart. C: Alan Alda, Jacqueline Bisset, Curt Jurgens, Barbara Parkins.

Moon of the Wolf (1972). ABC-TV. D: Daniel Petrie. S: Alvin Sapinsley. From the novel by Leslie H. Whitten. C: David Janssen, Barbara Rush, Bradford Dillman.

Mortuary (1981). Artists Releasing. D: Howard Avedis. S: Howard Avedis, Marlene Schmidt. C: Mary McDonough, Lynda Day George, Christopher George, Bill Paxton.

Motel Hell (1980). United Artists. D: Kevin Connor. S: Robert Jaffe, Steven-Charles Jaffe. C: Rory Calhoun, Paul Linke, Nancy Parsons, Nina Axelrod.

My Bloody Valentine (1981). Paramount. D: George Mihalka. S: John Beaird. C: Paul Kelman, Lori Hallier, Neil Affleck.

Nightcomers, The (1971). Arco Embassy. D: Michael Winner. S: Michael Hastings. C: Marlon Brando, Stephanie Beacham, Thora Mird.

Night Cries (1978). ABC-TV. D: Richard Lang. S: Brian Taggert. C: Susan Saint James, Michael Parks, William Conrad.

Night of the Living Dead (1968). Image 10/Walter Reade. D: George A. Romero. S: John A. Russo, George A. Romero. C: Judith O'Dea, Duane Jones.

Night School (1980). Paramount. D: Ken Hughes. S: Ruth Avergon. C: Rachel Ward, Leonard Mann, Drew Snyder, Joseph R. Sicari.

Night Slaves (1970). ABC-TV. D: Ted Post. S: Everett Chambers, Robert Specht. From the novel by Jerry Sohl. C: James Franciscus, Lee Grant, Scott Marlowe, Andrew Prine, Leslie Nielsen.

Night Stalker, The (1972). ABC-TV. D: John L. Moxey. S: Richard Matheson. C: Darren McGavin, Carol Lynley, Simon Oakland, Ralph Meeker.

Night Strangler, The (1973). ABC-TV. D: Dan Curtis. S: Richard Matheson. C: Darren McGavin, JoAnn Pflug, Simon Oakland, Scott Brady, Wally Cox.

Nightmare on Elm Street, A (1984). New Line. D: Wes Craven. S: Wes Craven. C: Amanda Wyss, Heather Langenkamp, Ronee Blakely.

Norliss Tapes, The (1973). NBC-TV. D: Dan Curtis. S: William F. Nolan. C: Roy Thinnes, Don Porter, Angie Dickinson, Claude Akins.

Nosferatu the Vampyre (1979). Twentieth Century-Fox. D: Werner Herzog. S: Werner Herzog. C: Klaus Kinski, Bruno Ganz, Isabelle Adjani.

Of Unknown Origin (1983). Warner Brothers. D: George Pan Cosmatos. S: Brian Taggert. From the novel, *The Visitor,* by Chauncey Parker III. C: Peter Weller, Jennifer Dale, Lawrence Dane.

Omen, The (1976). Twentieth Century-Fox. D: Richard Donner. S: David Seltzer. C: Gregory Peck, Lee Remick, David Warner.

Other, The (1972). Fox. D: Robert Mulligan. S: Thomas Tryon. From the novel by Thomas Tryon. C: Uta Hagen, Diana Muldaur, Chris Udvarnoky, Martin Udvarnoky.

Picnic at Hanging Rock (1975). Sugarfoot Productions. D: Peter Weir. S: Cliff Green. From the novel by Joan Lindsay. C: Rachel Roberts, Dominic Guard, Vivean Gray, Helen Morse.

Piranha (1978). New World/United Artists. D: Joe Dante. S: John Sayles. C: Bradford Dillman, Heather Menzies, Kevin McCarthy, Keenan Wynn.

Poltergeist (1982). MGM/United Artists. D: Tobe Hooper. S: Steven Spielberg, Michael Grais, Mark Victor. C: Craig T. Nelson, Jobeth Williams, Beatrice Straight, Dominique Dunne.

Possessed, The (1977). NBC-TV. D: Jerry Thorpe. S: John S. Young. C: James Farentino, Joan Hackett, Harrison Ford, Eugene Roche.

Possession of Joel Delaney, The (1972). Paramount. D: Waris Hussein. S: Matt Robinson, Grimes Grice. From the novel by Ramona Stewart. C: Perry King, Shirley MacLaine, Michael Holdern, David Elliott.

Prom Night (1980). Avco Embassy. D: Paul Lynch. S: William Gray. C: Leslie Nielsen, Jamie Lee Curtis, Casey Stevens.

Prophecy (1979). Paramount. D: John Frankenheimer. S: David Seltzer. C: Talia Shire, Robert Foxworth, Armand Assante, Richard Dysart.

Prowler, The (1981). Sandhurst. D: Joseph Zito. S: Glenn Leopold, Neal F. Barbera. C: Vicki Dawson, Christopher Goutman, Cindy Weintraub, Farley Granger.

Psycho II (1983). Universal. D: Richard Franklin. S: Tom Holland. C: Anthony Perkins, Vera Miles, Meg Tilly, Robert Loggia, Dennis Franz, Hugh Gillin.

Q—The Winged Serpent (1982). United Film. D: Larry Cohen. S: Larry Cohen. C: Michael Moriarty, Candy Clark, David Carradine, Richard Roundtree.

Rabid (1977). New World. D: David Cronenberg. S: David Cronenberg. C: Marilyn Chambers, Frank Moore, Joe Silver.

Re-Animator (1985). Empire. D: Stuart Gordon. S: Dennis Paoli, William J. Norris, Stuart Gordon. C: Bruce Abbott, Barbara Crampton, David Gale.

Return of Count Yorga, The (1971). American International. D: Bob Kelljean. S: Bob Kelljean, Yvonne Wilder. C: Robert Quarry, Mariette Hartley.

Revenge of the Stepford Wives (1980). NBC-TV. D: Robert Fuest. S: David Wiltse. C: Sharon Gless, Julie Kavner, Arthur Hill, Don Johnson.

Ritual of Evil (1970). NBC-TV. D: Robert Day. S: Robert Presnell, Jr. C: Louis Jourdan, Anne Baxter, Diane Hyland, John McMartin.

Rosemary's Baby (1968). Paramount. D: Roman Polanski. S: Roman Polanski. From the novel by Ira Levin. C: Mia Farrow, John Cassavetes, Ruth Gordon, Sidney Blackmur, Maurice Evans, Ralph Bellamy.

Ruby (1977). Dimension. D: Curtis Harrington. S: George Edwards, Barry Schneider. C: Piper Laurie, Stuart Whitman, Roger Davis, Fred Kohler.

'Salem's Lot (1979). CBS-TV. D: Tobe Hooper. S: Paul Monash. From the novel by Stephen King. C: David Soul, James Mason, Lance Kerwin, Reggie Nalder, Bonnie Bedelia.

Satan's School for Girls (1973). Spelling-Goldberg (TV). D: David Lowell Rich. S: Arthur A. Ross. C: Pamela Franklin, Kate Jackson, Jo Van Fleet, Roy Thinnes.

Satan's Triangle (1975). ABC-TV. D: Sutton Roley. S: William Read Woodfield. C: Kim Novak, Doug McClure, Alejandro Rey, Ed Lauter.

Savage Bees, The (1976). NBC-TV. D: Bruce Geller. S: Guerdon Trueblood. C: Ben Johnson, Michael Parks, Gretchen Corbett, Paul Hecht.

Savage Harvest (1981). Twentieth Century-Fox. D: Robert Collins. S: Robert Blees, Robert Collins. C: Tom Skerritt, Michelle Phillips, Shawn Stevens, Ann-Marie Martin.

Scanners (1981). Avco Embassy. D: David Cronenberg. S: David Cronenberg. C: Stephen Lack, Jennifer O'Neill, Patrick McGoohan, Michael Ironside.

Scream of the Wolf (1974). ABC-TV. D: Dan Curtis. S: Richard Matheson. C: Peter Graves, Clint Walker, Philip Carey, JoAnn Pflug.

Scream Pretty Peggy (1973). Universal (TV). D: Gordon Hessler. S: Jimmy Sangster, Arthur Hoffe. C: Bette Davis, Ted Bessell, Sian Barbara Allen.

Sender, The (1982). Paramount. D: Roger Christian. S: Thomas Baum. C: Kathryn Harrold, Zeljko Ivanek, Shirley Knight, Paul Freeman.

She Waits (1972). CBS-TV. D: Delbert Mann. S: Art Wallace. C: Patty Duke, David McCallum, Dorothy McGuire.

Shining, The (1980). Warner Brothers. D: Stanley Kubrick. S: Stanley Kubrick, Diane Johnson. From the novel by Stephen King. C: Jack Nicholson, Shelley Duvall, Danny Lloyd, Scatman Crothers.

Silver Bullet (1985). Paramount. D: Daniel Attias. S: Stephen King. From his novella, *Cycle of the Werewolf*. C: Gary Busey, Everett McGill.

Sins of Dorian Gray, The (1983). ABC-TV. D: Tony Maylam. S: Ken August and Peter Lawrence. C: Belinda Bauer, Anthony Perkins, Joseph Bottoms, Michael Ironside.

Sisters (1973). American International. D: Brian De Palma. S: Brian De Palma, Louisa Rose. C: Margot Kidder, Jennifer Salt, Charles Durning.

Slumber Party Massacre (1982). Santa Fe Productions. D: Amy Jones. S: Rita Mae Brown. C: Michele Michaels, Robin Stille, Michael Villela, Andre Honore.

Snowbeast (1977). NBC-TV. D: Herb Wallerstein. S: Joseph Stefano. C: Bo Svenson, Yvette Mimieux, Clint Walker, Robert Logan.

Someone Is Watching Me! (1978). Warner Brothers (TV). D. John Carpenter. S: John Carpenter. C: Laura Hutton, David Birney, Adrienne Barbeau, Charles Cyphers.

Something Evil (1972). CBS-TV. D: Steven Spielberg. S: Robert Clouse. C: Sandy Dennis, Darren McGavin, Ralph Bellamy, Jeff Corey.

Something Wicked This Way Comes (1983). Buena Vista. D: Jack Clayton. S: Ray Bradbury. From the novel by Ray Bradbury. C: Jason Robards, Jonathan Pryce, Diane Ladd, Pam Grier.

Spectre (1977). NBC-TV. D: Clive Donner. S: Gene Rodenberry, Samuel Peeples. C: Robert Culp, Gig Young, John Hurt, Ann Bell.

Spell, The (1977). NBC-TV. D: Lee Philips. S: Brian Taggart. C: Lee Grant, James Olson, Susan Myers.

Strange Behavior (1981). World Northal. D: Michael Laughlin. S: Michael Laughlin, William Condon. C: Louise Fletcher, Michael Murphy, Dan Shor, Fiona Lewis.

Strange Invaders (1983). Orion. D: Michael Laughlin. S: Michael Laughlin, William Condon. C: Paul LeMat, Nancy Allen, Diana Scarwid, Louise Fletcher, Wallace Shawn, Fiona Lewis, Kenneth Tobey.

Stranger in Our House (1978). Inter Planetary (TV). D: Wes Craven. S: Glenn M. Benest, Max A. Keller. From the novel, *Summer of Fear,* by Lois Duncan. C: Linda Blair, Lee Purcell, Carol Lawrence, Jeff East.

Stranger Within, The (1974). ABC-TV. D: Lee Philips. S: Richard Matheson. C: Barbara Eden, George Grizzard, Nehemiah Persoff.

Stuff, The (1985). New World. D: Larry Cohen. S: Larry Cohen. C: Michael Moriarty, Garrett Morris, Andrea Marcovicci.

Swarm, The (1978). Warner Brothers. D: Irwin Allen. S: Stirling Silliphant. From the novel by Arthur Herzog. C: Michael Caine, Katherine Ross, Richard Widmark, Richard Chamberlain, Olivia de Havilland.

Targets (1968). Paramount. D: Peter Bogdanovich. S: Peter Bogdanovich. C: Boris Karloff, Tim O'Kelly, James Brown, Sandy Baron, Peter Bogdanovich.

Tenant, The (1976). Paramount. D: Roman Polanski. S: Roman Polanski, Gerard Brach. From the novel, *La Locataire Chimerique,* by Roland Topor. C: Roman Polanski, Isabelle Adjani, Shelley Winters, Melvyn Douglas.

Terminator, The (1984). Orion. D: James Cameron. S: James Cameron, Gale Anne Hurd. C: Arnold Schwarzenegger, Michael Biehn, Linda Hamilton, Paul Winfield.

Terror Train (1980). Twentieth Century-Fox. D: Roger Spottiswoode. S: T. Y. Drake. C: Ben Johnson, Jamie Lee Curtis, Timothy Webber, David Copperfield.

Texas Chain Saw Massacre, The (1974). New Line/Bryanston. D: Tobe Hooper. S: Tobe Hooper, Kim Henkel. C: Marilyn Burns, Allen Danziger, Gunnar Hanse.

Thing, The (1982). Universal. D: John Carpenter. S: Bill Lancaster. From the story, "Who Goes There?" by John W. Campbell, Jr. C: Kurt Russell, A. Wilford Brimsley, T. K. Carter, David Clennon, David Keith.

Transylvania 6-5000 (1986). New World. D: Rudy DeLuca. S: Rudy DeLuca. C: Jeff Goldblum, Ed Begley, Jr., Joseph Bologna.

Troll (1986). Empire. D: John Buechler. S: Ed Naha. C: Michael Moriarty, Shelley Hack, Noah Hathaway.

Vampire (1979). ABC-TV. D: E. W. Swackhammer. S: Steven Bochco, Michael Kozoll. C: Jason Miller, E. G. Marshall, Richard Lynch, Kathryn Harrold, Jessica Walter.

Velvet Vampire, The (1971). New World. D: Stephanie Rothman. S: Maurice Jules, Stephanie Rothman. C: Michael Blodgett, Sherry Miles.

Videodrome (1983). Universal. D: David Cronenberg. S: David Cronenberg. C: James Woods, Deborah Harry, Sonja Smits, Peter Dvorsky.

Visiting Hours (1982). Twentieth Century-Fox. D: Jean-Claude Lord. S: Brian Taggert. C: Lee Grant, William Shatner, Michael Ironside, Linda Purl.

When a Stranger Calls (1979). Columbia. D: Fred Walton. S: Fred Walton, Steve Feke. C: Carol Kane, Charles Durning, Colleen Dewhurst, Tony Beckley.

When Michael Calls (1972). ABC-TV. D: Philip Leacock. S: James Bridges. From the novel by John Farris. C: Ben Gazzara, Elizabeth Ashley, Michael Douglas.

Wolfen (1981). Warner Brothers/Orion. D: Michael Wadleigh. S: Michael Wadleigh, David Eyre. From the novel by Whitley Streiber. C: Albert Finney, Edward James Olmos, Gregory Hines, Diane Venora.

Annotated Bibliography

This annotated bibliography covers books and articles published since 1968 that focus on specific horror films released during this period, explore general issues concerning horror as a popular film genre, or examine the history of the American horror film. (Items preceded by an * are reprinted in this collection.) I have attempted to be as comprehensive as possible, with the following exceptions.

(1) For the most part, I have not cited reviews of individual films published in newspapers, trade magazines, film journals, or general interest magazines, and I have included only a few particularly informative examples of the many interviews that have been published in recent years. Virtually all of the major movie reviewers, like Pauline Kael and Andrew Sarris, have on occasion discussed highly publicized, big-budget horror movies and the films of directors like Brian De Palma and Stanley Kubrick. Of particular interest are Carrie Rickey's reviews in the *Village Voice* and the Boston *Herald,* which chart with wit and insight the evolution of the genre in the late 1970s and 1980s. For a more complete listing of reviews and interviews with individual filmmakers and actors, see two indispensable reference works, the *International Index to Film Periodicals* and *Film Literature Index.*

(2) I have included only a few representative examples of the type of articles that appear in French film periodicals and in American "fanzines" like *Cinéfantastique, Fangoria, Gore Creatures, Midnight Marquee, Cinema Macabre,* and *Fantastic Films.* For all their reliance on industry gossip and recycled press releases and their fetishization of special effects, these fanzines often contain informative interviews and a good deal of interesting material about the production of individual films.

(3) Though I have listed works that examine the history of the genre or that compare the classic and the contemporary horror film, I have omitted the vast number of recent articles and books that are *solely* devoted to *Psycho, The Birds, Peeping Tom, Vampyr,* and other horror films that were released before 1968 and to James Whale and other directors of classic horror films.

"The Filming of *Altered States.*" *Cinéfantastique* 11, no. 2 (Fall 1981):16-37. Detailed discussion of the production of *Altered States.*

Allen, Tom. "Knight of the Living Dead." *Village Voice,* 23 Apr. 1979, 1, 44-46. Romero's career as an independent filmmaker, with particular reference to *Dawn of the Dead.*

Armstrong, Michael. "Some Like It Chilled." *Films and Filming* 17 (Feb. 1971):28–34; (Mar. 1971):32–37; (Apr. 1971):37–42; (May 1971):77–82. Surveys the genre in terms of "basic horror themes" like the undead and "metamorphosis."

Asselle, Giovanna, and Behroze Gandhy. "*Dressed to Kill.*" *Screen* 23, no. 3–4 (Sept.–Oct. 1982):137–43. Examines the response of feminists and film critics to *Dressed to Kill.*

Babington, Bruce. "Twice a Victim: Carrie Meets the BFI." *Screen* 24, no. 2 (1983):4–18. Challenges the reductive, one-sided reading of *Carrie* offered by Serafina Bathrick and by the Educational Department of the British Film Institute.

Barker, Martin, ed. *The Video Nasties: Freedom and Censorship in the Media.* London: Pluto Press, 1984. Collection of essays on the ideological implications of the British Video Recordings bill, which censors violent horror films like *I Spit on Your Grave.*

Bathrick, Serafina Kent. "Ragtime: The Horror of Growing up Female." *Jump Cut* 14 (Mar. 1977):9–10. Critique of the sexist "biologism" and "bewildered fascination with female power" in De Palma's *Carrie.*

Bérard, Yves. "Les morts-vivants." *Avant-Scène du Cinéma* 187 (1 May 1977):23–38. Zombies, vampires, mummies, and other forms of the living dead in horror films.

Beylie, Claude, Jacques Goimard, and Michel Capdenac. "Fantastic Story." *Ecran* 17 (July–Aug. 1973):2–22. Theoretical and critical introduction to the "fantastic" as a genre in American and European film.

Biskind, Peter. "Between the Teeth." *Jump Cut* 9 (Oct.–Dec. 1975):1, 26. Contrasts the "comforting liberalism" and sexual imagery in novel and film versions of *Jaws.*

Boss, Pete. "Vile Bodies and Bad Medicine." *Screen* 27, no. 1 (1986):14–24. The representation of institutionalized medicine, the "fear of technological conspiracy," and the "discourse of bodily destruction" in modern horror.

Bowles, Stephen E. "*The Exorcist* and *Jaws.*" *Literature/Film Quarterly* 4 (1976): 196–214. Extended comparison of *The Exorcist* and *Jaws* as examples of popular filmmaking and as adaptations of best-selling novels.

Braudy, Leo. "Genre and the Resurrection of the Past." In *Shadows of the Magic Lamp: Fantasy and Science Fiction in Film,* edited by George Slusser and Eric S. Rabkin, 1–13. Carbondale: Southern Illinois University Press, 1985. Includes a discussion of how the images and motifs of horror have invaded other contemporary film genres.

Brighton, Lew. "Saturn in Retrograde or The Texas Jump Cut." *Film Journal* 2, no. 4 (1975):24–27. Review of *The Texas Chain Saw Massacre.*

Broeske, Pat H. "Killing Is Alive and Well in Hollywood." *Los Angeles Times,* 2 Sept. 1984, 19–22. Survey of the "gore" film industry.

Brophy, Philip. "Horrality—The Textuality of Contemporary Horror Films." *Screen* 27, no. 1 (1986):2–13. On the distinguishing characteristics of contemporary horror, including its emphasis on the "act of showing" and its "perverse sense of humor."

Brosnan, John. *The Horror People.* New York: New American Library, 1977. Biographical essays on British and American actors, directors, writers, and producers who have worked in the genre. Includes interviews.

Brown, Royal S. "*Dressed to Kill:* Myth and Fantasy in the Horror/Suspense Genre." *Film/Psychology Review* 4 (Summer–Fall 1980):169–82. Violence, sexual stereotypes, narcissism, doubling, and voyeurism in *Dressed to Kill, Carrie,* and other horror films.

Bunnell, Charlene. "The Gothic: A Literary Genre's Transition to Film." In *Planks of Reason,* edited by Barry Keith Grant, 79–100. Metuchen, N.J.: Scarecrow Press, 1984. Elements of gothic literature in two adaptations, *The Haunting* and *The Shining.*

Butler, Ivan. *Horror in the Cinema.* New York: Warner Books, 1970. Descriptive history of the genre through Polanski's *Repulsion,* based on the contrast between "lurid sensationalism" and the "restrained" suggestiveness of "atmospheric" horror.

Campbell, Mary B. "Biological Alchemy and the Films of David Cronenberg." In *Planks of Reason,* edited by Barry Keith Grant, 307–20. Metuchen, N.J.: Scarecrow Press, 1984. Interprets the "fear of the mindlessly autonomous Life Force" in Cronenberg's films in light of the alchemical tradition.

Canby, Vincent. "Chilling Truths about Scaring." *New York Times,* 21 Jan. 1979, sec. 2, 13, 18. The relative merits of three "Hitchcockian" films: *Halloween, The Last Wave,* and *Invasion of the Body Snatchers* (1978).

Carroll, Noel. "Nightmare and the Horror Film: The Symbolic Biology of Fantastic Beings." *Film Quarterly* 34, no. 3 (Spring 1981):16–25. Discusses the "basic plot structures" and the "archaic, conflicting impulses" expressed in the horror film.

Chase, Donald. "The Cult Movie Comes of Age: An Interview with George A. Romero and Richard P. Rubinstein." *Millimeter* 7, no. 10 (Oct. 1979):200–11. Interview on the production and distribution of *Dawn of the Dead.*

Chute, David. "Dante's Inferno." *Film Comment* 20, no. 3 (May–June 1984):22–27. Comedy and horror in *Gremlins* and Dante's other films. Includes an interview with Dante.

Chute, David. "He Came from Within." *Film Comment* 16, no. 2 (Mar.–Apr. 1980):36–39, 42. Science, satire, and sexuality in *The Brood* and Cronenberg's other horror films.

Chute, David. "Tom Savini: Maniac." *Film Comment* 17, no. 4 (July–Aug. 1981): 24–27. Surveys Savini's special effects work in films like *Friday the 13th* and *Dawn of the Dead.*

Cohn, Lawrence. "Horror, Sci-Fi Pix Earn 37% of Rentals." *Variety,* 19 Nov. 1980, 5, 32. Commercial success of horror and science fiction films during the 1970s.

Cook, David A. "American Horror: *The Shining.*" *Literature/Film Quarterly* 12 no. 1 (1984):2–4. America's "murderous system of economic exploitation" as the "true horror" in *The Shining* (1980).

Daniels, Les. *Living in Fear: A History of Horror in the Mass Media.* New York:

Scribner's, 1975. Historical survey of horror in literature, pulp magazines, comic books, radio, television, and film. Includes several classic horror stories.

Dadoun, Roger. "Fetishism in the Horror Film." *Enclitic* 1, no. 2 (1979):39–63. Valuable — and difficult — psychoanalytic study of fetishism and the maternal, principally in classic vampire films.

Davis-Genelli, Lyn, and Tom Davis-Genelli. "*Alien:* A Myth of Survival." *Film/Psychological Review* 4 (Summer–Fall 1980):235–41. *Alien* as a struggle for survival involving the masculine and the feminine "principle."

Derry, Charles. *Dark Dreams: A Psychological History of the Modern Horror Film.* New York: A. S. Barnes and Company, 1977. Surveys three subgenres from the 1960s into the 1970s: the horror of personality, of Armageddon, and of the demonic. Includes several interviews.

Dettman, Bruce, and Michael Bedford. *The Horror Factory: The Horror Films of Universal, 1931–1955.* New York: Gordon Press, 1976. Film-by-film history of Universal's horror films, with plot summaries and evaluative comments.

Dickstein, Morris. "The Aesthetics of Fright." *American Film* 5 (Sept. 1980):32–37, 56–59. The horror film as a "subcultural" genre that addresses and "neutralizes" elemental fears and social anxieties.

*Dillard, R. H. W. "Drawing the Circle: A Devolution of Values in Three Horror Films." *Film Journal* 2, no. 2 (1973):6–35. Detailed examination of the aesthetic and moral values of *Frankenstein* (1931), *The Wolf Man,* and *Night of the Living Dead.*

Dillard, R. H. W. "Even a Man Who Is Pure at Heart: Poetry and Danger in the Horror Film." In *Man and the Movies,* edited by W. R. Robinson, 60–96. Baltimore, Md.: Penguin, 1969. Valuable discussion of classic Hollywood horror films as twentieth-century morality plays in which we encounter the "dark truths of sin and death."

Dillard, R. H. W. *Horror Films.* New York: Monarch Press, 1976. Narrowly focused, but detailed and insightful examination of "moral consciousness" and the "devolution of values" in *Frankenstein* (1931), *The Wolf Man, Night of the Living Dead,* and *Fellini-Satyricon.*

Ebert, Roger. "Why Movie Audiences Aren't Safe Anymore." *American Film* 6, no. 5 (Mar. 1981):54–56. Criticism of *Friday the 13th* and other "women-in-danger" films that encourage the audience to assume the point of view of the "nonspecific male killing force."

Ehlers, Leigh A. "*Carrie:* Book and Film." *Literature/Film Quarterly* 9 (1981):32–39. Contrasts the novel and film versions of *Carrie* in terms of their presentation of rationality and repression.

Evans, Walter. "Monster Movies and Rites of Initiation." *Journal of Popular Film* 4 (1975):124–42. Functional and formal parallels between the initiation rites of premodern societies and movies featuring vampires and other monsters.

Evans, Walter. "Monster Movies: A Sexual Theory." *Journal of Popular Film* 2 (Fall 1973):353–65. Adolescent sexuality and the theme of "horrible and mysterious psychological and physical change" in classic American monster movies.

Everson, William K. *Classics of the Horror Film.* Secaucus, N.J.: Citadel, 1974.

Focuses on the pre-1950 period, emphasizing background information and the aesthetics of suggestion and indirection.

Eyles, Allen, ed. *The House of Horror: The Story of Hammer Films.* London: Lorrimer, 1973. Film-by-film history of Hammer's horror films, with interviews and plot summaries.

Figenshu, Tom. "Screams of a Summer Night." *Film Comment* 15, no. 5 (Sept.-Oct. 1979):49-53. The role of structure, mood, and the creature in *Dracula* (1979), *The Amityville Horror,* and *Alien.*

*Fischer, Lucy, and Marcia Landy. " 'Eyes of Laura Mars': A Binocular Critique." *Screen* 23, no. 3-4 (Sept.-Oct. 1982):4-19. Detailed study of "male-dominated vision," self-reflexivity, and "cultural hostility toward women" in *Eyes of Laura Mars.*

Fisher, Richard. "*Sisters:* A Filmic Critique." *Filmmakers Newsletter* 6 (Sept. 1973): 22-24. Voyeurism, split-screen techniques, and parallels with Hitchcock in *Sisters.*

Fowler, Douglas. "*Alien, The Thing* and the Principles of Terror." *Studies in Popular Culture* 4 (1981):16-23. "Pleasurable terror" and the "primal" struggle for survival in *Alien* and *The Thing.*

Fox, Julian. "The Golden Age of Terror." *Films and Filming* 22 (June 1976): 16-23; (July 1976):18-24; (Aug. 1976):20-24; (Sept. 1976):20-25; (Oct. 1976): 18-25. Surveys horror films from 1930-36, praising them for their stylization, "tactful avoidance of the explicit," skillful direction, and pitiable monsters.

Frentz, Thomas S., and Thomas B. Farrell. "Conversion of America's Consciousness: The Rhetoric of *The Exorcist.*" *Quarterly Journal of Speech* 61, no. 1 (Feb. 1975):40-47. The victory of "transcendent Christian faith" over Positivism in *The Exorcist.*

Friedman, Lester D. " 'Canyons of Nightmare': The Jewish Horror Film." In *Planks of Reason,* edited by Barry Keith Grant, 126-52. Metuchen, N.J.: Scarecrow Press, 1984. Jewish characters as victims and monsters in horror films and *Young Frankenstein* as parodic horror reflecting a "Jewish sense of comic alienation."

Gagne, Paul R. "*Ghost Story:* From Novel to Film." *Cinéfantastique* 12, no. 1 (Feb. 1982):20-39. Discusses the adaptation of Peter Straub's novel *Ghost Story* for the screen.

Gans, Herbert J. "*The Exorcist:* A Devilish Attack on Women." *Social Policy* 5 (May-June 1974):71-73. *The Exorcist* as "an attack on social change," focused in particular on women who attempt to move beyond "traditional roles."

Garel, Alain. "Permanence de Dracula." *Image et Son* 345 (Dec. 1979):12-16. Badham's *Dracula* (1979) in the context of earlier vampire films.

Garis, Mick. "A Panel Discussion of Fear on Film." *Fangoria* 19 (1982): 30-33; 20 (1982):26-29. Transcription of a television program featuring John Landis, John Carpenter, and David Cronenberg.

Giles, Dennis. "Conditions of Pleasure in Horror Cinema." In *Planks of Reason,* edited by Barry Keith Grant, 38-52. Metuchen, N.J.: Scarecrow Press, 1984.

Study of the genre from the point of view of contemporary reception theory, emphasizing the horror film's reliance on "the pleasure of not seeing."

Glut, Donald F. *Classic Movie Monsters.* Metuchen, N.J.: Scarecrow Press, 1978. Encyclopedic survey of the appearances of the wolf man, the mummy, and other classic movie monsters.

Glut, Donald F. *The Dracula Book.* Metuchen, N.J.: Scarecrow Press, 1975. Encyclopedic survey of the various incarnations of Count Dracula in fiction, film, theater, and television.

Glut, Donald F. *The Frankenstein Legend.* Metuchen, N.J.: Scarecrow Press, 1973. Encyclopedic survey of the many versions of the Frankenstein story in literature, film, television, and other media.

Goldstein, Richard. "The Horror! The Horror!" *Village Voice,* 27 Nov. 1984, 77. Contrasts the emphasis on "social disintegration" in modern horror with the reassuring social cohesion in monster movies of the 1950s.

Gordon, Norman G. "Family Structure and Dynamics in De Palma's Horror Films." *Psychoanalytic Review* 70 (Fall 1983):435–42. Psychoanalytic reading of sexual desire and the disintegration of the nuclear family in De Palma's films.

Gordon, Norman G., and Anaruth Gordon. "Controversial Issues in De Palma's *Dressed to Kill.*" *Psychoanalytic Review* 69 (Winter 1982):559–66. De Palma's "bleak, hedonistic view of human nature" and his "typically masculine view of the fusion of sex and violence" in *Dressed to Kill.*

Gordon, Norman G., and Anaruth Gordon. "De Palma's Dreams: Terror and Trauma." *Dreamworks* 3, no. 2 (1983):139–49. Examination of the "dream states" in De Palma's horror films as "cinematic equivalents of the night terror."

Grant, Barry Keith, ed. *Planks of Reason: Essays on the Horror Film.* Metuchen, N.J.: Scarecrow Press, 1984. Important anthology that includes original and reprinted essays on specific classic and modern films and subgenres as well as more general speculations about the genre. Includes bibliography.

Greenberg, Harvey R. "The Fractures of Desire: Psychoanalytic Notes on *Alien* and the Contemporary 'Cruel' Horror Film." *Psychoanalytic Review* 70 (Summer 1983):241–67. *Alien* and other recent "cruel" horror films as embodiments of the "primordial selfishness" and the "fractures of ego-desire" that are characteristic of our era.

Greenberg, Harvey R. *The Movies on Your Mind.* New York: E. P. Dutton/Saturday Review Press, 1975. Includes extended psychoanalytic analysis of American horror films, from *Frankenstein* (1931) through *The Exorcist.*

Greenspun, Roger. "Carrie, and Sally and Leatherface among the Film Buffs." *Film Comment* 13, no. 1 (Jan.–Feb. 1977):14–17. Discussion of *The Texas Chain Saw Massacre* and *Carrie* that serves as a response to critics of violent horror films.

Handling, Piers, ed. *The Shape of Rage: The Films of David Cronenberg.* Toronto: General Publishing Co., 1983. Collection of essays on Cronenberg's horror films. Includes an interview.

Heath, Stephen. "*Jaws,* Ideology and Film Theory." In *Popular Film and Televi-*

sion, 200–205. London: British Film Institute, 1981. The ideology and "signifying practice" of *Jaws* as a "filmic system."

Henry, Michael. "Histoires de l'oeil: de *Fury* aux *Yeux de Laura Mars.*" *Positif* 217 (Apr. 1979): 69–72. Vision, the artist, and the monstrous in *The Fury* and *Eyes of Laura Mars.*

Hoile, Christopher. "The Uncanny and the Fairy Tale in Kubrick's *The Shining.*" *Literature/Film Quarterly* 2, no. 1 (1984):5–12. Animism and "oedipal tensions" in *The Shining.*

Huss, Roy, and T. J. Ross, eds. *Focus on the Horror Film.* Englewood Cliffs, N.J.: Prentice-Hall, 1972. Collection of essays and reviews that discuss classic films of Gothic horror, monster movies, and psychological thrillers from the 1920s to the late 1960s. Includes annotated bibliography.

Hutchinson, Tom. *Horror and Fantasy in the Cinema.* London: Studio Vista, 1974. Overview of the genre that groups horror films with films of science fiction and fantasy.

Jones, Alan. "Argento." *Cinéfantastique* 13, no. 6 (Sept. 1983):20–21. Introduction to the career of the Italian producer and director, Dario Argento.

Kapsis, Robert E. "Dressed to Kill." *American Film* 7, no. 5 (Mar. 1982):52–56. Commercial success, marketing strategies, and MPAA rating of horror films from 1978–81.

Kawin, Bruce F. "Children of the Light." In *Shadows of the Magic Lamp: Fantasy and Science Fiction in Film,* edited by George Slusser and Eric S. Rabkin, 14–29. Carbondale: Southern Illinois University Press, 1985. The "good" horror film, which "shows us something that we need to see," defined in opposition to science fiction and to the brutalizing, "bad" horror film, like *Friday the 13th.*

*Kawin, Bruce F. Review of *The Funhouse* and *The Howling. Film Quarterly* 35, no. 1 (Fall 1981):25–31. The fate of the "first victim" in the reflexive horror of *The Funhouse* and *The Howling.*

Kawin, Bruce. "The Mummy's Pool." *Dreamworks* 1, no. 4 (Summer 1981):291–301. Insightful exploration of the connections among nightmares, dreams, visionary seeing, ritual, and horror films, with particular reference to *The Wolf Man* and *The Mummy's Ghost.*

Keeler, Greg. "*The Shining:* Ted Kramer Has a Nightmare." *Journal of Popular Film and Television* 8, no. 4 (Winter 1981):2–8. *The Shining* as "negative correlative" to the image of the family, marriage, and vocation in films like *Kramer vs. Kramer.*

Kelley, Bill. "*'Salem's Lot:* Filming Horror for Television." *Cinéfantastique* 9, no. 2 (Winter 1979):9–21. Interviews and production information about the making of a made-for-television horror film.

Kellner, Douglas. "Fear and Trembling in the Age of Reagan: Notes on *Poltergeist.*" *Socialist Review* 13, no. 3 (May–June 1983):121–31. "Transcendent occultism" and the articulation of anxieties of the middle class in *Poltergeist.*

Kennedy, Harlan. "Things That Go Howl in the Id." *Film Comment* 18, no. 2 (1982):37–39. Surveys the themes of split-personality, conspiracy, and "sudden slaughter" that link *Friday the 13th* and other horror films with films like *Southern Comfort* and *Blow Out.*

*Kinder, Marsha, and Beverle Houston. "Seeing Is Believing: *The Exorcist* and *Don't Look Now.*" *Cinema* 34 (1974):22–33. Detailed examination of *The Exorcist* and *Don't Look Now.*

King, Stephen. *Danse Macabre.* New York: Everest House, 1981. Includes a discussion of the "universal" and the "sociopolitical" fears expressed in American horror movies from 1950–80.

Koch, Stephen. "Fashions in Pornography." *Harpers* 253 (Nov. 1976):108–11. Attack on the "hard-core pornography of violence" in "exploitation" films like *The Texas Chain Saw Massacre.*

Larsen, Ernest. "Hi-Tech Horror." *Jump Cut* 21 (Nov. 1979):1, 12, 30. The "struggle against technology" in and the ideological implications of *Alien* and *Dawn of the Dead.*

Lavery, David. "The Horror Film and the Horror of Film." *Film Criticism* 7 (1982): 47–55. *Don't Look Now* discussed in relation to the phenomenological film theory of Roger Munier.

Lemkin, Jonathan. "Archetypal Landscapes and *Jaws.*" In *Planks of Reason,* edited by Barry Keith Grant, 277–89. Metuchen, N.J.: Scarecrow Press, 1984. American archetypes of the wilderness and the community in *Jaws.*

Lenne, Gérard. "La proie et le monstre." *Ecran* 28 (Aug.–Sept. 1974):65–69. Principal types of female characters in films of horror and the fantastic.

London, Rose. *Zombie: The Living Dead.* New York: Bounty Books, 1976. Survey of vampire, mummy, and zombie films.

Losano, Wayne A. "The Vampire Rises Again in Films of the Seventies." *Film Journal* 2, no. 2 (1973):60–62. Increasingly explicit violence and sex in vampire films of the early 1970s as reflection of the "desensitization of the modern audience."

Lowry, Ed, and Louis Black. "Cinema of Apocalypse." *Take One* 7, no. 6 (May 1979):17–18. *Dawn of the Dead* and the apocalyptic tradition in horror films of the 1970s.

Lowry, Edward. "Genre and Enunciation: The Case of Horror." *Journal of Film and Video* 36, no. 2 (Spring 1984):13–20, 72. Argues that horror must be understood as a "mode of address" that depends on a "sado-masochistic relationship" between audience and film.

Mackey, Mary. "The Meat Hook Mama, the Nice Girl, and Butch Cassidy in Drag." *Jump Cut* 14 (Mar. 1977):12–14. The female victim and violence against women in *The Texas Chain Saw Massacre* and other films.

Manchel, Frank. *Terrors of the Screen.* Englewood Cliffs, N.J.: Prentice-Hall, 1970. Historical survey of the genre, emphasizing the pre-1950 period.

Mank, Gregory William. *It's Alive! The Classic Cinema Saga of Frankenstein.* New York: A. S. Barnes, 1981. Detailed survey of Universal's series of Frankenstein films, including interviews, plot summaries, and extensive production information.

Maslin, Janet. "Bloodbaths Debase Movies and Audiences." *New York Times,*

21 Nov. 1982, sec. 2, 1, 13. Critique of films like *Slumber Party Massacre* as debasing, derivative, "impersonal bloodbaths" and "violent pornography."

Maslin, Janet. "Tired Blood Claims the Horror Film as a Fresh Victim." *New York Times,* 1 Nov. 1981, sec. 2, 15, 23. Criticism of the predictability and much-emphasized gore in *Nightmare* and other films of the "slice-'em-up genre."

McConnell, Frank D. *The Spoken Seen: Film and the Romantic Imagination.* Baltimore, Md.: Johns Hopkins University Press, 1975. Includes a discussion of the sociopolitical and sexual implications of horror films, with particular reference to *Creature from the Black Lagoon.*

McConnell, Frank. "Rough Beasts Slouching." *Kenyon Review* 1 (1970):109–120. Evolution of horror from *Frankenstein* (1931) and *Dracula* (1931) — with their ties to nineteenth-century American literature — through the monster movies of the 1950s.

Naha, Ed. *Horrors from Screen to Scream.* New York: Avon, 1975. Selective annotated filmography.

Neale, Stephen. *Genre.* London: British Film Institute, 1980. Theory of film genre (based on recent trends in semiotics, psychoanalysis, and Marxist criticism) that includes several references to the horror film.

Neale, Steve. "*Halloween:* Suspense, Aggression and the Look." *Framework* 14 (Spring 1981):25–29. Detailed consideration of violence, suspense, sexuality, point of view, and the role of the viewer in *Halloween.*

Nelson, Thomas Allen. *Kubrick: Inside a Film Artist's Maze.* Bloomington: Indiana University Press, 1982. Includes a detailed comparison of the novel and film versions of *The Shining* and an analysis of the "mazelike designs" of Kubrick's films.

Pannill, Linda. "The Woman Artist as Creature and Creator." *Journal of Popular Culture* 16, no. 2 (Fall 1982):26–29. The female monster and the woman artist in *Eyes of Laura Mars* and other horror films.

Pattison, Barrie. *The Seal of Dracula.* New York: Bounty Books, 1975. Survey of vampire films.

Peters, Nancy Joyce. "Backyard Bombs and Invisible Rays: Horror Movies on Television." *Cultural Correspondences* 10–11 (Fall 1979):39–42. The "unrepressed image" and the "poetic" transformation of reality in horror films.

Pirie, David. *A Heritage of Horror: The English Gothic Cinema, 1946–1972.* New York: Avon, 1974. Critical history of British horror films, with particular attention to Hammer's Dracula and Frankenstein films and to the careers of directors like Terence Fisher and Michael Reeves.

Pirie, David. *The Vampire Cinema.* London: Hamlyn, 1977. Comprehensive historical survey of the vampire film.

Polan, Dana. "Eros and Syphilization." *Tabloid: A Review of Mass Culture and Everyday Life* 5 (Winter 1982):31–34. Nihilism, the threat of "libidinal vitality," and reactionary ideology in contemporary horror films.

Prawer, S. S. *Caligari's Children: The Film as Tale of Terror.* New York: Oxford University Press, 1980. Survey of horror film in the context of literature of the uncanny, with particular emphasis on the aesthetics of suggestion and indirection as embodied in films like *Caligari* and *Vampyr.*

Pym, John. Review of *Invasion of the Body Snatchers* (1978). *Sight and Sound* 48, no. 2 (Spring 1979):128-29. Contrasts the 1978 remake with the 1956 version of *Invasion of the Body Snatchers.*

Rafferty, Terrence. "De Palma's American Dreams." *Sight and Sound* 53, no. 2 (Spring 1984):142-46. Nightmare and the "helpless, sensitive observer" in De Palma's films from *Carrie* to *Scarface.*

Rebello, Stephen. "*Cat People:* Paul Schrader Changes His Spots." *American Film* 7, no. 6 (1982):38-45. Information on the production of *Cat People* (1982).

Reed, Joseph. "Subgenres in Horror Pictures: The Pentagram, Faust, and Philoctetes." In *Planks of Reason,* edited by Barry Keith Grant, 101-12. Metuchen, N.J.: Scarecrow Press, 1984. The nature and role of subgenre in horror, focusing on films that feature versions of Frankenstein, the Wolfman, the Mad Doctor, and Jekyll/Hyde.

Rickey, Carrie. "Make Mine Cronenberg." *Village Voice,* 1 Feb. 1983, 62-65. *Videodrome* in the context of Cronenberg's previous "biochemical horror comedies."

Rockett, W. H. "The Door Ajar: Structure and Convention in Horror Films That Would Terrify." *Journal of Popular Film and Television* 10, no. 3 (Fall 1982):130-36. In praise of suggestive, open-ended horror films that reverse genre expectations and abandon "strict Aristotelian narrative conventions."

Rockett, Will H. "Landscape and Manscape: Reflection and Distortion in Horror Films." *Post Script* 3 (1983):19-34. Expressionist influences, the "pathetic fallacy," and the "uncanny" in the set design and architecture of horror films.

Rodowick, D. N. "The Enemy Within: The Economy of Violence in *The Hills Have Eyes.*" In *Planks of Reason,* edited by Barry Keith Grant, 321-30. Metuchen, N.J.: Scarecrow Press, 1984. The "ideology of violence" and the correspondences between the monstrous and the bourgeois family in *The Hills Have Eyes.*

Ross, Philippe. "Le Gore: Boursouflure Sanglante du Cinéma Bis." *La Revue du Cinéma* 373 (June 1982):81-98. The history, principal films and directors, and conventional elements of the "gore" film as a subgenre of horror.

Rubey, Dan. "The Jaws in the Mirror." *Jump Cut* 10/11 (1976):20-23. *Jaws* as reflective of the "shared concerns and fears of our society."

Rubinstein, Richard. "The Making of *Sisters.*" *Filmmaker's Newsletter* 6 (Sept. 1973):25-30. Interview with De Palma about *Sisters* and Hitchcock.

Russell, Sharon. "The Witch in Film." *Film Reader* 3 (1978):80-89. The witch as mythic "product of male fears" in folklore and film. Includes a filmography.

Sabatier, Jean-Marie. "1976: le point sur le cinéma 'fantastique.'" *Revue de Cinéma* 303 (Feb. 1976):48-74. Extended survey of the role of the "fantastic" in films of the 1960s and 1970s.

Sammon, Paul M. "David Cronenberg." *Cinéfantastique* 10, no. 4 (Spring 1981): 21-34. Survey of Cronenberg's career. Includes interview.

Schatz, Thomas. *Old Hollywood/New Hollywood: Ritual, Art, and Industry.* Ann Arbor, Mich.: UMI Research Press, 1983. Includes a discussion of the influence of *Psycho* and *The Birds* on the modern American horror film.

Schupp, Patrick. "Les monstres de l'été." *Séquences* 98 (Oct. 1979):27-32. Ecological and apocalyptic nightmares in recent horror films.

Scott, Ridley. "The Filming of *Alien.*" *American Cinematographer* 60 (Aug. 1979): 772-73, 808, 842-44. Detailed information on the production of *Alien*.

Scott, Tony. "Romero: An Interview with the Director of *Night of the Living Dead.*" *Cinéfantastique* 2, no. 3 (1973):8-15. Informative interview covering *Night of the Living Dead* and Romero's films through *The Crazies*.

Sharrett, Christopher. " 'Fairy Tales for the Apocalypse': Wes Craven on the Horror Film." *Literature/Film Quarterly* 13 (1985):139-47. Informative interview on the ideological import of Craven's films.

Sharrett, Christopher. "The Idea of Apocalypse in *The Texas Chain Saw Massacre.*" In *Planks of Reason,* edited by Barry Keith Grant, 255-76. Metuchen, N.J.: Scarecrow Press, 1984. Detailed study of the "modernist" version of the apocalyptic vision in *The Texas Chain Saw Massacre*.

Simpson, Mike. "The Horror Genre: *Texas Chain Saw Massacre.*" *Filmmakers Newsletter* 8 (Aug. 1975):24-28. Information about the production of *The Texas Chain Saw Massacre*.

Slusser, George. "Fantasy, Science Fiction, Mystery, Horror." In *Shadows of the Magic Lamp: Fantasy and Science Fiction in Film,* edited by George Slusser and Eric S. Rabkin, 208-30. Carbondale: Southern Illinois University Press, 1985. Reassessment of the value of genre criticism, focusing on the relations among horror, science fiction, and fantasy.

Snyder, Stephen. "Family Life and Leisure Culture in *The Shining.*" *Film Criticism* 6 (Fall 1982):4-13. The "leisure culture syndrome," isolationism, and the fate of the creative imagination in *The Shining*.

Sobchack, Vivian Carol. *The Limits of Infinity: The American Science Fiction Film, 1950-75.* New York: A. S. Barnes, 1980. Includes a discussion of the relationship between horror and science fiction films.

Stanley, John. *The Creature Features Movie Guide.* Rev. ed. New York: Warner Books, 1984. Capsule reviews and partial production credits for over 3,000 films.

Stein, Elliott. "Have Horror Films Gone Too Far?" *New York Times,* 20 June 1982, sec. 2, 1, 21. Questions whether children are affected by the explicit "emphasis on violence, blood and gore" in modern horror films.

Surmacz, Gary Anthony. "Anatomy of a Horror Film." *Cinéfantastique* 4, no. 1 (1975):14-27. Detailed interview with the producers and the screenwriter of *Night of the Living Dead*.

Tarratt, Margaret. "Monsters from the Id." *Films and Filming* 17 (Dec. 1970): 38-42; (Jan. 1971):40-42. Freudian reading of the conflict between civilization and the id in *The Thing, The Bride of Frankenstein,* and other horror/science fiction films.

Telotte, J. P. *Dreams of Darkness: Fantasy and the Films of Val Lewton.* Urbana: University of Illinois Press, 1985. Detailed study of Lewton's horror/fantasy films.

Telotte, J. P. "Faith and Idolatry in the Horror Film." *Literature/Film Quarterly* 8 (1980):143-55. Perception and "audience participation" in films like *Halloween* and *Psycho*.

Telotte, J. P. "Human Artifice and the Science Fiction Film." *Film Quarterly* 36,

no. 3 (1983):44-51. Doubles, replicants, and the threat to human nature in
Alien, The Thing (1982), and other recent films.

Telotte, J. P. "The Doubles of Fantasy and the Space of Desire." *Film Criticism*
7 (1982):56-68. Fascination with and fear of the double in a series of films
from *Frankenstein* (1931) to *The Thing* (1982).

*Telotte, J. P. "Through a Pumpkin's Eye: The Reflexive Nature of Horror."
Literature/Film Quarterly 10 (1982):139-49. Voyeurism, "narcissistic vision,"
and the role of the spectator in *Halloween*.

Thomson, David. "Cats: Paul Schrader Interviewed." *Film Comment* 18, no. 2
(Mar.-Apr. 1982):49-52. Interview about *Cat People*.

Thomson, David. *Overexposures: The Crisis in American Filmmaking*. New York:
William Morrow, 1981. Includes essays on voyeurism and the "dynamics of
terror" in *Jaws, Carrie, Halloween,* and *The Shining*.

Twitchell, James B. *Dreadful Pleasures: An Anatomy of Modern Horror*. New
York: Oxford University Press, 1985. Important study of horror as a ritualistic form that helps guide the adolescent audience through "the complicated
passage from onanism to reproductive sexuality." Particular emphasis on the
representation of incest and "family romance" in the myths of Frankenstein,
the vampire, and the werewolf as they appear in nineteenth-century literature and twentieth-century film.

Twitchell, James B. "*Frankenstein* and the Anatomy of Horror." *Georgia Review*
37, no. 1 (Spring 1983):41-78. Includes a discussion of the sexual themes of
Rocky Horror Picture Show examined in the context of Mary Shelley's novel
and film versions of *Frankenstein*.

Ursini, James, and Alain Silver. *The Vampire Film*. New York: A. S. Barnes, 1975.
Surveys the various forms the male and female vampire have taken in film,
with particular emphasis on Hammer's vampire films of the 1960s and early
1970s.

Van Wert, William. "*The Exorcist:* Ritual or Therapy?" *Jump Cut* 1 (May-June
1974):3-5. Review that considers the role of ritual in *The Exorcist*.

Waller, Gregory A. "Disorientation and Point of View in Nicolas Roeg's *Don't
Look Now*." *Proceedings of the Purdue Conference on Film* 6 (1982):68-74.
Roeg's manipulation of point of view in *Don't Look Now*.

Waller, Gregory A. *The Living and the Undead: From Stoker's Dracula to Romero's
Dawn of the Dead*. Urbana: University of Illinois Press, 1986. Detailed study
of the story of the violent confrontation between the living and the undead,
with particular emphasis on the film adaptations of *Dracula* and Romero's
living dead films.

Waller, Gregory A. "Seeing It Through: Closure in Four Horror Films." *Proceedings of the Purdue Conference on Film* 7 (1983):17-24. Resolution and closure
in *Frankenstein* (1931), *Nosferatu* (1922), *Dracula* (1979), and *The Funhouse*.

Waller, Gregory A. "Sex and the Beast Within." *Proceedings of the Second Annual
Film Conference of Kent State University* (1984):9-13. Sexual identity and
transformation in *The Howling* and *Cat People* (1982).

Wexman, Virginia Wright. *Roman Polanski*. Boston: Twayne, 1985. Includes a
discussion of *Rosemary's Baby* and Polanski's other horror films.

White, Dennis L. "The Poetics of Horror: More than Meets the Eye." *Cinema Journal* 10, no. 2 (Spring 1971):1-18. Interesting survey of the principal fears (of powerlessness, of the id, for example) evoked and dramatized in horror films from *Caligari* through the 1960s.

Williams, Linda. "When the Woman Looks." In *Re-Vision: Essays in Feminist Film Criticism,* edited by Mary Ann Doane, Patricia Mellencamp, and Linda Williams, 83-99. Frederick, Md.: American Film Institute, 1984. First-rate discussion of the "look of horror" and the "affinity between monster and woman" in classic and recent horror films.

Williams, Tony. "American Cinema in the '70s: Family Horror." *Movie,* 27/28 (1981):117-26. The monster and the monstrous family as product and embodiment of Vietnam era America in the films of Romero, Craven, and others.

Williams, Tony. "Cohen on Cohen." *Sight and Sound* 53, no. 1 (Winter 1983-1984): 21-25. Interview with Larry Cohen covering his work in horror and non-horror films.

Williams, Tony. "Horror in the Family." *Focus on Film* 36 (Oct. 1980):14-20. Horror and the American family in "satanic movies" and the films of De Palma, Cohen, Craven, Romero, and other directors.

Willis, Donald C. *Horror and Science Fiction Films II.* Metuchen, N.J.: Scarecrow Press, 1982. Very useful filmography of over 2,300 films, half of which were released between 1971-81. Many of the listings include critical annotation as well as complete credits.

Wilson, William. "Riding the Crest of the Horror Wave." *New York Times,* 11 May 1980, sec. 6, 42-48, 54, 63. Survey of Stephen King's career that includes information about Kubrick's adaptation of *The Shining.*

Winter, Douglas E. *Stephen King: The Art of Darkness.* New York: New American Library, 1984. Includes interviews with King and information about the film adaptations of King's novels.

Wolf, Leonard. "In Horror Movies, Some Things Are Sacred." *New York Times,* 4 April 1976, sec. 2, 1, 19. Tradition and "lurking religious content" in horror films.

Wood, Robin, and Richard Lippe, eds. *American Nightmare: Essays on the Horror Film.* Toronto: Festival of Festivals, 1979. Invaluable collection of original and reprinted essays including Wood's "Introduction to the American Horror Film" and studies of, for example, *Nosferatu, Jaws, Sisters,* and the films of Larry Cohen.

Wood, Robin. "The American Family Comedy: From *Meet Me in St. Louis* to *The Texas Chain Saw Massacre.*" *Wide Angle* 3, no. 2 (1979):5-11. Links American family comedies of the 1940s like *Meet Me in St. Louis* and horror films involving the family.

*Wood, Robin. "Beauty Bests the Beast." *American Film* 8, no. 10 (Sept. 1983): 63-65. Discussion of *Eyes of a Stranger* and other films in the context of "violence-against-women" movies.

Wood, Robin. "Burying the Undead: The Use and Obsolescence of Count Dracula." *Mosaic* 16 (Winter/Spring 1983):175-87. Comparison of Stoker's novel with film versions of *Dracula,* including Badham's 1979 film.

Wood, Robin. *Hollywood from Vietnam to Reagan.* New York: Columbia University Press, 1986. Includes a number of Wood's previously published essays on American horror films and directors like De Palma, Romero, and Cohen.

Wood, Robin. "Neglected Nightmares." *Film Comment* 16, no. 2 (Mar.-Apr. 1980): 24-32. The ideological implications of generally overlooked films by Romero, Craven, Rothman, and Clark.

Wood, Robin. "Return of the Repressed." *Film Comment* 14, no. 4 (July-Aug. 1978):25-32. Influential discussion of the relationship between normality and the monster in horror films, focusing on the cultural significance and the recurring motifs of the genre.

Yakir, Dan. "Morning Becomes Romero." *Film Comment* 15, no. 3 (May-June 1979):60-65. Interview covering *Dawn of the Dead* and Romero's earlier horror films.

Ziegler, Robert E. "Killing Space: The Dialectic in John Carpenter's Films." *Georgia Review* 37, no. 4 (Winter 1983):770-86. The presentation of evil and the "violation and profanation" of home and self in Carpenter's films.

Zimmerman, Bonnie. "Daughters of Darkness: Lesbian Vampires." *Jump Cut* 25-26 (1981):23-24. Feminist reading of film treatments of the "lesbian vampire myth."

Index

Unless otherwise indicated, all titles in italics refer to feature films or made-for-television movies.

UNIVERSITY OF ILLINOIS PRESS
1325 SOUTH OAK STREET
CHAMPAIGN, ILLINOIS 61820-6903
WWW.PRESS.UILLINOIS.EDU